Windows NT Administration
Single Systems to Heterogeneous Networks

Marshall Brain

Shay Woodard

P T R Prentice Hall

Englewood Cliffs, New Jersey 07632

Library of Congress Cataloging-in-Publication Data

```
Brain, Marshall.
    Windows NT administration : single systems to heterogeneous
    networks / Marshall Brain, Shay Woodard.
      p.  cm,
    Includes index.
    ISBN 0-13-176694-5
    1. Operating systems (Computers) 2. Windows NT. I. Woodard,
    Shay.  II. Title.
QA76.76.063B719  1994                                   93-42506
004.6--dc20                                             CIP
```

Editorial/production supervision and interior design: *Dit Mosco*
Cover design: *Tommyboy Graphics*
Cover photo: *Uniphoto* ©David Ryan
Manufacturing Manager: *Alexis Heydt*
Acquisitions editor: *Mike Meehan*

©1994 by P T R Prentice Hall
Prentice-Hall, Inc.
A Paramount Communications Company
Englewood Cliffs, New Jersey 07632

The publisher offers discounts on this book when ordered in bulk quantities. For more information, contact:

Corporate Sales Department
PTR Prentice Hall
113 Sylvan Avenue
Englewood Cliffs, NJ 07632

Phone: 201-592-2863
Fax: 201-592-2249

Printed in the United States of America
10 9 8 7 6 5 4 3 2 1

ISBN 0-13-176694-5

Prentice-Hall International (UK) Limited, *London*
Prentice-Hall of Australia Pty. Limited, *Sydney*
Prentice-Hall Canada Inc., *Toronto*
Prentice-Hall Hispanoamericana, S.A., *Mexico*
Prentice-Hall of India Private Limited, *New Delhi*
Prentice-Hall of Japan, Inc., *Tokyo*
Simon & Schuster Asia Pte. Ltd., *Singapore*
Editora Prentice-Hall do Brasil, Ltda., *Rio de Janeiro*

CONTENTS

PREFACE

Who Needs This Book?

This book examines the administration of Windows NT systems and networks. A Windows NT configuration can range anywhere from a single machine sitting on your desk at home to a 200-node heterogeneous network inside a large Fortune 500 company. The goal of this book is to cover the whole spectrum, introducing you to the administration tools and networking capabilities built into Windows NT so that you can begin to design and implement effective computing environments. Many different types of people will find this book to be valuable:

- *Owners of single NT systems*

  If you have an NT machine of your own, either at the office or in your home, then you need to log in as the administrator of the machine on occasion to perform administrative tasks. You will do this to create new user accounts (so associates can share your machine), to back up your hard disk, to add new equipment to your machine, and so on. If this is your first opportunity to work on a machine that has accounts and administration facilities, then you probably have some basic questions like "What are accounts?", "Why shouldn't I log in as administrator all the time?", and "What benefits do I gain from the different administration tools?". Part 1 of this book focuses on basic, single-machine administration tasks, and discusses the fundamental issues and vocabulary that you must understand to administrate your machine properly.

- *The "computer person" in a small business or department*
  If you have been designated the "computer person" in a small company or in a department of a larger company, then you have a number of varied responsibilities ranging from installing network cable to showing someone how to format a floppy disk. Windows NT will make your life easier. It contains many features that help you network your machines together and easily share disks, printers, and e-mail. You will have to log in as the administrator to activate many of these features. Part 2 of this book describes how to administrate small and medium-sized NT networks.

- *An administrator in a large company planning to build a large NT network from scratch.*
  If you are about to install a large Windows NT network, then there are a number of design decisions you will face. How should you arrange and distribute your printers? Should you give everyone a local hard disk or use large disk servers? How should you implement accounts, centrally with a Domain Controller or in a distributed fashion? How do you take advantage of facilities available in NT to make administration of a large network easier? Part 2 of this book discusses the design and implementation of NT networks.

- *An administrator in a large company planning to integrate NT into an existing network.*
  If you have an existing network, it might be a Windows for Workgroups system, a collection of UNIX machines connected via Transmission Control Protocol/Internet Protocol (TCP/IP), OS/2 machines, or some combination. Windows NT works well with all of these systems. Part 2 of this book describes how to link Windows NT to other systems on the network so that all the different pieces work in harmony.

- *A new administrator who has inherited an NT network of some type.*
  If you have just inherited a Windows NT network, then you may be feeling a bit overloaded. This book will help you to learn the concepts and principles important to NT network administration starting at the beginning. Part 1 of the book will teach you the basic tools used to administrate an NT system. Part 2 will teach you the fundamentals of

small network configurations, and also discuss many of the issues faced by your predecessor, thus allowing you to understand the decisions the predecessor made. Once you have finished the book you will be able to expand the network and keep improving it.

No matter what your position on the Windows NT learning curve, you can use this book to better utilize your single NT machine or to interconnect large numbers of NT machines.

The Design of This Book

This book is designed to follow the natural development of a Windows NT network in the workplace. A company typically starts by installing one or two NT machines in individual offices. In a small company, for example, the owner might install Windows NT on one or two company-owned machines. In a larger company, individuals might install NT on the machines in their offices to take advantage of certain NT applications. The machines are probably managed by the people who own them. Part 1 of this book teaches you the concepts important to single-machine administration. You will learn about all of the administrative tools that come with NT and see how they are used.

As more NT machines are added (e.g., as the small business grows or as more people install NT in a large company) it becomes advantageous to connect the machines together on a network to share resources and information. Part 2 of the book discusses how to share disks and printers, how to create e-mail Post Offices, how to configure a small network, and so on.

In a large company, NT typically has to intercommunicate with many different types of machines on a heterogeneous network. The network may contain UNIX machines, Novell servers, large e-mail systems, Internet connections, and so on. Part 2 also discusses intercommunication between NT and other systems in a large network.

If you have never seen NT before, you can start at the beginning of this book and learn everything about NT administration by following this natural progression. If you are already familiar with NT or network administration, then you can jump to the middle of the book and pull out the specific information you need.

Prerequisites

This book assumes that you already know how to use the basic tools in Windows NT, tools like the File Manager, the Program Manager, and the Control Panel. If you are not familiar with these tools then please refer to the first book in this series entitled, "Using Windows NT: The Essentials for Professionals."

The Philosophy Behind This Book

Network administration can be either a joy or a chore, depending on how well the system meets the needs of its users, and how agreeable the system makes life for the administrator. If the system expands appropriately as the needs of the users expand, and if the system helps the administrator with day-to-day tasks, then administration can be quite pleasant. If the system also helps the administrator to fix problems quickly as they arise, then it is even better because the administrator is never left standing before a crowd of angry users.

Windows NT contains a number of tools that make administration easier, and it also allows you to handle quite a few normal administrative tasks remotely. NT will help you to design systems that are uniquely suited to the needs of your users. For example, an NT network can be configured as a client/server system, as a peer-to-peer network, or as a mixture of the two philosophies.

This book shows you how to use the administration tools built into Windows NT to build systems that meet the needs of your users. It also helps you to understand the design decisions that you will have to make as you implement your network.

Contents

This book consists of two parts, and follows a logical progression from stand-alone NT machines to larger corporate networks. Chapter 1 presents an overview of Windows NT, explains why it was created, and shows how you can use its capabilities to design an effective network for your company. Chapter 1 also introduces you to much of the vocabulary used in Windows NT and network administration in general.

In Part 1 you learn about the administrative tools shipped with Windows NT in a single machine context. These tools allow you to create accounts and groups, manage your disk space by adding new drives and partitioning them, and back up your drives. You also learn about certain tools hidden in the Control Panel that allow you, when logged on as administrator, to set the time and date, control virtual memory space, customize the behavior of the system, and so on. All of these tools are needed whether you are administrating one NT machine or a thousand. In this part of the book the tools are presented in a single-machine context. If you have your own machine and want to administrate it effectively, or if you are new to NT administration, then this is a good place to start.

Part 1

Chapter 2   The User Manager

Chapter 3   Installing Printers

Chapter 4   Backing Up Disks

Chapter 5   Uninterruptable Power Supplies

Chapter 6   Managing Disks

Chapter 7   Advanced Features and System Tuning

Chapter 8   Event Monitoring

Chapter 9   Performance Monitoring

Whenever two or more NT machines have gathered within a cable-run of each other, you will want to network them together. Windows NT was meant to network. It has a number of features and facilities that are available only when a network is available. In Part 2 you will learn how to connect NT machines to a network, how to share hard disks over the net, how to install and share printers, and how to create and manage an e-mail Post Office for the network so that users can communicate with one another. As your network becomes larger, you will also learn about dedicated disk servers and user Domains. Part 2 is useful when you are setting up homogeneous NT networks in a small business or department.

Part 2

Chapter 10   Designing and Creating a Network

Chapter 11   Sharing Disks and Printers

Chapter 12   Implementing Electronic Mail

Chapter 13   Domains and Servers

In a large company NT is just one part of a much larger picture. NT machines must coexist on a heterogeneous network that may contain UNIX machines and workstations, Internet connections, and so on. Part 2 of the book continues and discusses how to integrate NT into this sort of environment, and how to use NT to communicate with different machines. For example, NT has commands built into it that allow easy connections to TCP/IP machines. Third party software allows you to mount Network File System (NFS) volumes. You may also want to integrate NT workstations into a larger e-mail system and eventually provide Internet access. Part 2 discusses these issues and shows you how to use NT to access other facilities on the network.

Chapter 14   Connecting to TCP/IP Machines

Chapter 15   Other Connections

By the end of the book you will be familiar with all of the different administrative capabilities built into Windows NT.

Questions and Comments

If you have any questions or comments, or if you have suggestions that you think would help to improve the quality of this book, we would like to hear from you. We prefer e-mail, but if you are not connected you can reach us via U.S. mail at the following address:

Interface Technologies
P.O. Box 841
Zebulon, NC 27597

Appendix D contains instructions on reaching us electronically. For example, we offer an automatic-response e-mail service that lets you download updates and corrections to this book, as well as supplemental material, free of charge. If you currently do not have an e-mail account, you may wish to consider enrolling in a service like CompuServe or MCI mail so you can send and receive messages on the Internet.

Acknowledgments

Several people helped with the creation of this book, and we would like to take a moment to thank them for their help and effort.

Mike Meehan made all of these books possible, and we are grateful for his never-ending support and encouragement. He is the main reason this project has worked.

Roger Hopper at Conner Peripherals went out of his way on several occasions to help us with the Tape Backup chapter in this book. Conner is the supplier of the Tape Backup software for Windows NT, and also sells an advanced product separately.

We met Tonya van Dam and Mike Nash from Microsoft at Comdex, and they were very helpful in answering questions we had on the Advanced Server product at a time when not much other information was available.

Rob Ward helped with the Disk Manager chapter by supplying several spare SCSI drives that he had. These drives, being empty, allowed us to go through several destroy and rebuild cycles without worrying about losing anything important.

Sean Hennessey from Airco in RTP, NC allowed us to hook into his company's Novell network and experiment with it. We started working on this chapter at a time when the Novell requester for NT was quite buggy, and Sean demonstrated a good bit of patience. It turned out that patience was for naught: The Novell requester did not ship with the final product. But that does not diminish Sean's contribution.

Lance Lovette also showed a lot of patience as we dismantled his machine repeatedly to experiment with different adapters, disk configurations, drivers, and so on.

Three reviewers, Ken Beck, Jack Beidler, and Phil Bourne, contributed significantly to this book by forcing us to examine unclear sections and rewrite parts of the book that did not adequately explain important concepts. Their comments have significantly improved this book. Philip Meese of Mercury Technologies also contributed to this book with his comments and questions.

Sandy Brain helped immensely with her biweekly cookie shipments. A proper blood sugar level is important to any writing endeavor.

Finally, Dit Mosco has pushed all of these books through production, and we would like to thank her for her persistence and good humor throughout the process.

AN INTRODUCTION TO WINDOWS NT ADMINISTRATION

This chapter introduces you to the Windows NT philosophy, the vocabulary, and concepts behind NT administration, and the basic issues that you face when designing and implementing NT networks. The chapter is designed to meet the needs of several different types of people. For example, if you are coming from a UNIX, VMS, or mainframe background, then you understand many of the basic administration concepts but may be unfamiliar with the network computing model and the Windows product line. On the other hand, if you are coming from an MS-DOS or Windows background, then the concepts of accounts, groups, and user rights are probably unfamiliar to you. You may be wondering why a system has to be "administered" in the first place. There were never any accounts in DOS and everything worked just fine.

This chapter will answer many of your questions and give you the vocabulary and understanding you need to effectively administrate NT systems and networks.

1.1 Understanding Windows NT in the Workplace

Workplace computing has undergone a rapid and remarkable change in the last 10 years or so. Prior to 1980, mainframes and minicomputers controlled the marketplace, and they all offered a fairly standard configuration. A company or department would purchase a large and expensive central machine and then place a terminal on each worker's desk. The central machine contained all the computing resources. All hard disk space, CPU power, and memory were controlled by this one machine.

The mainframe or minicomputer was expensive and had unique environmental demands, so it lived in a room of its own away from everyone else. Its needs were tended to by a group of technicians. Generally there was only one computer per department or company because of these requirements. Most companies also had a special department, normally called the Management Information Services (MIS) department, that handled all system programming. When someone wanted a program they submitted a request to the MIS department.

Around 1980, and especially around 1983 when the IBM PC came out in a reasonable configuration, the corporate computing environment began to change. Personal computers started appearing everywhere. These machines were popular for several reasons:

- They had a low entry cost. Anyone with a spare $2,000–$4,000 in the department budget could buy one.
- They were easy to use and maintain relative to mainframes and mini-computers.
- The user was no longer dependent on the MIS department. Instead of waiting for MIS to create a program, an individual could now purchase software to spontaneously create special reports or capabilities very quickly.

Because of its advantages, the personal computing model has come to dominate the business computing environment. Unfortunately there are several significant problems with this model:

- A personal computer by itself is rather wasteful. Each machine must have its own printer, for example, and this printer generally sits idle most of the time.
- There is no easy way to share information among machines. In a business environment, this is a significant handicap because people must usually work together to get tasks accomplished.
- Personal computers offer little or no security for the information they hold. Anyone with access to the machine can view all of its data.
- People who own the computers end up wasting a tremendous amount of time on "administrative tasks" such as adding and upgrading software, backing up the hard disk, installing new hardware, and configuring and adjusting the operating system. These tasks have nothing to do with the job description of the person who owns the machine, and

therefore that person is wasting time and probably performing the job non-optimally.

Several systems evolved to solve some of these problems. Local area networks, for example, help machines share information and printers. Server systems, such as Novell Netware, allow data to be centralized in larger machines so that it can be backed up and secured properly. Many of the fundamental problems remain however. It is still difficult to secure information on individual machines, to upgrade software, to back up distributed data, and so on.

In the meantime, another phenomenon was occurring elsewhere in the scientific and academic communities: Workstation computing. In these environments, technically sophisticated users each own a powerful workstation, and the machines communicate with one another on high-speed networks. Workstation networks are typically found in engineering firms, universities, and financial institutions. When configured correctly a workstation environment has a number of advantages. A workstation network is secure and it is very easy to share data, printers, e-mail, and so on. They tend to be much more complicated than PC networks, however, especially from an administration standpoint.

The goal of Windows NT is to provide a complete solution for the workplace computing environment by combining the best features of the personal computer with the best features of a workstation network. NT lowers network administration costs by making it possible to perform many common administration tasks remotely. A large company can therefore dedicate one person (or a small department) to administration, and that person can handle most common administrative tasks anywhere on the network from his or her office.

A properly configured NT machine is as easy to use as a PC, because NT has a user interface that is very similar to Windows 3.1. On the other hand, it has all of the power and security of a workstation network, while being much easier to administrate. Windows NT is the best of both worlds.

1.2 A Brief History of Windows NT

If you are coming from a UNIX or mainframe background then you may be unfamiliar with the Microsoft Windows family. Or you may have heard about it and always considered it to be a toy. Suddenly Windows and Windows NT are everywhere, and you might be wondering how that happened. This section will give you an overview of the history of Windows so you can understand the evolution of NT. Windows NT is a complete, modern operating system that uses the familiar Windows 3.1 Graphical User Interface (GUI) as its primary method of communication with the user.

Currently there are several familiar GUIs on the market: The Macintosh system from Apple Computer (the system that started the whole trend toward GUIs) running on Apple's proprietary hardware, the Windows family from Microsoft running on generic PC hardware, the Motif system running on high-end workstations under UNIX, OS/2 on PC hardware, the Next Step system, the Amiga, and so on. All of these systems do generally the same thing in generally the same way, at least from a user's perspective. For example, a typical user could sit down on any of these systems and create a memo, paint a picture, or send e-mail without a lot of difficulty. Also, all these systems are moving toward each other at a rapid pace. They are borrowing features back and forth so quickly that they may all be exactly alike eventually.

The Microsoft Windows family, by any capitalistic measure, is the most successful of these systems. Windows will run on almost any piece of PC-compatible hardware, so it has been installed on millions of machines and is used by millions of people daily. Because of its success, Microsoft has released several different Windows products to appeal to specific sub-audiences among its throng of users.

The first product of the three is plain Windows, or "Windows 3.1." After several years of fits and starts, Microsoft finally got Windows "right" in version 3.1, and sales of the product have been massive. Windows 3.1 standardized the Windows user interface and now all products in the Windows family share the interface seen in 3.1. Windows 3.1 is the "entry level" product intended for single user installations found in the home or small business environment. See Figure 1.1.

The intermediate product is "Windows for Workgroups." Windows for Workgroups looks just like Windows 3.1 to the user, but it contains extra programs and features that let it exploit small local area networks. A Windows for Workgroups system can easily share directories, disks, and printers among several interconnected machines. The system also allows for personal intercommunication using e-mail and chat programs. It is therefore intended for small

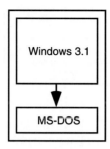

Figure 1.1
A single-user Windows 3.1 setup.

or intermediately sized groups of PCs typically seen in a small business or a department of a larger company. See Figure 1.2.

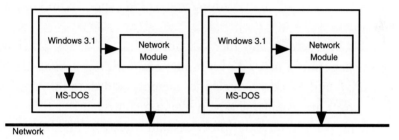

Figure 1.2
A multiuser Windows for Workgroups setup.

Windows 3.1 and Windows for Workgroups are built on top of MS-DOS, the Microsoft operating system for PC-class machines. This layering is a liability because MS-DOS is primitive by today's standards. MS-DOS has a very simple file system with limited features and no security. MS-DOS version 6.0 offers none of the capabilities the user would expect to find in a "real" operating system; features such as virtual memory, multiple processes, inter-process communication, and so on. Windows takes care of some of these problems itself as best it can. For example, it offers a good memory management system and cooperative multitasking. But because it is built on DOS the system is fragile, and the file management facilities are poor. The system is also permanently attached to PC-compatible hardware. There is really no easy way to move it to other platforms.

Windows NT is Microsoft's answer to these problems. It is a complete and modern operating system built from the ground up as a total solution to

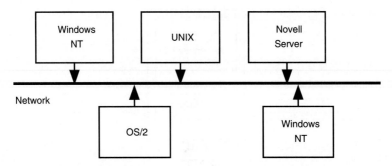

Figure 1.3
Windows NT on a heterogeneous network.

workplace computing. There are no separate modules and there is no DOS, as shown in Figure 1.3. It offers everything you would expect to find in a modern operating system:

- 32-bit instructions and memory addressing: Like any other modern workstation, NT uses a 32-bit numeric and address format. Unlike older DOS and Windows machine, memory addressing is "flat," so you can create arrays as large as you like in memory.
- Preemptive multitasking (processes and threads): The Macintosh and Microsoft Windows 3.1 use *cooperative multitasking*, in which applications yield the processor to one another at each application's discretion. Windows NT, like UNIX, instead uses *preemptive multitasking*. Under this system, CPU time is automatically allocated to each application (called a *process*). In addition, applications can divide themselves up into separate *threads* of execution. An application might do this in order to perform a lengthy calculation in the background without affecting the user interface.
- Symmetric Multiprocessing: An NT machine can contain more than one CPU. In a multiprocessor machine, NT will allocate different threads to different CPUs to take full advantage of all CPU power available. In addition, NT is itself multi-threaded, and its different threads can run on separate processors.
- Multiple platforms (Intel, MIPS, Alpha, etc.): NT is designed to run on a variety of processor architectures. At the time of this book's publication, NT had been ported to Intel 80x86 machines, MIPS platforms, and DEC's Alpha chips. Unlike UNIX, which looks different

depending on whose hardware it is running on, NT looks exactly the same to both the user and the programmer no matter which sort of architecture is running it.

- Remote procedure calls: NT supports Open Software Foundation (OSF)-style Remote Procedures Calls (RPCs), which can be used to easily build client/server applications that run efficiently on a network.

- Total network support (TCP/IP, NetBIOS Extended User Interface (NetBEUI), etc.): Windows NT is designed to run on a network, and supports a native format for communication with other NT machines as well as Windows for Workgroups systems and machines running TCP/IP protocols.

- C2 certified security: When using the NT File System (NTFS), Windows NT creates a secure system. All users must log in with an account name and password. Files and directories on the disk are protected by Access Control Lists (ACLs). Applications are isolated from one another in memory so that the crash of one does not affect any of the others.

- DOS and Portable Operating System Interface (POSIX) support: Windows NT, regardless of the platform, can run DOS applications using the MS-DOS prompt, a command-based interface to NT's capabilities. The MS-DOS prompt simulates MS-DOS on PC systems, using the same commands as DOS does on a PC. However, the MS-DOS prompt is completely simulated, so it looks exactly the same on any CPU architecture. You can also execute POSIX and character-mode OS/2 applications in this environment.

As you can see, NT's capabilities are patterned along the lines of an operating system like UNIX, and in several cases features such as RPCs were borrowed directly and completely from the UNIX world.

Microsoft has covered all of the power in Windows NT with the familiar Windows 3.1 interface found in the other Windows products. This decision means that anyone familiar with previous versions of Windows can use NT right out of the box. Everything looks identical. The only real additions that the user sees when comparing NT to the Windows for Workgroups interface are the security features in the File Manager and the logon screen that ensures that those security features work.

From an administrative standpoint however, NT contains a wealth of new features. NT attempts to completely separate "use" of the system from "administration" of the system so that users do not have to waste their time on administrative tasks. A user may "own" the machine on his or her desktop, but that does not mean that the user wants to spend time backing up the hard disks, installing software, or configuring the network. Those administrative tasks are better left to a trained administrator. NT therefore provides separate administrative tools that allow remote access.

1.3 What Is an Administrator?

If you have spent your life working on a stand-alone machine, such as a PC-compatible or a Macintosh, then you may have several very fundamental questions about system administration:

- What is an administrator?
- What is an administrative task?
- What is an administrative account?
- Why does NT need accounts?
- What are user rights?

This section will help to answer these questions for you and explain why NT separates administrative tasks from user tasks.

People buy computers to *use* them—computers help to get work done more efficiently. The user wants to create spreadsheets, edit documents, copy files, and so on. A typical user does not want to worry about the computer hardware itself, or the software, or the operating system. The user also wants to be able to ignore the details of the network. Copying files back and forth over the network is fine, but no user wants to have to think about cable runs, routers, and network traffic loads.

All of the activities performed on a computer that have nothing to do with getting a job done are called *administrative tasks*. The most common administrative tasks are listed below:

- Installing the machine and operating system, and getting everything up and running
- Installing and upgrading software
- Installing and upgrading hardware (e.g., new disks, printers, etc.)
- Backing up the hard disk

- Designing, installing, maintaining, and upgrading a network
- Implementing an e-mail system
- Securing the data on the system

None of these tasks actually accomplish anything useful as far as a normal user is concerned; they just get in the way. Many of these tasks require specialized knowledge that most users do not have. Administrative tasks are better left to a person (or a group of people in a large company) trained in performing them. NT makes all of these tasks easier by providing specialized administration tools, most of which can be used remotely over the network.

The last item in the list is extremely important. One of the biggest problems with personal computers today is the lack of security for the data stored on these systems. If you have a normal personal computer sitting on your desk, then anyone can come along and look at any of the information you have stored on the machine. This is especially a problem when several people share the same machine. There is no privacy for the individual users because the hard disk is wide open and unsecured. Also, there is no way to protect the operating system itself from intentional or accidental damage. You have probably seen or heard about a new user who comes along and erases the root directory, thereby crippling the entire machine. Or a program, either a normal program run amok or a virus intending to do damage, gets out of control and erases or damages parts of the operating system so the machine no longer boots. In order to solve these problems a system must be secure.

User accounts, in combination with a secure file system, create a secure machine. On a Windows NT machine, each user must have an account and a password to do anything on the machine. When the machine powers up, it forces the user to log in. Without an account and a password the machine is inoperable. If the machine's hard disk uses NTFS, the user's account gives the user access to only certain areas of the hard disk. For example, users are normally able to read and write files in their *home directories* (the personal directories assigned to them when their accounts are created). They may also access certain applications. However, there is no way for the user to erase or damage those applications.

Users can choose to let other people see or modify the files in their home directories. However, normal users cannot do anything else if the administrator secures everything properly. For example, normal users cannot modify the op-

erating system, or erase an application directory, or destroy or read other people's files, unless they have explicit permission to do so (see Appendix G for a
security checklist). These security features make NT an extremely stable operating system, and they also allow people sharing a machine to keep their work
private. That privacy applies not only when people are working on an individual machine, but also when a hard disk is shared with others over the network.

The administrator controls the security of the system by creating accounts
that give people access to a machine, and by setting the *rights* that each user has.
The administrator can give someone very limited access to the machine, or total control. For example, an administrator can set up an account so that the
user is able to log in and run just one application. Alternatively, the administrator could give an account full administrative privileges. User rights are described in Chapter 2.

The NT system recognizes certain accounts as *administrative accounts* and
gives the owner of the account administrative privileges. The owner can essentially do anything anywhere. All administrative tools are available, and the user
can freely look at any area of the hard disk on the machine. This of course gives
the owner of an administrative account the ability to wreak havoc, and you
therefore do not want to give administration privileges to anyone who does not
fully understand the use of the tools and facilities available.

1.4 The Evolution of an NT Network

Windows NT is meant to be used on a network. Built-in features in the
File Manager, Print Manager, and the operating system itself make it extremely
easy to use disks and printers that are attached to other NT machines on the
net. NT also contains facilities that allow you to communicate with other types
of machines. For example, TCP/IP commands like `telnet` and `ftp` are
available on all NT machines, so it is easy to access UNIX machines. All of
these capabilities together make it extremely easy to design and implement NT
networks or attach NT machines to existing networks.

A typical network naturally evolves through a set of recognizable phases.
Every now and again you may hear someone say, "I need to purchase and install
1,000 NT workstations and a network for my customer service reps in Q3,"
but it is far more common for networks to start small and grow over time. The
different phases of network growth are described in the following sections.

1.4.1   Phase One — A Single Machine

A typical NT network starts with just one machine. For example, a person starts a small business and buys a machine, or someone in a large company purchases Windows NT to run a special NT application important to his or her job. In a single-machine configuration like this, the person who owns the machine acts as its administrator. The owner adds new software, creates new accounts to share the machine with other people, installs a printer, and so on.

Many of the administrative features built into NT are very useful in a single-machine situation. For example, the Backup tool makes it extremely easy to back up your hard disk. If you are using the machine in your home, you can use the User Manager tool to create a separate account for your children and limit them to just the games directory if you like.

1.4.2   Phase Two — A Peer-to-Peer Network

A small business grows and purchases new machines. A lone NT user in a large company may convince others that they should convert to NT. Now several NT machines exist in close proximity to one another. By networking the machines together the users can share data on their hard disks, as well as printers and backup devices. Figure 1.4 shows a typical small NT network.

In a network like this, each machine will normally have an administrator account and an account for the person who "owns" the machine. If a machine is shared by several people then the machine will have accounts for each user. If users want to modify or customize their machines, then they log in as the administrator and change things on their own. The arrangement is normally informal. All of the disks are available on the network, and the printer is shared by everyone. One person might back up the entire network to tape each night or at the end of the week.

This sort of network is often called a "Peer-to-Peer" network. All machines are equal to their "peers." The owner of each computer controls the access to resources on his or her machine, and there is little or no central management.

1.4.3   Phase Three — The Proto-Administrator

As the network grows and more machines connect into it, the needs of the network users change. One person is designated as the "computer person" and

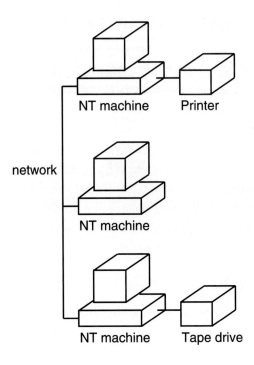

Figure 1.4
A small NT network.

users are instructed to "Call Jane when something doesn't work right." That person becomes the de facto *network administrator*. Generally, the administrator is in charge of installing new hardware and software, adding machines to the network, fixing problems and sending machines in for repair, backing up the system, and so on. With less than ten machines on a network the activities of the administrator generally do not constitute a full time job, and the computer person is able to continue with other activities without too many disturbances.

At this point in the evolution of the system, e-mail capability becomes desirable. An e-mail system gives users a new way to communicate, and also makes it easy to transfer documents between users. You can also use groupware software like Schedule+ in conjunction with the e-mail system (see the book "Using Windows NT: The Essentials for Professionals" in this series for more information), and this is a further incentive to add e-mail.

NT makes the implementation of an e-mail system extremely easy. One machine is designated as the *Post Office* for the network, and all of the other users attach to it. This machine will lose the disk space required to store e-mail messages, but beyond that it is normally unaffected by the processing overhead of e-mail tasks and can be used as a normal workstation. It simply needs to run NT 24 hours a day so that it can handle e-mail requests at any time.

Give one person control

No matter how small your network, put one person in charge of administering it so that all activities on the network are coordinated and synchronized. For example, even if there are only three machines on the net, put one person in charge of backing up the network and adding accounts. If you don't do this, people will "do their own thing" and this will often lead to naming conflicts, network problems, duplicated files on the network, and so on. Let one knowledgeable person know everything that is happening on the net so that problems are avoided.

1.4.4   Phase Four — A Full-scale System

At some point a network becomes big enough for the company to justify employing a full-time person to administrate it. This person often wears many hats initially, and is probably in charge of designing network expansions, making purchasing decisions on equipment and software, backing up the entire network, training new users, managing all of the accounts, repairing, replacing, and maintaining the existing equipment, and upgrading software packages network-wide. As the network continues to grow, a single administrator turns into a department as people are hired to specialize in these individual tasks.

Several things start to happen when a network extends beyond the few-machine level. First, the one-user-one-machine account model often becomes cumbersome. The problem is especially acute in academic environments, where a group of students or faculty members share a pool of machines located in a lab or a computer room. The administrator is forced to maintain and synchronize large account lists on each individual machine. For example, when a new user needs an account, the administrator must add the account on every machine that the user might potentially use. In addition, each user's profile (the screen colors, icon arrangements, and so on, chosen by the user) is different on each individual machine. If the user changes the screen color on one machine, for example, the change is not reflected on any of the others. NT can solve this problem using a *Domain Controller:* a single machine that holds a single account list that is accessed remotely whenever someone logs in. The machine holding the account list is the account server for the network. Now each person is known by a single account, and this arrangement makes the assignment of disk and printer privileges much simpler and cleaner. Domains are discussed in Chapter 13.

Another problem that arises on growing networks involves hard disk usage inefficiencies. For example, imagine a network with ten machines, each of which has its own 500 MB hard disk. Also imagine that, on average, each hard disk has 200 MB of free space at the moment. That's 2 Gigabytes of unused space. If someone wanted to create a 1 Gigabyte database file however, it is not possible to do so because the disk space is fragmented across many machines. In a case like this it is often beneficial to create a machine that acts as a disk server or a database server for the network. Each user machine might contain a small local hard disk just big enough to hold the operating system and swap space. All other files are stored on the server. This arrangement often makes more efficient use of available disk drives. Server configurations are discussed in Chapters 10 and 13.

On a large network, printers may be centralized at the server machines, or they may be distributed across the network on individual machines. There is not any inherent advantage to either approach, although there may be specific advantages to one approach or another at your site. See Chapters 5 and 11 for details on printers.

UNIX, mainframe, and VMS users are accustomed to the concept of terminals and terminal servers. For example, a single UNIX machine might support 20 dumb terminals connected by serial lines, or 10 X terminals connected on the network. NT has no equivalent configuration; each machine must be a complete computer running NT. The machine must have a hard disk that holds (at a minimum) the operating system files, temp space, and the virtual memory swap file. A 150–200 MB disk drive in such a machine is appropriate. Low-end machines capable of running NT are extremely inexpensive now, and these machines can work with high-end servers to form cost-effective arrangements. See Chapter 10 for details.

Networks grow over time. You might start with five machines on the net, but as the company grows so does the network. The other thing that grows is network traffic. The more machines that you put on a single network segment, the more loaded the network becomes. Eventually, file transfers and printing become so slow that people notice the degradation and complain. The solution to the problem is to segment the network into individual subnets consisting of 20 to 30 machines each. The segments are then connected back together using a router. See Chapter 14 for a more detailed discussion.

1.4.5   Phase Five — Heterogeneous Networks

A large company, especially one that has been around for awhile, does not have the luxury of installing a homogeneous NT network consisting only of NT machines. Other departments may have UNIX machines, OS/2 machines, PCs running Windows for Workgroups, and so on.

In general, NT makes inter-environment communication very easy. For example, NT already contains the commands necessary to communicate with existing TCP/IP machines such as UNIX workstations. Chapters 14 and 15 of this book discuss the different issues involved in connecting NT to other systems.

1.5 Tools Available to the Administrator

Windows NT contains a number of tools that support you in your administrative tasks. These tools are listed below:

- The User Manager: Lets you add user accounts, assign rights to users, and form groups of users that make file and printer security easier. This tool also lets you choose user actions that you want to track for security reasons.

- The Print Manager: Lets you connect printers either locally to a machine or remotely through the network, and assign drivers to interface the printer to NT. The Print Manager also lets you secure printers so that only designated users can access them.

- The Disk Administrator: Lets you add disks to your NT system and modify the partition tables of the different drives connected to your machine. Additional capabilities include the ability to set up volume sets and stripe sets.

- The File Manager: Lets you change the permissions on files and directories of drives formatted with NTFS.
- The Tape Backup program: Lets you back up your hard disk onto tape and later restore data from tape after a disk crash or mistake. It is also useful for archiving and transferring data.
- The Control Panel: Contains a number of administrative tools that let you enable, disable, and tune different capabilities on your machine such as services, uninterruptable power supplies, and network communications.
- The Event Viewer: Lets you view a variety of events generated by the operating system, applications, and security activities.
- The Performance Monitor: Using counters built into the operating system, allows you to view a wide variety of performance indicators on every aspect of your machine's performance.

1.6 Installing Windows NT

Appendix B discusses the installation of Windows NT. Once you have completed installation, you can restart the machine. It will come up with the following characteristics:

- It will have three accounts: the administrator account, your personal account, and a guest account.
- It will have the directories shown in Figure 1.5.

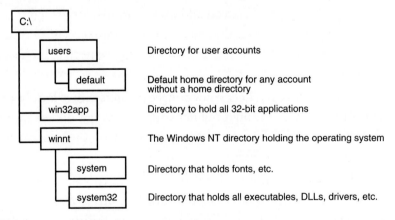

Figure 1.5
The Windows NT Directory setup.

- If you had a network card in the machine during NT's installation, the system has network support for the NT native protocol. You can communicate with other NT machines on the network immediately. You will need to add other protocols separately as described in Chapter 14.
- If you requested it, NT installed a printer driver and the printer is ready to go.

One of your most important tasks as an administrator will be to modify and tune this initial system until it perfectly matches your needs. Equally important is making the system comfortable for other users. This book will help you do that.

1.7 Conclusion

If you are new to network administration, you may have found yourself intrigued by the scope of the field. It at first seems that all you have to do is plug machines together with a network cable, but you are probably now realizing that an effective network is something you must design to best meet the needs of your particular users.

The following sections will teach you about NT administration. The book starts at the beginning by showing you how to administrate a single machine. Then it moves to small networks, larger homogeneous networks, and finally heterogeneous networks. This logical progression will allow you to see and understand the entire NT administration picture.

PART

Part One introduces you to the basics of Windows NT administration by showing you the administration tools in a single-machine environment. You can use these tools on your own machine to learn about the different capabilities available.

SINGLE-MACHINE ADMINISTRATION

THE USER MANAGER

Once you have installed NT, one of the first things you need to do is examine and tune your user account. You may also want to create new accounts so that you can share your machine with other users. In this chapter you will learn about accounts, groups, and user rights, and you will also learn how to create and manipulate accounts and groups using the User Manager.

If you have not yet installed Windows NT, see Appendix B for more information.

2.1 Overview: Accounts, Groups, and Rights

In order to use an NT machine, you must have an *account* on the machine. Accounts are the key to security in Windows NT because they identify each user to the system and tell NT what an individual is allowed to do. Every NT machine maintains an account list that identifies the valid users of that particular machine. Alternatively, an NT Advanced Server on the network can manage an account list shared by many NT machines. This option is described in more detail in Chapter 13.

Every NT machine starts with three accounts, all of which are created during the installation process. The first account is the administrator account, the second is a guest account, and the third is an initial user account. One of your primary jobs as an administrator is to create new accounts for other users as the need arises, and assign user rights to those accounts.

An account identifies a user to the system and to other users. A user's account stores several specific pieces of information about the user. For example, the account record stores the name of the account, the user's password, and the user's full name and description. It also stores the path to the *home directory* for the user. The home directory is the default directory for the user, the directory the user is "in" right after logging onto the system. This is generally the directory in which the user does his or her work.

Each account belongs to one or more *groups*. All NT machines have six predefined groups, and the administrator can create other groups for special situations. Groups do two things:

1.   They assign *rights* to an account.
2.   They group accounts together to make permissions easier to assign in the File Manager and the Print Manager.

For example, an account that is a member of the "guests" group (a predefined NT group available on all NT machines) gives the user the right to log on to and use that particular NT machine, but the person using the account can do little else. For example, the user of an account that is a member of the guests group cannot set the system time. There is a right named "Change the system time," and the guest group does not have this right. On the other hand, a person whose account is included in the "Power Users" group (another predefined NT group) can do almost anything on the system. See Figure 2.1.

Table 2.1 contains a list of the six predefined groups available in Windows NT. Tables 2.2 and 2.3 contain lists that show all of the individual rights that are available for assignment on an NT machine, and the rights that are assigned to each predefined NT group. Table 2.4 shows advanced user rights. Advanced rights are rarely granted to anyone other than programmers in special coding situations. When programmers need an advanced right, they know it and will ask for it.

The rights shown in Table 2.2 can be selectively granted or denied to a user by the administrator. There are also a number of built-in capabilities granted to different groups that are preassigned and unchangeable. These capabilities are listed in Table 2.5.

Administrators can perform any of the tasks shown in Table 2.5. Power users can perform all of them except for assigning user rights, overriding workstation locks, and formatting the hard disk. In addition, a power user cannot

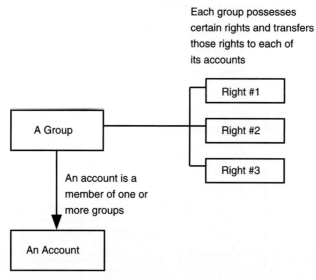

Figure 2.1
The relationships between accounts, groups, and rights.

Table 2.1   Pre-defined Groups

Administrators	People needing full administrative privileges
Backup Operators	People who need to operate backup devices
Guests	Infrequent or unusual users of the system
Power Users	Knowledgeable people who need nearly full access
Replicator	Used with file replication features of the advanced server—never assigned to a user
Users	People who need to use the machine

Table 2.2   Normal Rights

Access this computer from the network
Everyone
Power Users
Administrators
Back up files and directories
Administrators
Backup Operators
Change the system time
Administrators
Power Users

Table 2.2   Normal Rights (Continued)

Force shutdown from a remote system
Administrators
Power Users
Log on locally
Everyone
Administrators
Backup Operators
Guests
Power Users
Users
Manage auditing and Security log
Administrators
Restore files and directories
Administrators
Backup Operators
Shut down the system
Everyone
Administrators
Backup Operators
Power Users
Users
Take ownership of files and other objects
Administrators

Table 2.3   Rights by Group

Administrators
All of the rights in Table 2.2
Power Users
Access this computer from the network
Change the system time
Force shutdown from a remote system
Log on locally
Shut down the system

Table 2.3   Rights by Group (Continued)

Backup Operators
Back up files and directories
Log on locally
Restore files and directories
Shut down the system
Users
Log on locally
Shut down the system
Guests
Log on locally

Table 2.4   Advanced User Rights

Act as part of the operating system
Bypass traverse checking
Create a page file
Create a token object
Create permanent shared objects
Debug programs
Generate security audits
Increase quotas
Increase scheduling priorities
Load and unload device drivers
Lock pages in memory
Log on as a service
Modify firmware environment values

Table 2.5   Built-in Capabilities

Assign user rights
Create and manage user accounts
Create and manage local groups
Create common groups in the Program Manager
Format the workstation's hard disk
Keep local profile
Lock the workstation

Table 2.5   Built-in Capabilities (Continued)

Override a lock on a workstation
Share and stop sharing directories
Share and stop sharing printers

delete or modify accounts or groups created by the administrator. A user can create local groups and manage them, but has none of the other abilities listed in Table 2.5. Backup operators can keep a local profile. Anyone can lock a workstation.

When someone logs into an NT machine with the administrator account or with an account that is a member of the administrator's group, that person can do absolutely anything to any part of the system. The administrator can examine any directory on the hard disk, can add and remove disk partitions, can share portions of the hard disk on the network, and can control access to the printers. The administrator account should therefore be used sparingly. Because it allows access to everything, it is possible to damage the operating system itself, for example, by deleting the wrong file in the operating system directory.

A normal user account has fewer privileges, and you are therefore less likely to harm the system when logged in as a user (provided that the system is using a secure and properly configured file system—see Appendix G). Even if you own your NT machine and can therefore use both the administrator and user accounts whenever you like, it is a good practice to use the administrator account only when you have a specific need to do so. For example, you might log on as the administrator to create a new account for a friend. For normal day-to-day activities you should log on as a normal user or a power user.

Groups and accounts are used by the File Manager to control access to files. If your machine's hard disk is formatted with NTFS, then each file and directory has an access control list that controls which groups and individual users can access them. The owner of the file or directory can specifically choose which users and groups may use the file, and exactly what the user or group can do. See Appendix A for more information. The Print Manager contains the same sort of control mechanisms for printers.

Here is a summary of the terms discussed above:

• Account: An account identifies a specific user to the system.

- User rights: Rights determine what a user is able to do on the system. For example, if a group has the "Shut down the system" right, and an account belongs to that group, then the owner of the account has the right to shut down the system.

- Group: A group has associated with it both accounts and user rights. Every account generally belongs to at least one group. Every group generally has at least one user right associated with it, although it is common to create a group having no user rights that exists strictly to assign file permissions in the File Manager.

- File permissions: Permission to access a file can be granted to an individual account or to a group. The assignment of file permissions is normally done in the File Manager. For example, a user might give a co-worker access to one of his or her directories. It is common for the administrator to create a new group and assign several accounts to it so that the administrator can easily give everyone in the group access to a directory. It would be possible for the administrator to give 10 individual accounts access to a directory one by one, but this is tedious and much more easily handled by creating a group containing the 10 users.

Administrative Strategy

Using groups to assign permissions

Use groups to link related accounts together. For example, you might form a group containing all of the programmer accounts so that you can give all of the programmers access to the directories containing the compilers and libraries. You might create another group containing the accounts of all of the sales people so that you can give this group access to a directory containing sales information. The programmer for the sales department would be a member of both of these groups and would therefore be able to access both directories.

As an administrator, one of your primary responsibilities is to create accounts for new users, and to place these accounts in the appropriate groups. Each person who uses an NT machine should have his or her own individual account. This makes it possible to track machine use very specifically. You may also want to create new groups. For example, if a collection of users log on to the machine to write C++ programs, you might create a group called "program-mers." You can then assign special user rights to this group, and you can also use the group in the File Manager to give that set of users access to special di-rectories and applications needed to write C++ programs.

2.2 Creating New Accounts

Let's say that you own your NT machine, and a friend of yours asks to use it to write a report while you are on vacation. Since you are the owner of the machine you have access to the administrator's account, your user account, and the guest account. You have several options:

- You can give your friend the password to the administrator account and let your friend do absolutely anything with the machine. The problem with this approach is that it is possible for your friend to make a mis-take and destroy the operating system. You have probably watched, or heard of, a new user making a mistake and accidentally erasing the en-tire hard disk. Because of the possibility of accidental or purposeful damage or tampering, you should keep the administrator's account to yourself.

- You can give your friend access to your personal user account. This is safer than the first approach because the user cannot damage the oper-ating system. On the other hand, your friend can now read and/or damage your personal files. You should therefore keep your personal ac-count to yourself.

- You can tell your friend about the guest account. This is an acceptable approach from a security standpoint because only the files in the `\users\default` directory will be visible to your friend, and about the only thing that he or she can do is log on and work with files in that directory (provided you are using NTFS on your system and have set permissions properly. See Section 2.9). That may create problems of its own however. A guest, for example, may not be able to shut down the system, and you may want your friend to have more access than a guest.

- You can create a new account specifically for your friend, and assign your friend's account to an appropriate group. In the process, you can create a private home directory for your friend in which he or she can privately create new files and directories.

The last approach is clearly the best one. It lets you give your friend exactly what he or she needs from the machine. You can also create a personal home directory so that his or her work is private. It only takes a minute to create a new account for somebody, and the security and privacy advantages of doing so clearly make it the best approach when you want to give someone access to your machine.

Administrative Strategy

Create new accounts for new users

   If you have administrative privileges on your machine, it is unwise to give another user access to the administrative account or your personal account. It opens the door to tampering and accidental damage. Instead, create a new account for the user and assign that user whatever rights he or she specifically needs.

To create a new account, log on as the administrator. In the Program Manager find the Administrative Tools group and open the User Manager. This application allows you to create new accounts and groups, and to assign new user rights. Figure 2.2 shows a screen dump of this tool during use shortly after installation of NT.

```
┌──────────────────────── User Manager ──────────────────── ▼ ▲ ┐
│  User   Policies   Options   Help                                │
│ ┌─────────────┬──────────────┬──────────────────────────────┐   │
│ │ Username    │ Full Name    │ Description                   │   │
│ ├─────────────┴──────────────┴──────────────────────────────┤   │
│ │ 👤 Administrator                      Built-in account for administering the computer/doma│
│ │ 👤 brain                                                   │   │
│ │ 👤 Guest                              Built-in account for guest access to the computer/do│
│ │                                                            │   │
│ ├─────────────┬──────────────────────────────────────────────┤  │
│ │ Groups      │ Description                                   │  │
│ ├─────────────┴──────────────────────────────────────────────┤  │
│ │ 👥 Administrators    Members can fully administer the computer/domain │
│ │ 👥 Backup Operators  Members can bypass file security to back up files│
│ │ 👥 Guests            Users granted guest access to the computer/domain│
│ │ 👥 Power Users       Members can share directories and printers       │
│ │ 👥 Replicator        Supports file replication in a domain            │
│ │ 👥 Users             Ordinary users                                   │
│ └───────────────────────────────────────────────────────────────┘
```

Figure 2.2
The User Manager.

The upper list in Figure 2.2 shows all existing user accounts on the machine. This machine has accounts for the administrator, guests, and a user named Brain. The administrator account has a password that was created by the person who performed the installation. The user account Brain has a name and password also created during installation. The guest account has no password initially, although it is easy to change. Simply double click on the guest account and type a password and confirmation password into the appropriate spaces. See below for more information.

The lower list in Figure 2.2 shows the list of all available groups. NT installs six standard groups initially, as described in Section 2.1. You can then create new groups as the need arises. See Section 2.4 for more information.

To create a new account, select the **New User** option from the **User** menu. You will see a dialog like the one shown in Figure 2.3. In this dialog you specify

```
┌──────────────────────────────────────────────────────────────┐
│ ▭                          New User                            │
├──────────────────────────────────────────────────────────────┤
│  Username:     [                              ]    ┌────────┐  │
│                                                    │   OK   │  │
│  Full Name:    [                              ]    └────────┘  │
│                                                    ┌────────┐  │
│  Description:  [                              ]    │ Cancel │  │
│                                                    └────────┘  │
│  Password:     [                              ]    ┌────────┐  │
│  Confirm                                           │  Help  │  │
│  Password:     [                              ]    └────────┘  │
│                                                                │
│  ☐ User Must Change Password at Next Logon                     │
│  ☐ User Cannot Change Password                                 │
│  ☐ Password Never Expires                                      │
│  ☐ Account Disabled                                            │
│                                                                │
│   ┌────────┐  ┌────────┐                                       │
│   │  Groups │  │ Profile │                                     │
│   └────────┘  └────────┘                                       │
└──────────────────────────────────────────────────────────────┘
```

Figure 2.3
The New User dialog.

the new user name (also known as the logon ID), the full name of the user, a description of the user, and the user's initial password. You can also specify four conditions on the account in the check boxes at the bottom of the dialog.

- The **User Must Change Password at Next Logon** check box forces the user to create a new password for the account when logging in for the first time. This option allows the administrator to use a default password when creating the account. The user must change it to a new password immediately after logging in the first time.

- The **User Cannot Change Password** option prevents the user from changing the password. This option is useful on an account like the guest account, which may be shared by several users.
- The **Password Never Expires** option lets the user keep his or her password as long as desired. If you do not enable this option, the user must change the password on the schedule dictated by the Account Policies dialog. See Section 2.7.
- The **Account Disabled** check box turns off the account without deleting it. This option is useful if a user will be on vacation for three months and you want to make sure the account is secure. You might also use it if you wanted, for example, to disable the guest account for a period of time.

Administrative Strategy

Passwords for new accounts

You have two choices when creating passwords for a new account. First, you can ask the user for his or her initial password and use that. The disadvantages to this approach are: 1) There is a security risk whenever someone tells you a password and you write it down, and 2) You may not be able to get in touch with the user before you create the account. Second, you can use a default password like "PASSWORD," or leave the password blank. You can then force the user to change the password using the **User Must Change Password at Next Logon** check box.

Two buttons at the bottom of the new user dialog in Figure 2.3 allow you to assign the new account to a group and to customize the user's profile. The **Groups** button is important: The group or groups of which the user is a member determines the user's rights on the system. By default a new user belongs to the Users group. When you click on the **Groups** button you will see a dialog like the one shown in Figure 2.4.

Different users need to belong to different groups depending on how they will use the machine. The list below offers some guidelines in choosing the appropriate group for a new user.

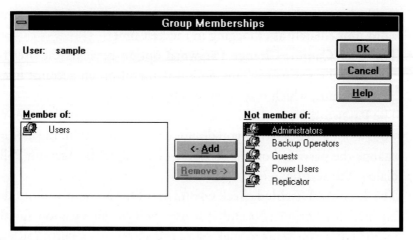

Figure 2.4
The Groups dialog.

- A member of the **Administrators** group can do anything to the machine at any time. Therefore, there are few good reasons to make a user a member of this group. As mentioned previously, full administrative privileges should be guarded.

- A member of the **Power Users** group can work with the machine as though he or she is the owner of it. Quite a few administrative powers are granted to the Power User group, but there are enough restrictions to prevent security problems. For example, a power user can create and modify new accounts, but cannot delete or edit accounts created by the administrator. A power user cannot take ownership of files, preventing the user from tampering with other user's files. A power user cannot modify the Security log. A power user can share printers and drives. In most cases where you want the user to have administrative powers, the Power User group is the appropriate choice.

- A member of the **Users** group can log on, do his or her work, and log back out. In addition, a user can shut down the system.

- A member of the **Backup Operators** group is like a user, but can also backup and restore files and directories. A backup operator is therefore a potential security risk and should be chosen carefully.

- A member of the **Guest** group has almost the same privileges as a user. If you permit guest logons, you can selectively lock guests out of different parts of the system by changing guest access to things like the printer, files, and so on.

- The **Replicator** group is special. See Section 13.6 for details. You should never make a user a member of this group.

If the new user belongs in the Users group, then you need do nothing: NT automatically places all new users in the Users group by default. If you want to make the user a member of a different group, you should click on the "Users" group in the left hand list and click the **Remove** button to eliminate user privileges. Then choose a new group and press the **Add** button. You can also create your own groups as discussed in Section 2.4.

The **Profile** button in Figure 2.3 lets you enter a *logon script* and *home directory* for the user, as shown in Figure 2.5. The logon script causes a batch file to execute each time the user logs in. The home directory gives the user a personal work area that is used as the default directory when the user logs in or starts an application.

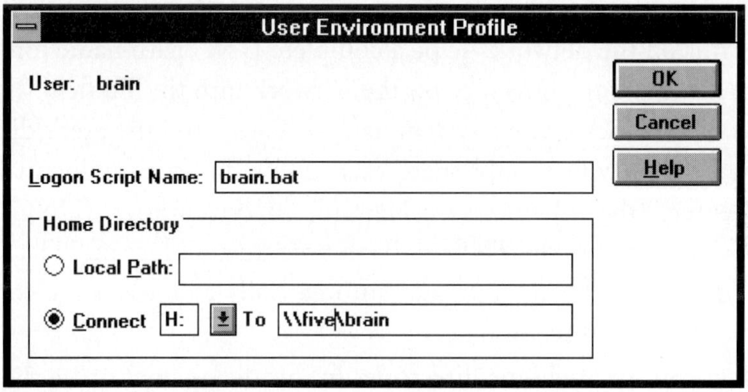

```
┌──────────────────────────────────────────────────────────────┐
│ ▬       │        User Environment Profile              │
├──────────────────────────────────────────────────────────────┤
│                                                  ┌──────────┐  │
│  User:   brain                                   │   OK     │  │
│                                                  └──────────┘  │
│                                                  ┌──────────┐  │
│                                                  │  Cancel  │  │
│                                                  └──────────┘  │
│  Logon Script Name: │brain.bat           │      ┌──────────┐  │
│                                                  │  Help    │  │
│  ┌─Home Directory────────────────────────┐      └──────────┘  │
│  │  ○ Local Path: │                   │                      │
│  │                                                             │
│  │  ◉ Connect  │H:│ │▼│ To │\\five\brain         │          │
│  └─────────────────────────────────────────┘                 │
└──────────────────────────────────────────────────────────────┘
```

Figure 2.5
The Profile dialog.

NT creates a directory called `users` during installation, generally at `c:\users`. Initially that directory contains one subdirectory named `default`. It is the default directory for guest accounts and any other account that does not have a home directory. You can create additional subdirectories in the `users` directory for each new user. By keeping all user directories in one place like this, it makes it extremely easy to back up all user accounts. See Section 10.4 for more information on choosing the best location for home directories.

Home directories can be placed either on the local hard disk, or on a network drive. In either case the system will create the directory that you specify in this dialog, provided that the file names and paths are valid. Alternatively, you can use the File Manager to create the directory, and then type the path name of the new directory into the Profile dialog. Enter the entire path name, including the drive letter or system name, into the appropriate field.

For example, if you want to create a new home directory for the user "jones" on the local hard disk, you would type `c:\users\jones` into the **Local Path** field. You could also type `c:\users\%USERNAME%` into the **Local Path** field. `%USERNAME%` is a variable that represents the user name for the account. When used in this way, NT substitutes the account's user name automatically.

If instead you want to create the user's home directory on a drive located elsewhere on the network, click on the **Connect** option, and choose a drive letter for the user's home directory. When the user logs in, the user will see the chosen drive letter in the File Manager, or at the MS-DOS prompt, as a separate drive. That drive will be associated strictly with the user's home directory, wherever it is on the network. Type a complete UNC path name for the location of the user's home directory on the network into the **To** field. For example, if the drive is located on a system named "sales," and the user's directory is shared as "jones" (you should share each user's directory individually), you would enter the Universal Naming Convention (UNC) name `\\sales\jones` into the **To** field. Each time the user logs in, NT creates the specified drive letter for the user and automatically establishes the connection to the remote home directory.

When you specify home directories in this dialog, make sure that the file names and path names used are valid. Don't use invalid characters. If the directory is on a DOS File Allocation Table (FAT) file system, do not use names outside the 8-dot-3 naming convention. For example, if the user name has more than eight characters in it, and you use the `%USERNAME%` placeholder, the home directory will not get created. The system will generate an error when it tries to create the home directory, and you will have to go back and create it by hand.

The logon script is a batch file that is executed whenever the user logs on. It has a function similar to the Startup group in the Program Manager, but because it is a batch file it can contain, for example, branching and looping state-

Home directories

Every user should have their own home directory. If you are using NTFS, then you may want to secure each home directory so that each user is the only person who can initially use it. Home directories should be clustered together in one place (e.g., under the `c:\users` directory) to make backing them up and inspecting them easier. You may also want to attach each user's home directory to a specific drive letter when they log on. For example, you might elect to have every user see an H drive ("H" for Home) at log on. Use the **Connect** option to do this.

ments. You place all logon scripts in the Windows NT replicator import script directory (e.g., `c:\winnt\system32\repl\import\ scripts` if you followed the normal installation procedure. See Section 13.6 for information about the replicator), and they can be unique for each user or shared by many. Type only the file name of the script into the **Logon Script Name** field. NT will automatically look for it in the Windows NT directory. If you want to let the user have control over the startup script, you can place a call to a second batch file (placed in the user's home directory) in the original script.

Once you have specified all of the parameters for the new account and pressed the **OK** button in Figure 2.3, NT will create the new account. The user can log on as soon as you log out.

To later modify or customize an existing user account, you use the same tools. For example, you will want to modify your personal user account, as described in Section 2.3. You can either double click on the user's account in the account list of the User Manager, or single click to select it and then choose the **Properties** option in the **User** menu. You can change the logon ID of an account using the **Rename** option in the **User** menu. It is also possible to create a new account by copying an existing account and modifying it. Select an existing account and then choose the **Copy** option in the **User** menu. Modify the copy as appropriate. To delete an existing account, select the account and then choose the **Delete** option in the **File** menu.

A user account generally receives its user rights from the group or groups to which it belongs. For example, if an account is a member of the Power Users

Log on scripts

As the administrator, you can use Logon Scripts in many different ways to customize the system for yourself or other users. For example, you could have it automatically start up Notepad (or other applications) with a certain file that contains a message of the day. You could have a Logon Script scan the user's directory for unneeded files and delete them to conserve space. You could have it automatically form network connections for specific users (using the `net use` command). You could have it send a message to another machine on the network so that you know when a certain user has logged in (using the `net send` command). See Chapter 10 for more information on the network. If you want users to be able to have their own logon scripts, along with the ability to modify them, then you can enter as the last line in the original script a path that will call a second script in the user's home directory:

```
call %HOMEPATH%\logon
```

Now the users can create their own logon scripts that execute after your initial script.

Creating multiple accounts

If you need to create a number of accounts that are similar, create a single account to act as a template and then copy it for each new account in the set. See Section 2.6 for details.

group, then the account has all of the user rights associated with the Power Users group. If an account is a member of more than one group, then the account has the rights of all groups to which it belongs. It is also possible to assign rights one at a time to an individual account. To do this, select the **User Rights** option in the **Policies** menu. You will see a dialog similar to the one shown in Figure 2.8.

You can choose a specific right in the combo box at the top of the dialog, and then click the **Add** button to reveal a dialog displaying all of the different groups available. If you click the **Show Users** button and scroll down to select an individual user, then that individual user will receive the right chosen. See Section 2.5 for further information on assigning rights to an individual or group.

2.3 Customizing Your User Account

One of the first things that you will want to do as administrator is customize your personal user account. NT created this account for you when you first installed the system. You will log on using this account whenever you plan to *use* your machine. If you log on with the administrator's account all of the time, you risk damaging the operating system or applications by inadvertently modifying or erasing critical files. It is a good idea to reserve your use of the administrator's account for administrative tasks such as creating new accounts, tuning the system, and so on.

There are several things you can do to customize your account. As discussed in the previous section, you can:

- Update your user name and description
- Change the group that you belong to so you have more user rights
- Create a home directory
- Create a logon script

To change your personal account, log on as the administrator. Start the User Manager application by finding its icon in the Administration Tools group of the Program Manager. You will see a window displaying a list of accounts as well as a list of available groups. See Figure 2.2 for an example. Double click on your user account. A new window will appear displaying your account information, as shown in Figure 2.3. Your user name is fixed (use the **Rename** option in the **User** menu to rename an account), but everything else in the window is changeable and easily modified. See Section 2.2 for a complete description of each field.

To change your user rights, you can do one of two things. The easiest is to click on the **Groups** button, where you will see that your account is a member of the Administrators group. It is a good idea to use a different group for your personal account to keep a mental division between "using" the system and "administering" it. Click on "Administrators" and then click the **Remove** button. Now click on the Power Users or Users group and click the **Add** button. A member of the Power Users group can do almost anything that an administrator can do, as seen in Section 2.1. A normal user has less privileges. It is also possible to add specific rights to your account individually, or to create a new group for yourself with certain rights. See Section 2.5 for details. Click the **OK** button to return to your account information when you are done adjusting your group memberships.

To modify your home directory and logon script, click the **Profile** button. The logon script is similar to the Startup group in the Program Manager. It is a batch file executed whenever you log on. The logon script file must be placed in the replicators import directory: Enter the name of the file (not the path, just the name) into the **Logon Script** field, as described in the previous section. Your home directory is the default directory used whenever any application program displays a File Open or Save As dialog. It generally contains all of your work when logged in as a user, although it is possible to use other directories as well. The home directory can reside on your local system or on a remote system. NT created a directory called "Users" during installation, and you should place all new user directories underneath it in the directory tree. See Section 2.2 for details on creating a home directory.

Now log off as the administrator by either pressing **Ctrl-Alt-Del** and clicking the **Logoff** button, or by choosing the **Logoff** option in the **File** menu of the Program Manager. Log on under your customized user account and see how it feels. Whenever you wish to change this account, log back on as the administrator and adjust it as desired.

2.4 Creating a New Group

Windows NT ships with six predefined groups. These groups have common sets of user rights associated with them. For example, the Guest group contains just the right to log on to the system, while the Power User group contains the right to do almost anything short of violating certain security barriers. See Section 2.1 for a complete list of the associations. A user's account receives its rights depending on the group to which it belongs.

Groups are also used in the File Manager and Print Manager to grant file and printer permissions. See Chapter 11 and Appendix A. You therefore will create new groups for one of two reasons:

- You have a specific set of user rights, not reflected in any of the current groups, that you want to assign to one or more users.

- You have a specific group of users that need access to the same set of files or directories, and it is easier to grant that access by giving it to a single group rather than each user individually.

In the second case, the new group may or may not have any user rights associated with it. If not, then users assigned to the new group will also need to be members of another group, such as Users or Power Users, that does have user rights. The rights of a specific user are a combination of all of the rights found in all groups to which the user belongs.

Creating a new group is a straightforward process. Select the **New Local Group** option from the **User** menu. You will see a dialog similar to the one shown in Figure 2.6.

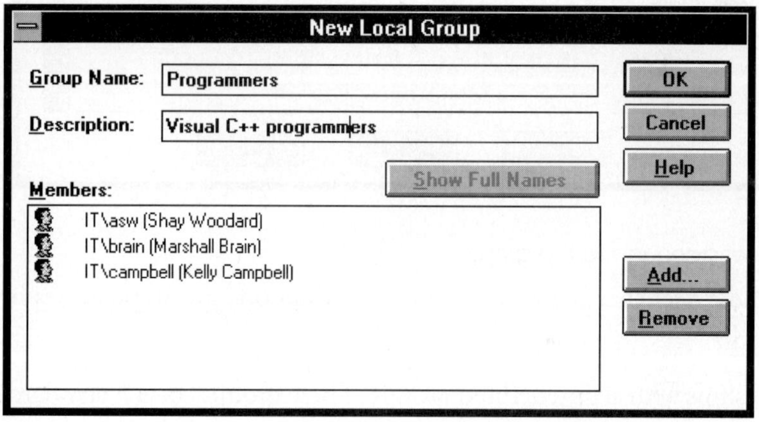

Figure 2.6
Creating a new local group.

This dialog lets you create and describe a new group. You can then add users to the group by pressing the **Add** button. This button presents a dialog like the one shown in Figure 2.7.

You can select user accounts from the current machine, or if the machine is a member of a Domain you can select from the account list on the Domain server as well. See Chapter 13. Once you have added all of your users, the group is complete. See the next section for adding new user rights to the group.

2.5 Assigning New Rights to an Account or a Group

You can assign user rights to an individual account or, more commonly, to a group. Each member of the group acquires any rights assigned to the

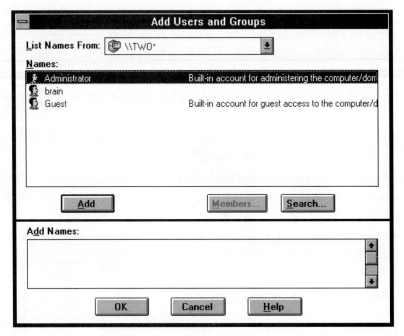

Figure 2.7
Adding user accounts to the group.

group, and a user that is a member of more than one group possesses multiple group rights.

NT ships with six predefined groups. These groups cover a standard mix of user rights. The rights assigned to each of the standard groups are listed in Section 2.1. To give rights to a group that you have created, or to an individual user, choose the **User Rights** option in the **Policies** menu. You will see the User Rights Policy dialog as shown in Figure 2.8. The combo box labeled **Right** lets you choose the right that you wish to assign. The **Show Advanced User Rights** check box at the bottom of the dialog lets you augment this list with advanced rights generally appropriate only for programmers and administrators.

Click the **Add** button to select the user or group that should receive the right. A dialog similar to the one shown in Figure 2.9 will appear. By default it shows only groups. Click on the **Show Users** button to include individual account names in the list if you want to assign a right to a specific user. You can also select a Domain server on your network (see Chapter 13) using the combo box at the top of the dialog to include other user lists.

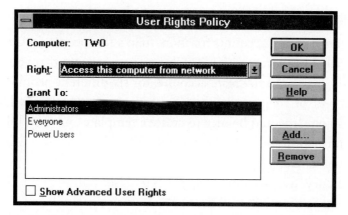

Figure 2.8
The User Rights Policy dialog allows you to assign rights to groups or users.

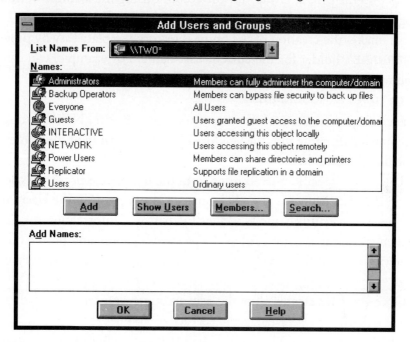

Figure 2.9
The Add Users and Groups dialog.

Click on one or more groups or users and then click the **Add** button. Your selections will appear in the list at the bottom of the dialog. Click **OK** when you have added all appropriate selections to the list. The chosen right will be assigned to each group or account that you picked.

2.6 Creating and Managing Uniform Accounts

If you are creating accounts for more than a few people, it can be bothersome to set all of the parameters for each new user account that you create. For example, you may need to create accounts for six different people in the sales department. All of them probably require the same access privileges, logon script, and so on. It would be nice to create a template and then fill in just the personal information for each new account. The User Manager will let you do just that using its **Copy** option.

Create a new user account using the **New User** option in the **Users** menu, as described in Section 2.2. Call the new account, which will be your template, something generic like "sales." Leave the personal information for the account blank. Set up the proper groups for the account using the **Groups** button. Set the logon script and the home directory using the **Profile** button.

NT makes the creation of the home directory template easy by providing a `%USERNAME%` holder for the current user name. For example, you can type the following string into the home directory field:

```
c:\users\%USERNAME%
```

Each time you create an account from the template, NT will substitute the account's user name into the %USERNAME% portion of the home directory field and create the new home directory.

To create a specific user account from the template, select the "sales" account in the User Manager and click on the **Copy** option in the **Users** menu. Fill in the new account name as well as the personal information for the new user, then create the account. All of the password, group, and profile information previously established will get copied, and a new home directory will be created.

Once you have created all of the sales accounts, you can later modify them as a set as well. In the User Manager select each of the sales accounts by Ctrl-clicking (hold down the control key and click the left mouse button) on them so that all are highlighted. Choose the **Properties** option in the **User** menu. Any changes that you make here will apply to all of the users that you have selected.

2.7 Changing Policies

The **Account** option in the **Policies** menu lets you set several options that determine the behavior of passwords on your system. Users change their pass-

Creating and managing a set of accounts

If you have a set of users that all need identical accounts and identical privileges, then you should create an account template to make the creation of the accounts easier. You should also create a new group and make all of the users a member of that group. You can then grant all of the users in the group access to appropriate files and directories, as well as printers, quite easily. If you ever need to modify the accounts for the set of users, do it by Ctrl-clicking on all of them in the User Manager window and choosing the **Properties** option. You will save a tremendous amount of time.

Creating hundreds of accounts

Let's say that you need to create a set of 100 accounts with the same characteristics. (If you have this many users, you should definitely be using the NT Advanced Server. See Chapter 13). The easiest way to create this many accounts is to place all the user information in a spreadsheet or text file, and then use some form of Macro Recorder to copy and paste each piece of user information from the spreadsheet into the User Manager. The fields in the User Manager will accept the Ctrl-V keystroke as a paste operation. This technique allows you to rapidly create any number of accounts. The initial release of NT does not contain the normal Macro Recorder found in other versions of Windows, so check your spreadsheet or look for third party tools.

words by typing **Ctrl-Alt-Del** while logged in and choosing the **Change Password** option in the resulting dialog box. The Account Policy dialog is shown in Figure 2.10.

You can set four behaviors from this dialog:

- Maximum Password Age
- Minimum Password Age
- Minimum Password Length
- Password Uniqueness

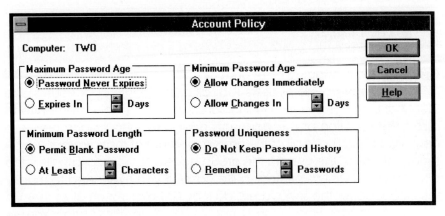

Figure 2.10
The Account Policy dialog.

Maximum Password Age controls how often your system's users have to change their passwords. If the time limit on the account's password is approaching or has actually expired when a user logs into the machine, a dialog box advises the user to change the password.

Minimum Password Age controls how often a user is allowed to change a password. You use this time period in conjunction with **Password Uniqueness.** If your goal is to require a unique password then you should not allow immediate changes. See below for more information.

Minimum Password Length forces users to create passwords of a certain length or greater. A good value is six or more characters if you want users to enter effective passwords.

Password Uniqueness requires users to choose unique passwords when they change passwords. This is done using a history list of previously used passwords, and it forces the user to choose a unique password at each forced password change. If the system did not retain a password history, then when a password expired (as controlled by **Maximum Password Age**), the user could simply reuse the current password or alternate between two passwords, effectively bypassing the intent of required password changes.

In conjunction with **Password Uniqueness,** you should set **Minimum Password Age** to one or more days so that the user actually has to use the new password for some period of time. If a minimum age is not set, and the password history is set to five, for example, the user could immediately change the password five times and again bypass the intent of **Password Uniqueness.**

Administrative Strategy

Password security

Passwords are probably the most important part of the NT security system. If your users have weak passwords, then the security of the system is jeopardized. A weak password is one that is short or non-existent, or static. For example, if users can have null passwords or one character passwords, or if they can keep the same password for two years, then it is much easier for someone to break in. You should set the password policies for your system in a way that encourages users to create effective passwords and to change their passwords with some frequency.

You should also educate users about the importance of passwords so they understand what the security systems in Windows NT are trying to accomplish. NT has several security goals:

- Prevent unauthorized use of the computer and its data
- Prevent theft of data or applications
- Prevent tampering and mistakes from damaging NT or applications
- Provide privacy for individual users
- Document the activities of users in log files for accountability reasons

If users do not secure their individual accounts with effective passwords, then these security goals are compromised.

Using the four password policy fields you can help users create strong passwords. For example, you might set the maximum age to 30 days, so users must change their passwords every month. You might also set the password history list so that it remembers 50 prior passwords for each user, effectively forcing the user to choose a unique password every time. You could then set minimum password age to two days to prevent the user from bypassing the history list. Finally, you can set the minimum password length to six characters to make sure that users do not create short or null passwords that are easy for passers-by to observe.

2.8 Auditing System Usage

Windows NT can track a wide range of user activities and store them in a Security log. You use the Event Viewer (Chapter 8) to examine the log. For example, you can have NT log unsuccessful logon events, file accesses, attempts to shutdown the machine, and so on, and then use the information to check for security threats. You might notice a rash of unsuccessful logon attempts at a certain time, and use that information to catch someone trying to break into the system.

The following successful and failed activities can be logged by NT:

- Logon and Logoff: If you note repeated failures to log on, it probably means that someone is trying to log on over and over again to discover someone's password. If you note the behavior is at certain times or on a certain machine, it may be possible for you to catch the person in the act the next time it happens.

- File and Object Access: You can track failed file accesses and use this information to note if certain users are trying to get into files or directories where they do not belong.

- Use of User Rights: If you note that someone is trying to make use of certain user rights, it may mean that the user is trying to tamper with things, or that you need to give that user more rights than he or she currently possesses.

- User and Group Management: This option tracks use of the User Manager. If you have given other users administrative privileges then you can use this option to track new accounts, or changes to groups and accounts that might create security problems in the future.

- Security Policy Changes: You can use this option to detect if users are trying to tamper with security features, or to note if other administrators are creating security leaks.

- Restart and Shutdown: This option tracks successful and unsuccessful shutdown attempts. These attempts may indicate that someone is trying to shutdown the system to reboot it under a different operating system.

- Process Tracking: This option tracks program activation and exit, handle duplication, and so on.

Initially NT is set to record no security events. You can change this behavior by selecting the **Audit** option in the **Policies** menu of the Audit Policy dialog, as shown in Figure 2.11. In this dialog you determine which events you are interested in, and whether you want to track successes, failures, or both. You set the maximum size of the Security log in the Event Viewer. See Chapter 8.

```
┌─────────────────────────────────────────────────────────┐
│ ─                        Audit Policy                      │
├─────────────────────────────────────────────────────────┤
│  Computer:   TWO                           ┌──────────┐   │
│   ○ Do Not Audit                           │    OK    │   │
│                                            └──────────┘   │
│  ┌─◉ Audit These Events:───────────────┐   ┌──────────┐   │
│                            Success  Failure│  Cancel  │   │
│   Logon and Logoff            ⊠       ⊠    └──────────┘   │
│   File and Object Access      ⊠       ⊠    ┌──────────┐   │
│   Use of User Rights          ⊠       □    │   Help   │   │
│   User and Group Management   ⊠       □    └──────────┘   │
│   Security Policy Changes     □       □                   │
│   Restart, Shutdown, and System  □    □                   │
│   Process Tracking            □       □                   │
└─────────────────────────────────────────────────────────┘
```

Figure 2.11
The Audit Policy dialog.

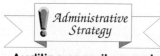

> ! *Administrative Strategy*
>
> **Auditing security events**
>
> Set the Audit Policy in the User Manager to record events that might be useful to you in checking security breaches or inappropriate user behavior. For example, you might want to track unsuccessful logon attempts because that may indicate that someone is trying to crack the system. Or you may want to track attempts to shut down the system because that may show that someone is trying to reboot the machine under DOS. See Appendix G for more information on security policies.

2.9 Setting up Initial File Permissions

When Windows NT installs itself on an NTFS disk partition, it installs a standard set of directories as shown in Section 1.6. These directories, and the files they contain, all have permissions set on them. You will want to check the default permissions and change them if they are too lenient.

As discussed in Appendix A, NTFS allows you to attach extremely specific permissions to directories and individual files. In the case of the operating system files, you probably want to assign permissions that prevent normal users from modifying or deleting any file in the Windows NT directory, or in any application directory. Most users do, however, need to be able to look at, execute, and read the files. Otherwise the user has no way to run any of the programs or to access system resources.

The administrator account can either retain full access on all directories, or it can minimize its own access as well. The latter option has the advantage of protecting the operating system, but forces you, as the administrator, to adjust the permissions every time you want to change something.

Giving the entire NT system directory (c:\winnt) read and execute privileges for everyone is sufficient to allow full use of the system without allowing users any way to delete or modify important system files. Give each user exclusive full access to their own home directories.

2.10 Examples

Let's say you have a lone Windows NT machine in a lab, and you are in charge of administrating the machine. Here are the requirements for the machine:
- Five of the technicians in the lab need to share the computer.
- All five of them need to be able to access a directory that holds daily lab results.
- Two of the technicians need to access a special application directory and its data directory to operate one of the pieces of equipment in the lab. However, you want to prevent the other three technicians from accessing the application because it is very easy for an inexperienced operator to damage the equipment.
- Outside graduate students occasionally visit the lab for a day, and at the end of the day they are asked to write a quick one-page report. These grad students should not be allowed to read or modify any of the files on the machine.

Your job is to configure the machine so that these requirements are met. First of all, in order to meet the third and fourth requirements, the machine needs to have an NTFS partition so you can secure files. If the hard disk has a FAT partition instead, you need to convert it to NTFS. See Chapter 6 for information on creating new partitions.

Next, decide on account names for each of the five users and decide where you will put their home directories. The `c:\users` directory is probably the best place for these directories.

Start the User Manager. The easiest way to create the five accounts is to create an account template as described in Section 2.6. In the template place a default password in the password fields and mark the **Change Password immediately** field. In the **Home Directory** field of the user profile, type `c:\users\%USERNAME%`. You may also want to create a logon script for the users. See Section 2.2 for details. Each of the new users can be a member of the Users group.

Copy the template five times, adding in the personal information for each user. You might want to then log on to each account and tune it appropriately on a per-user basis. For example, you might want to delete the Administrative Tools group from the Program Manager of each account, or add in Program Manager icons for different applications used in the lab. See Appendix F. Note that the NT Advanced Server completely automates these steps with the Profile Editor. See Chapter 13 for details.

Now make sure that the directories holding the special application and data are not available to normal users. Do this using the **Security** menu of the File Manager, as described in Appendix A. To handle the third requirement, create a new group and make the two technicians members of the group. Using the File Manager again, set the permissions on the application and data directories so that the new group can access them.

Probably the best way to handle the graduate students is to use the guest account. With the File Manager, make sure that guests have no access to any directory on the hard disk that contains sensitive information. Mark the **Password Never Changes** check box for the guest account in the User Manager. Then give students the guest password and account name whenever they need to use the machine. They can save their reports onto personal floppy disks.

You may want to make an experienced user in the lab a member of the Power Users group to offload some of the administrative tasks onto someone else. You might also want to designate a backup operator in charge of backing up the machine to tape each night. Make that person a member of the Backup Operators group. See Chapter 4.

You may have security concerns about this machine, especially since it is in an open lab and attached to sensitive equipment. Use the Auditing features described in Section 2.8 to track certain types of behavior. See Chapter 8, as well as Appendix G, for guidance in reading the Security log.

2.11 Conclusion

Accounts are important in a single-machine situation because they let you control access to your machine and protect its security. In a network situation they become even more important because accounts allow multiple users on the net to share drives and files in a secure way. Part 2 of this book discusses several different ways to create accounts on the network.

INSTALLING PRINTERS

Once NT is running and you have adjusted your user account so that it is comfortable, the next thing you need is a printer. With a user account and a printer, you can do most of your day-to-day work. On a stand-alone NT machine used by a single person, this may be all that you ever need to do as the administrator.

In this chapter you will learn how to attach a printer to an NT machine and customize the way that users interact with it. In Chapter 11 you will learn how to share the printer on the network.

3.1 Overview

The Print Manager provides access to printers both on the local machine and over the network. It provides a number of advanced features including time-based and personnel-based access permissions, spooling, priorities, printer queue manipulation, and printer pooling. It supports an incredibly wide variety of printing devices.

From an administrator's standpoint, there are several tasks that you must perform with the Print Manager before users on a given machine can access local printers. First, you must "create" the printer: You must connect the printer to the machine, select a proper device driver to control it, and customize the printer's behavior. You must then grant access to the printer, or deny access to it, for certain users and groups.

You will find that NT makes printer administration easy. It provides a facility for administrating all printers over the network, as discussed in Chapter

11. It also makes it possible to give printer administration privileges to other users and groups. You will quite often grant the user of a private NT machine printer administration privileges, so that the user can customize the printer to his or her liking without needing you to intervene.

3.2 Installing a Printer

Windows NT supports an extremely wide range of printers using printer device drivers. NT comes with drivers for hundreds of different printers, and manufacturers can also supply new drivers with the printers they ship. You can install the printer either during the installation of NT or afterwards.

When you install a printer you are required to do two things. First, you must select an appropriate printer driver so that Windows NT and the printer can communicate. Second, you need to physically cable the printer to one of the ports on the machine. You can connect the printer either to an available serial port or to a parallel port. To begin the process, look at your printer and find out its manufacturer and model number. If it is a new printer, look in the box and see if the manufacturer supplied a diskette containing driver software. If not, it means either that:

- NT already recognizes the printer and has the driver on the distribution disk (there is a high probability that this is the case).
- You will have to do a little legwork to get the driver you need from the manufacturer.
- The printer is compatible with something else that NT already recognizes (e.g., most laser printers are compatible with an HP Laserjet II), so you can use that driver. Consult the printer's documentation.
- It is time to buy a new printer.

The time to check for drivers is *before* you purchase the printer. Windows 3.1 and Windows NT drivers are not compatible, so make sure that NT drivers are available.

To connect a printer, choose an appropriate cable and attach the printer to a port, either parallel or serial, on your machine. If you have a choice, parallel ports are faster and therefore preferred. If you have no experience with this sort of thing, try to contact the printer manufacturer or the manufacturer of your computer, or read the documentation that came with these machines for assistance with cabling.

Administrative Strategy

Using alternative printer drivers

Just about any printer, even if you do not have a specific NT driver for it, can be connected to Windows NT in some way. Generally, any printer has a native mode, but also supports emulation modes. For example, almost all inexpensive laser printers emulate the HP Laserjet II. Almost all dot matrix printers emulate an Epson MX-80. Postscript printers are usually roughly equivalent to one another, so if you are missing a specific PostScript driver for a printer you can often make it work with one of the other PostScript drivers shipped with NT (alternatively, you can send postscript output from the Print Manager to a file using one of the other PostScript drivers, and then send the resulting text file to the printer using the print command in the MS-DOS window). If nothing else, you can pick the plain-Jane "Generic" printer and use it to produce straight text output.

With the printer connected you are ready to perform the administrative task of "creating" it in Windows NT. When you create a printer, you tell NT about the printer and NT creates a printer queue for it. It is possible to create multiple queues for a single physical printer and then give those queues different characteristics.

Log on as the administrator and start the Print Manager application from the Main group in the Program Manager. Use the **Create Printer** option in the **Printer** menu. You will see a dialog like the one shown in Figure 3.1. This dialog lets you select a printer driver and otherwise configure the printer.

In the **Printer Name** field enter a name for the printer. This is the name that will identify the printer to people both on the local machine and on the network. The maximum length is 32 characters. In the **Description** field type a description that briefly summarizes the model, purpose, restrictions, etc., on the printer, up to 64 characters. Now choose a driver using the **Driver** combo box. If you have in your possession a diskette containing the manufacturer's NT driver for the printer, then find the **Other...** selection at the very bottom of the list. Otherwise look for the printer in the list, or choose a compatible printer.

In the **Print To** field select the appropriate port. Choose one of the serial ports if you connected the printer to a serial port (generally labeled COM1,

```
┌─────────────────────────────────────────────────────────────┐
│ ⊟                      Create Printer                         │
├─────────────────────────────────────────────────────────────┤
│                                                               │
│  Printer Name:  │mx-80                         │   ┌────────┐ │
│                                                   │   OK   │ │
│                                                   └────────┘ │
│  Driver:        │Epson MX-80              │ ▼│    ┌────────┐ │
│                                                   │ Cancel │ │
│                                                   └────────┘ │
│  Description:   │old Epson MX-80          │        ┌────────┐ │
│                                                   │ Setup..│ │
│                                                   └────────┘ │
│                                                   ┌────────┐ │
│  Print to:      │LPT1:                    │ ▼│    │Details.│ │
│                                                   └────────┘ │
│      ┌─ ☐ Share this printer on the network ──┐  ┌────────┐ │
│      │                                         │  │Settings│ │
│      │ Share Name: │                  │        │  └────────┘ │
│      │                                         │  ┌────────┐ │
│      │ Location:   │                  │        │  │  Help  │ │
│      └─────────────────────────────────────────┘  └────────┘ │
└─────────────────────────────────────────────────────────────┘
```

Figure 3.1
The Create Printer dialog.

COM2, etc.), or the proper parallel port if you connected it to a parallel port (generally labeled LPT1, LPT2, etc.). If the port you used is not listed, select the **Network Printer...** option in the list and name the port there. You can also choose to redirect the printer's output to a file if desired, rather than routing it to a physical port. Choose the **File** option. Every time you try to print something, you will be asked to enter a file name.

Administrative
Strategy

Printing to files

 In some cases, users may want to print a document to a file on one machine, and then take the printed output to another, different machine to actually print it. For example, users might want to produce PostScript files on an NT machine so that they can send a disk containing the PostScript output to a typesetter who has a 2,400 DPI Linotype PostScript printer attached to an Apple Macintosh. This is easy to do. In the Print Manager create a printer. Choose a PostScript driver (in our office we have had good luck with the "Digital PrintServer 40" driver in this exact situation). In the **Print To** field choose **File**. Now whenever users print to that printer, they will be asked to enter a file name for the PostScript output, and that file can be sent to the typesetter.

Once you select the port, press the **Settings** button in the Create Printer dialog. If you are using a parallel printer port you will see a dialog similar to the one shown in Figure 3.2. If you chose a serial port you will see a dialog similar to that shown in Figure 3.3. Update the fields as necessary to match your hardware. See the documentation for your printer, or contact the printer manufacturer, if you have problems with any of the settings.

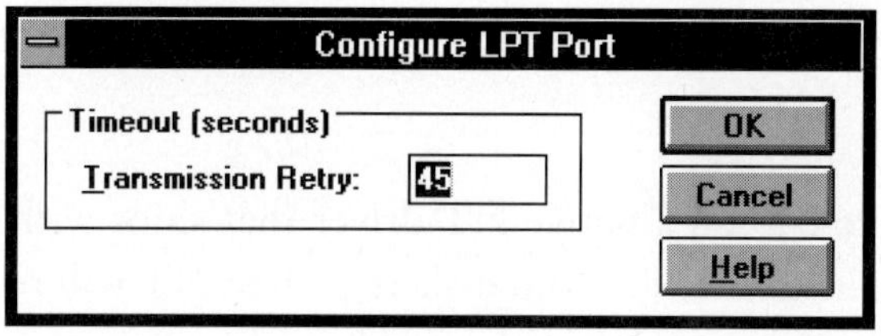

```
┌──────────────────────────────────────────┐
│ ─          Configure LPT Port             │
│ ┌Timeout (seconds)──────────┐  ┌────────┐ │
│ │ Transmission Retry:  [45] │  │   OK   │ │
│ │                           │  ├────────┤ │
│ └───────────────────────────┘  │ Cancel │ │
│                                 ├────────┤ │
│                                 │  Help  │ │
│                                 └────────┘ │
└──────────────────────────────────────────┘
```

Figure 3.2
The Configure LPT Port dialog.

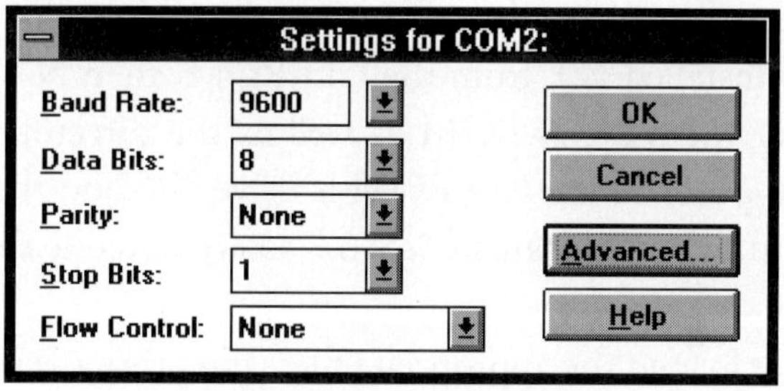

```
┌──────────────────────────────────────────┐
│ ─          Settings for COM2:             │
│  Baud Rate:  [9600]  ▼    ┌────────────┐  │
│  Data Bits:  [8]     ▼    │     OK     │  │
│  Parity:     [None]  ▼    │   Cancel   │  │
│  Stop Bits:  [1]     ▼    │ Advanced...│  │
│  Flow Control: [None] ▼   │    Help    │  │
│                           └────────────┘  │
└──────────────────────────────────────────┘
```

Figure 3.3
The settings for COM Port dialog.

The Create Printer dialog contains a section that allows you to share the printer on the network. This capability is discussed in Chapter 11. There are also a number of printer customizations that are available through the **Details** button, as described in the next section. It is easy to change printer properties at any time, so for now go ahead and create the printer by clicking on the **OK** button.

In most cases you will see a dialog like the one shown in Figure 3.4. The Print Manager uses this dialog to request the location of the drivers it needs. Answer this dialog as follows:

- If the manufacturer has supplied the driver on a diskette and you have chosen the **Other...** option in the **Driver** combo box, then insert the diskette and direct the dialog to the appropriate drive (A: or B:).

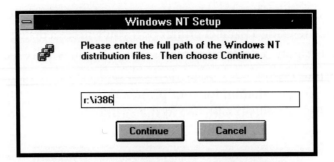

Figure 3.4
The Setup dialog.

- If you have chosen a native NT driver that ships with NT, and if you originally installed NT from diskettes, then NT will request a diskette. Enter the appropriate drive letter (A: or B:). When you click the **OK** button, the A: or B: Drive will spin and the system will ask you for one of the installation diskettes by number.

- If you have chosen a native NT driver that ships with NT, and if you originally installed NT from the CD-ROM, then NT needs both the drive letter for the CD-ROM as well as the directory that holds the drivers. In our case the CD-ROM is drive "R" and the directory containing the drivers is named "i386," so we entered `r:\i386` at the prompt.

Once NT has loaded the appropriate files, the printer is ready to use. You will see a new window for it representing its printer queue in the Print Manager. See the next section for customizations.

3.3 Customizing Printer Behavior

In the Print Manager, each printer that you have installed has a separate window. You can customize a printer at any time by selecting the printer's window in the Print Manager and then selecting the **Properties** button in the **Printer** menu. You will see a dialog identical to the Create Printer dialog shown in Figure 3.1.

3.3.1   The Details Dialog

Click on the **Details** button shown in Figure 3.1. The dialog shown in Figure 3.5 will appear.

Administrative Strategy

Finding printer drivers

If you do not know where the native drivers are on the CD-ROM, then in the dialog shown in Figure 3.4 type the root directory of the drive containing the CD-ROM (for example, R:\). The loader will fail on the first file it searches for and tell you the file's name. You can then switch to the File Manager and search for that file on the CD-ROM. Return to the Print Manager and try again.

(This is a special note to those of you who had to jump through several hoops to get NT to load in the first place, and now do not actually have access to the CD-ROM drive in NT mode. Type the root directory of your hard disk into the dialog. Let the loader fail and tell you the name of the file it wants. Now, shut down NT and switch to a mode that lets you read the CD-ROM drive. Copy the needed file from the CD-ROM to a floppy disk, restart NT, and create the printer again. It may take several repetitions of the process, but it will get the job done. The alternative is reinstallation.)

```
                        Printer Details - mx-80

Available From:  12:00 AM    To:  12:00 AM             OK

Separator File:  [                        ] [...]     Cancel

                                                     Job Defaults...
Print to Additional Ports:    Priority:   1            Help
LPT2:
LPT3:                         Print Processor:  WinPrint
COM1:
COM2:                         Default Datatype:  RAW
COM3:

   Delete Port               ☐ Print Directly to Ports
```

Figure 3.5
The Printer Details dialog.

The first thing that you can set in the Printer Details dialog is the printer availability. If the printer lives in a room that is open only between 9:00 AM and 5:00 PM, you can modify the **Available** fields to reflect this schedule.

You can also specify a separator file that is printed between jobs. NT provides several different files depending on the type of printer you have. The supplied separators are intended for PCL and PostScript printers and are named accordingly. To select a separator, click the "..." button to the right of the field. Change into the `c:\winnt\system32` directory and look for files having a ".sep" extension. Try several out. They are modifiable, but are written in special printing languages that require expertise to decode and edit. If you know the page description language for your printer you can, in theory, create any type of separator page you like using those supplied as examples.

It is also possible to *pool* printers using the **Print to additional ports** list. A printer pool is a set of identical printers connected to a single printer queue. The queue chooses the first available printer in the pool when it needs to print something. For example, say you have an excessive amount of printing taking place in a particular office, or that print jobs take quite awhile to complete and several people are generating output. In a situation like this you need several identical printers to meet the demand. You could set up all of the printers individually, but this places the responsibility for finding a free printer on the users.

A better option is to create a pool. Connect a set of identical printers to the same machine. Create a new printer as described in Section 3.2 and establish one of the ports as the main port in the **Create Printer** dialog. In the **Print to Additional Ports** list seen in Figure 3.5 select the ports for the remaining printers in the pool. The users will see the collection of printers as a single device in the Print Manager. When someone prints to the pool, NT will pick the first available printer for each print job in the queue. Pools do not work unless all of the printers in the pool are identical, because only one driver can be chosen for all of the printers in a pool.

The Print Manager automatically spools output to the hard disk. When you print, the output is collected by the Print Manager as quickly as possible, stored on disk, and then fed to the printer as a background task so you can continue with other work. If you want to bypass print spooling and print directly to a port, click on the **Print Directly to Ports** check box. There are several disadvantages to doing this, the main one being that you have to wait for the entire print job to complete each time you print something. Do not print directly to a port unless you need to meet specific constraints for your printing hardware.

NT allows you to create multiple print queues for the same physical printer. There are several reasons why you might choose to do this. For example, you might wish to allow other people on the network to print on your printer only in the morning because you are out of the office. In the afternoons, you want to have free access to the printer without interruptions from other users. To create this arrangement, create two separate printers that use the same physical printer and port using the **Create Printer** option. In one of the printers set the time limits as appropriate in the Details dialog. Share this printer on the network. See Chapter 11. Use the other printer yourself without any time con straints.

Another application of this technique uses the **Priority** field in the **Details** dialog. Create two printers for the same physical device, share one on the network with a low priority, and keep the high priority copy to yourself. In the **Priority** field, 1 is the lowest priority and 99 is the highest.

Administrative Strategy

Multiple printer queues
   It is possible and often useful to create multiple printer queues for the same physical printer under the Print Manager. You might set the properties of one of the windows to a different available time, or you might have two windows with different paper orientations or priorities. By sharing one printer on the network and keeping one for local users, you allow customized access to the printer by different users.

3.3.2   Document Properties Dialog

In the Printer Details dialog (Figure 3.5) is a **Job Defaults** button that opens the Document Properties dialog. This dialog allows you to modify printer characteristics such as the orientation of the paper (portrait or landscape), the default number of copies, the halftone behavior of the printer, and other options such as the resolution and color characteristics. See Figure 3.6.

3.3.3   Printer Setup Dialog

By pushing the **Setup** button in Figure 3.1, you arrive at the Printer Setup dialog as shown in Figure 3.7. This dialog allows you to set the types of forms found in each paper tray, the amount of memory in the printer, and the font cartridges loaded on the printer. This dialog looks different for different printers, depending on the capabilities of the printer.

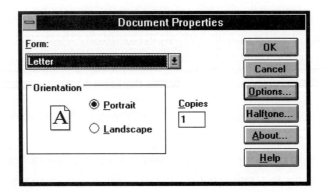

Figure 3.6
The Jobs Defaults dialog.

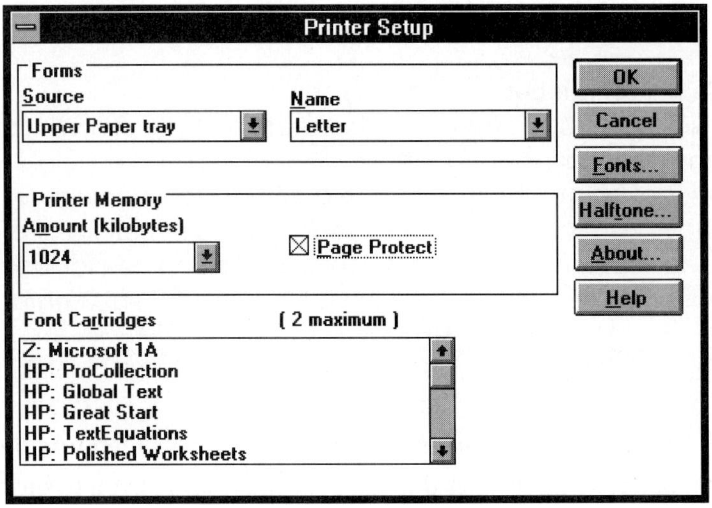

Figure 3.7
The Setup dialog.

NT comes with several forms of its own. You can also name and customize your own forms using the **Forms** option in the **Printer** menu. See Figure 3.8. To create a custom form, you select the size of the form and its margins, and give it a new name. For example, say you have an invoice that is 6 inches by 8 inches, and the top two inches contain your logo. You can easily create this invoice in the Forms dialog, call it "invoice," and then assign it to a paper tray in the Setup dialog above.

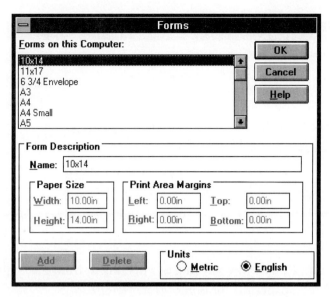

Figure 3.8
The Forms dialog.

3.4 Manipulating the Printer Queue

When a user has Print access to the printer, all that the user can do is print a file. When a user has Manage Documents access to a printer, the options in the **Document** menu of the Print Manager become available.

A user who has Full Control access to the printer can additionally change the order of documents in the printer queue, pause/resume/purge the printer queue, change printer properties, remove the printer, and change printer permissions. You will want to give users and groups various permissions depending on their requirements.

Document order in the print queue is easily changed simply by dragging the different documents to their desired location in the queue. The **Document** menu also offers the following options for manipulating documents:

- Remove Document: Deletes a specific document from the print queue. Select the document in the printer's window and then choose this option.
- Details: Allows the user to see a variety of information about the document, and to also set several parameters. See Figure 3.9. Select the document and then choose this option.
- Pause, Resume: Pauses and resumes the printing of a single document. Select the document and then choose this option.

```
┌──────────────────────────────────────────────────────────────┐
│ ▬                        Document Details                       │
├──────────────────────────────────────────────────────────────┤
│  Document Title:  Paintbrush - (Untitled)          ┌─────────┐ │
│                                                    │   OK    │ │
│  Status:      Printing        Pages:   1           └─────────┘ │
│                                                    ┌─────────┐ │
│  Size:        412044          Owner:   Administrator│ Cancel  │ │
│                                                    └─────────┘ │
│  Printed On:  mx-80           Notify:  ┌──────────┐┌─────────┐ │
│                                        │Administrator│  Help   │ │
│  Printed At:   9:51 AM        Priority:└──────────┘└─────────┘ │
│                                        ┌──────┐▲              │
│  Processor:   winprint                 │1     │▼              │
│                               Start Time:┌──────────┐▲        │
│  Datatype:    NT JNL 1.000             │12 : 00 AM │▼        │
│                               Until Time:┌──────────┐▲        │
│                                        │12 : 00 AM │▼        │
│                                        └──────────┘          │
└──────────────────────────────────────────────────────────────┘
```

Figure 3.9
The Details dialog.

- Restart: Restarts the printing of a document from the beginning in the event of a paper jam or other printer failure.

It is also possible for the administrator, a power user, the owner, or a user with Full Control permissions to pause and resume the printer itself in the **Print** menu or to purge the entire print queue.

3.5 Printer Security: Permissions and Auditing

Printers can have permissions in the same way that files can. For example, you can allow only certain individuals or groups to access a printer. You can also vary the *amount* of access that different users or groups have to a printer: You can let one user fully administrate a printer while another can do nothing more than print to it. To take advantage of permissions, choose a printer in the Print Manager and select the **Permissions** option from the **Security** menu. You will see a dialog like the one shown in Figure 3.10 for the chosen printer.

This dialog works in exactly the same way that it does in the File Manager. See Appendix A for details. You can add groups or specific users to the list using the **Add** button. For each user or group you can select permissions from the following set:

- No Access: The user or group is specifically denied access to the printer.
- Print: The user or group can print documents.
- Manage Documents: The user or group can print, and can also use options in the **Document** menu.

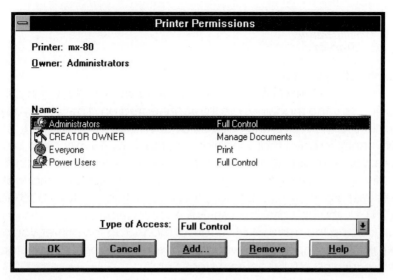

Figure 3.10
The Printer Permissions dialog.

- Full Access: The user has full administrative access to the printer, can change its properties and documents, can grant permissions to other users, remove the printer, change the order of documents in the printer queue, pause/resume/purge the printer queue, and so on.

If you are administering several personal machines that have printers, you will probably want to set up the printers yourself but then give the owners of each machine Full Access permissions to their private printer so they can adjust and customize things as they see fit. The other alternative is to restrict individual access by users and administrate the printers over the network to save yourself legwork. The **Server Viewer** option in the **Printer** menu allows remote administration, and is discussed in Chapter 11.

It is also possible to monitor printer use in the same way that it is possible to monitor user activities. See Section 2.8. Choose the **Audit** option in the **Security** menu to select the different printing events that you wish to audit. The selected events are stored in the Security log, and are easily viewed using the Event Viewer, as described in Chapter 8. Note that in order to use printer auditing, you must enable the auditing features in the User Manager first. See Section 1.5.

Printer auditing gives you the ability to find out exactly who is printing what when. You can audit everyone, or selected users or groups. You can audit for success or failure on five different types of activities:

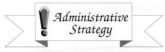

Administrating printers

You can administrate printers by walking around to each individual machine or, if the machines are interconnected on a network, you can administrate them over the network as described in Chapter 11. If your facility tends to have many individual printers tied to machines in user's offices, you probably want to consider giving each user control of his or her printer. To do that, you can either make the user a member of the Power User group (which also has other implications as described in Section 2.1), or you can give the user Full Access permissions on the printer. By off-loading the administrative task of managing the printer, you often make your life simpler. However, this approach will be unacceptable if your are running a fully secure system. See Appendix G.

- Print: An audit record is produced each time a user prints a document.
- Full Control: An audit record is produced each time the user changes job settings, shares a printer, changes printer properties, or pauses/restarts/moves/deletes documents.
- Delete: An audit record is produced each time the user deletes a printer.
- Change Permissions: An audit record is produced each time the user changes printer permissions.
- Take Ownership: An audit record is produced each time the user takes ownership of a printer.

Figure 3.11 shows a typical audit dialog. In this dialog you can add users or groups, and you can select exactly which activities you want to audit for each.

Each printer has an owner. The **Take Ownership** option in the **Security** menu allows you to take ownership of the printer. Generally you will want to make the administrator the owner of all printers. Administrators and users having Full Control access to the printer can take ownership of it. When a person takes ownership, he or she can do anything to the printer.

3.6 Examples

Let's say that you are the administrator for a small company that has not yet installed a network. You have three NT machines, each of which has its own

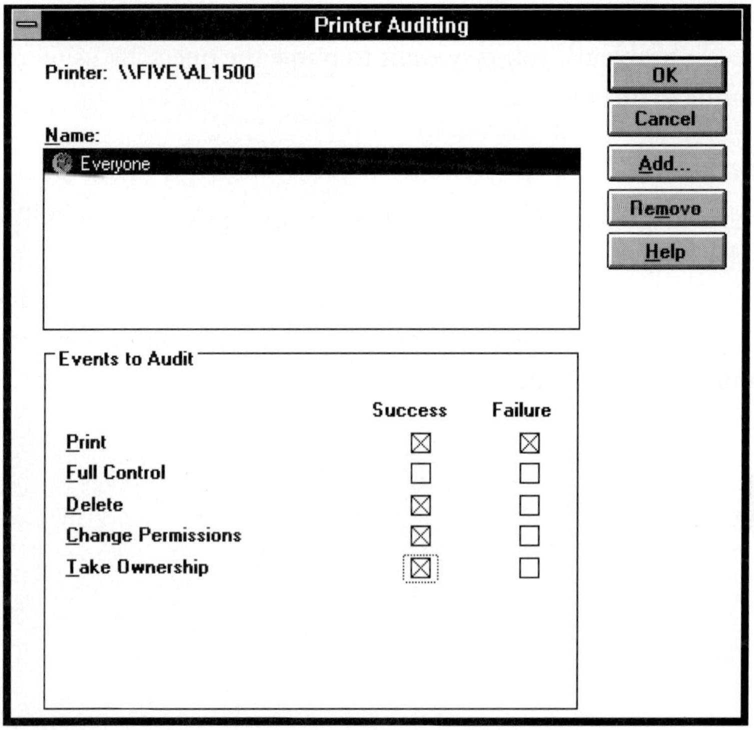

Figure 3.11
The Audit dialog.

printer, out in different users' offices. You will probably want to create each printer and then, if the users are fairly sophisticated, give each one Full Control permissions on their printers. For less sophisticated users, you will probably want to give them Manage Documents or Print permissions.

If security is an issue, you should audit everything that everyone does so that you can check for security breaches. You should give no one more than Manage Documents permissions. You will probably want to give certain users No Access permissions so that they cannot use a given printer.

Let's say that the company acquires a new NT machine for the order processing department. This machine uses a laser printer to produce invoices, packing slips, and receipts, and the load is greater than one printer can handle. You can purchase several identical printers and pool them together so that the load is balanced across all of the printers simultaneously.

One day you get called and a printer has hung, is printing garbage, or has a paper jam. You can turn the printer off, fix it, turn it back on, and then reprint the last document using the **Restart** option in the **Document** menu. In the case of severe problems, you may want to purge the queue by using the **Purge** option in the **Printer** menu.

3.7 Conclusion

In this chapter you have seen how to create a printer on an NT machine and you have also learned a number of customizations that make your printer more useful. Printers on a single machine are generally under-utilized however. In Part 2 of this book you will see how to share printers on the network so that you can increase their usefulness.

BACKING UP DISKS

4

One of the most important features of the Windows NT operating system is security. An NT machine, with appropriately configured NTFS partitions, is secure against theft of on-line data, as well as against accidental or malicious loss of data. For example, a new user cannot delete the operating system directory. System integrity is high because only the administrators can modify the operating system. This in turn leads to system reliability. Users can trust an NT machine.

But what if the hard disk crashes? Suddenly, the reliability of the operating system has been compromised by the hardware. NT solves this problem in two ways: It provides a convenient and easy tool to back up data on the hard disk to tape, and it also provides a simple tool for interfacing NT with an Uninterruptable Power Supply (UPS). With a UPS in place, one of the leading causes of hard disk failure is removed. This chapter discusses the Tape Backup tool, while the next chapter talks about the UPS management facilities.

4.1 Overview

The Windows NT Tape Backup program is a simple and straightforward tool written by Conner Software. It provides basic backup and restore services on a wide variety of high-capacity tape systems, and is more than adequate for backing up individual machines and small networks. If you need to back up a large network, or if you are looking for advanced features such as autonomous start times, repeatable network images and so on, you may wish to investigate alternative commercial products from Conner and others.

The Backup Program provided with NT resides in the Administrative Tools group in the Program Manager. It allows you to selectively back up an entire disk or disks, both on the local machine or over the network. You can also choose individual directories or files. It is possible to form a complete image, as well as incremental images.

If the data chosen requires more than one tape, then the program allows you to span tapes without difficulty. When a single backup requires more than one tape, a *catalog* is stored on the last tape. The catalog makes it easy for the backup program to display the directory of files on the tapes without having to scan the entire set. When the system needs the catalog, it will prompt you to insert the last tape in a collection. NT also allows you to build a partial catalog of an individual tape accidentally separated from its set, although this option is time consuming.

If a single backup session does not fill a tape, then it is possible to combine multiple *sets* on a single tape using the **Append** option. For example, if your system's hard disk fills one quarter of a 2 Gigabyte tape, you can append more than one backup session onto the unused end of the tape.

In order for your backup activities to be effective, they have to be done frequently and consistently, and they need to have some redundancy built into them. For example, if you back up your system once a month, then it is possible to lose up to a month's work after a disk crash. Even if you meticulously back your system up every day, however, you can still lose all your data if you lose the tapes. If the building burns down, you have nothing. It is therefore important to keep backup tapes off-site as well as on-site. The on-site copies are useful when a hard disk fails, while the off-site copies help you to recover from catastrophes.

A large company that understands the value of its data will typically have a complete backup plan. For example, every Saturday night the administrator makes two complete backups of the entire system or network. One copy gets stored locally, and the other is kept off-site. Then each weeknight the operator makes two incremental backups of the system (an incremental backup stores just those files that were modified that day). One copy is again stored off-site. If a hard disk fails, the company loses one day's work at most. In a bona fide catastrophe that destroys all on-site tapes, the effect is the same. Only a day's work is lost because of the off-site tapes.

You might also consider sending a weekly backup copy hundreds of miles away from your site. A hurricane or earthquake can destroy an entire city, and thus both copies of your data. There is a certain value to having copies of important data two thousand miles away.

In a large company, the system administrator will often hire operators or technicians to perform tape backups. These people need a certain subset of the administrator's rights in order to access files on a secure file system. NT therefore ships with a special group in the User Manager called the Backup Operators group. You can make those people who need access to the backup program members of this Backup Operators group.

Administrative Strategy

Storing your backup tapes

Do not store your backup tapes anywhere near the computer or tape drive that was used to create them. I once worked in a lab that was robbed, and the burglars stole the computer, the tape drive sitting next to it, and the backup tapes that were sitting on top of the tape drive. The lab had no other backups and lost everything.

4.2 Backing Up Your Hard Disk

To back up your hard disk, you need a tape drive and a tape. You also need to make sure that the tape drive was turned on and connected when Windows NT started. Otherwise, the tape drive's device drivers may not have loaded and initialized properly. If you experience problems, you might try shutting down the system and restarting it with the tape drive turned on. The first time you run the Tape Backup software, you will need to load a driver for your tape drive. See Section 7.2 for details.

If you have a single tape drive on the machine, the system will automatically default to it. If you have multiple drives and wish to select among them, choose the **Hardware Setup** option in the **Operations** menu of the Backup program. You will see a dialog like the one shown in Figure 4.1. Select the drive from the list.

To perform a backup, log on as administrator (or as a member of the backup operators group) and find the Backup application in the Administrative Tools group of the Program Manager. Double click on the Application icon and you will see a display similar to the one shown in Figure 4.2.

Figure 4.1
The Hardware Setup dialog.

Figure 4.2
The Backup program.

The window displays two icons. If you double click on the Drives icon you will see a list of drives, both local and networked, that are available on your machine. In Figure 4.3 the machine has a number of networked drives. In Figure 4.4 it has a single local hard disk. If there are drives on the network that you wish to back up, but they do not appear in the Drives window, then use the File Manager to connect to those drives. Exit and restart the backup program to make it aware of the new connections, or select the **Refresh** option in the **Window** menu.

To view the directory listing for a drive, double click on the Drive icon. You will see a new window that is strongly reminiscent of the File Manager, as

Figure 4.3
The Drives window.

shown in Figure 4.4. Options in the **Tree** and **View** menus let you adjust the view in the directory window to your specific preferences in a manner identical to that of the File Manager.

Before you create a backup tape, you must select the directories and files that you want to save. You do this using the check boxes that you see next to each drive, folder, and file. If you wish to back up an entire drive, click the check box next to the Drive icon. All of the check boxes next to each directory and file on that drive will activate as well. You may then choose to specifically deselect individual files you wish to exclude.

One file in particular that you should omit is `pagefile.sys` in the root directory. This is the paging file for Windows NT. If you select the **All File Details** option in the **View** menu you will find that this file has a minimum size of 20 MB, and is generally much larger. If the file is missing when NT starts, the system will automatically create it, so there is no need to waste the time or space necessary to back it up. You may know of other directories or files on the hard disk, such as temporary directories, swap directories, intermediate files, and so on, that you do not need to store on tape because they are useless or easy to restore from a CD-ROM or from another disk on the network.

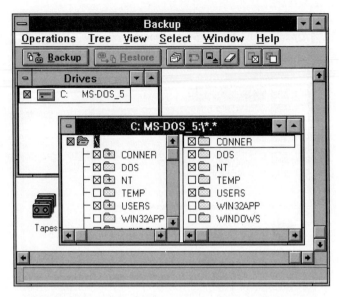

Figure 4.4
The view of an individual drive.

**Administrative
Strategy**

Single machine backups

There generally is no reason to back up most of the `c:\winnt`
directory. If the hard disk fails you will have to reinstall NT from scratch
anyway in order to get to the point where you can start the Tape Backup program. However, the `c:\winnt\system32\config` directory contains the configuration information about user accounts, file
permissions, etc., that are unique to your installation, and you will probably want to back it up.

Conversely, it is also possible to clear all of the check boxes for a drive and
then select individual files or directories to include in a backup set. To do this,
click on the drive's check box to clear it. This will clear the check boxes on all
directories and files for the drive. Now click on the individual items that you
want to copy to tape.

You can back up more than one drive to a tape. Each drive is stored on
tape as a *set*, each with its own description. Alternatively, you can back up each
drive individually to separate tapes. There is no real advantage to either ap-

proach, unless you want to be able to hand tapes for specific drives to certain individuals.

Once you have selected the drives, directories, and files that you want to include on the backup tape, insert a tape into the tape drive. It may buzz and whir for a bit, up to a minute depending on the drive. You can see what is on the tape by double clicking on the Tape icon seen in Figure 4.2 (for more information, see the next section). If the tape is not formatted (some tape configurations require formatting, while others do not) or if you want to erase the tape, you can select the **Erase Tape** option in the **Operations** menu. You will see a dialog like the one shown in Figure 4.5.

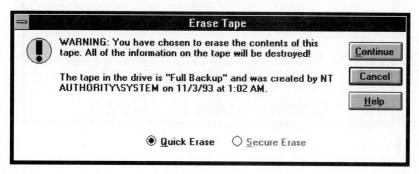

Figure 4.5
The Erase Tape dialog.

Now, select the **Backup** option in the **Operations** menu. You will see a dialog like that in Figure 4.6. With this dialog you select options and create descriptions for the tape you are about to create.

The **Tape Name** field lets you name the tape. The **Verify After Backup** check box causes the Backup program to create the tape and then rewind it and compare its contents with the files on the disk byte-by-byte. This doubles the time that it takes to create the tape, but guarantees that the data stored on it is valid.

The **Backup Local Registry** check box causes registry information to be saved onto the tape as well. The registry contains a variety of information about user configuration options and preferences. The registry contains the list of all user accounts, groups, profiles of each user's windows configuration, and so on.

The **Restrict Access to Owner** check box disallows people, besides the owner of the tape or an administrator, to restore the contents of the tape. The

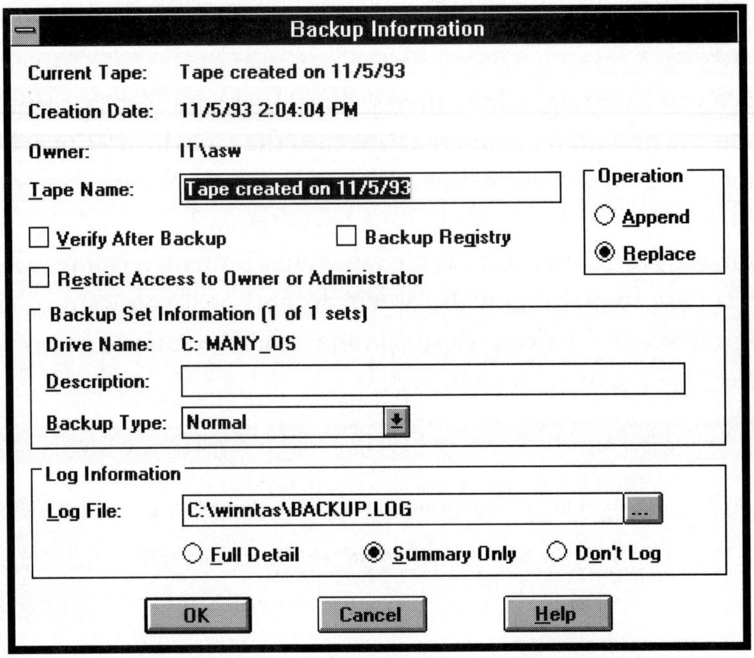

```
┌────────────────────────────────────────────────────────────┐
│ ▬                      Backup Information                    │
├────────────────────────────────────────────────────────────┤
│   Current Tape:    Tape created on 11/5/93                   │
│   Creation Date:   11/5/93 2:04:04 PM                        │
│   Owner:           IT\asw                                    │
│   Tape Name:   ┌──────────────────────────┐  ┌─ Operation ─┐ │
│                │Tape created on 11/5/93    │  │ ○ Append    │ │
│                └──────────────────────────┘  │             │ │
│   ☐ Verify After Backup      ☐ Backup Registry│ ◉ Replace  │ │
│   ☐ Restrict Access to Owner or Administrator └────────────┘ │
│   ┌─ Backup Set Information (1 of 1 sets) ──────────────────┐ │
│   │ Drive Name:   C: MANY_OS                                │ │
│   │ Description: ┌────────────────────────────────────────┐ │ │
│   │             └────────────────────────────────────────┘ │ │
│   │ Backup Type: │Normal              │▼│                   │ │
│   └──────────────────────────────────────────────────────── │ │
│   ┌─ Log Information ───────────────────────────────────────┐│
│   │ Log File:  │C:\winntas\BACKUP.LOG              │ │...│   ││
│   │          ○ Full Detail    ◉ Summary Only   ○ Don't Log  ││
│   └─────────────────────────────────────────────────────────┘│
│         ┌────────┐     ┌──────────┐     ┌────────┐           │
│         │   OK   │     │  Cancel  │     │  Help  │           │
│         └────────┘     └──────────┘     └────────┘           │
└────────────────────────────────────────────────────────────┘
```

Figure 4.6
The Backup dialog.

Operation radio box lets you decide whether you want to append the new backup to existing information on the tape, or to replace whatever is on the tape with the new information. If you have previously created a complete backup of a drive, it is common to append all incremental backups onto the same tape to keep them together.

In the **Backup Set Information** section you can describe each set and control the type of backup operation performed. Five different operations are possible. In order to understand them, you need to understand the concept of an "archive bit." Each file on the disk has associated with it a file name, time stamp, etc., as well as a set of four attribute bits. You can see the values of these four bits for any file by selecting the file in the File Manager and choosing the **Properties** option in the **File** menu. The bits are named "Archive," "Hidden," "Read Only," and "System." The archive bit is set any time a file is created or modified on the disk.

The backup program can optionally clear the archive bit when it saves the file to tape to indicate that it has been archived. This capability facilitates the creation of *incremental* backups. The first backup operation, at the beginning of the week for example, can store the contents of the entire drive and clear all the archive bits. The next backup operation the following day can find just those files that have the archive bit set (the modified files) and save them. An incremental backup is generally quite a bit faster than a normal backup because not many files change from day to day on a typical hard disk.

The different backup operations are listed below. See Section 4.6 for a description of how these different options affect recovery of data.

- Normal: All of the selected files are copied to tape, and their archive bits are cleared in the process.

- Copy: All of the selected files are copied to tape, but their archive bits remain unchanged.

- Incremental: All of the selected files whose archive bits are set are copied to tape, and their archive bits are cleared in the process.

- Differential: All of the selected files whose archive bits are set are copied to tape, but their archive bits remain unchanged.

- Daily Copy: All of the selected files whose archive bits are set, and whose time stamps indicate that they were last changed today, are copied to tape but their archive bits remain unchanged.

You may also choose to log this backup operation to a text file. Type in the file name and choose the level of detail you desire. The **Full Detail** option stores a complete log to disk; all file names copied to the tape end up in the log. The **Summary Only** options store only major operations, such as starting the backup and file failures, to the log file. The **Don't Log** option eliminates the log file.

Finally, choose whether to append this backup to the end of the current tape, or to start at the tape's beginning and replace everything. It is very common to do a Normal (or full) backup at the beginning of the week using the **Replace** option, and then append incremental backups to that same tape at the end of each day.

Once you have selected your options, click the **OK** button to begin the backup operation. You will see a progress dialog like the one shown in Figure 4.7 while the program writes the files to tape. If you want to cancel the operation midstream, click the **Cancel** button.

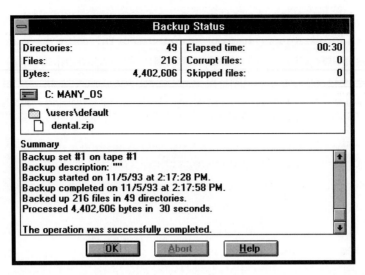

Figure 4.7
The Backup Status dialog.

If the backup operation needs to span multiple tapes, you will be prompted to change tapes when appropriate. Once the backup operation is complete, label and store the tape(s). It is important to keep all of the tapes in a spanning set together, since only the last tape in the set contains the catalog of directory information on the tape. It is possible to extract information from one tape in a spanning set, but the extraction process can take quite awhile. To do this, load the tape into the drive and select the **Catalog** option.

4.3 Restoring Information from a Tape

There are two reasons for restoring information from tape. In the first case, you or one of your users may have accidentally erased a directory or file and need to retrieve it from a tape. In the second case, you come in one morning to find that your hard disk has crashed and needs replacement. The second case presents a somewhat more severe and urgent problem. See the following section for a discussion.

To restore information from a tape, insert the tape in the tape drive and double click on the Tapes icon in Figure 4.1. You will see a display similar to the one shown in Figure 4.8. Double click on the Tape icon to reveal the sets stored on the tape. You may be prompted to insert the last tape in a spanning set of tapes so that catalog information can be retrieved.

Buying a tape drive

If you are going out to buy a tape drive, strongly consider storage capacity, data transfer time, and media cost in your buying decision. Do not look simply at price.

Say that you have a choice between a $500 cartridge drive using 200 MB tapes and a $1,500 Digital Audio Tape (DAT) drive using 2 GB DAT tapes, and you want to back up 1 Gigabyte of disk space. Buy the DAT drive. Sitting around for an hour waiting to change the cartridge tape becomes extremely unpleasant after just a few days, and that unpleasantness lowers the frequency of your backups. It is much nicer to be able to plug in a tape and walk away knowing that the backup will finish on its own. Also, the DAT tapes are so much cheaper and faster that, in the long run, the DAT drive is actually cheaper than the cartridge drive.

We consider the money we spent on our DAT drive to be some of our best-spent money in recent memory. Our backup frequency went up by a factor of ten because the drive is so fast and the tapes are so cheap. It is also very easy and inexpensive to ship large data sets to other sites on DAT tapes.

Backup tapes as portable media

The Tape Backup package provided with Windows NT is so easy to use that you may want to use tapes as a form of high capacity floppy disk for saving old versions of documents, distributing code and data, or archiving important but not currently needed files. For example, if you need to send 200 MB of information to a colleague in Brazil, and if you both use, for example, 4mm DAT tape drives, a DAT tape (at $10 to $15) is probably the cheapest way to send the information.

Double click on one of the sets and you will see the familiar File Manager type of display discussed in the previous section and shown in Figure 4.9. Using the check boxes next to each of the directories and files, you can select individual items to recover, or click on the check box next to the set to recover every-

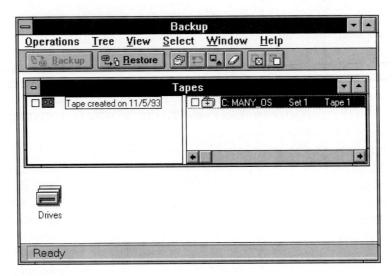

Figure 4.8
The Tapes window.

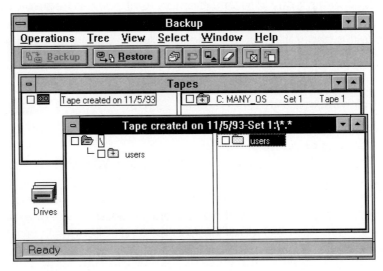

Figure 4.9
The view of an individual tape.

thing in it. Once you have selected the files to recover, choose the **Restore** option in the **Operations** menu. A Restore dialog like the one shown in Figure 4.10 will appear.

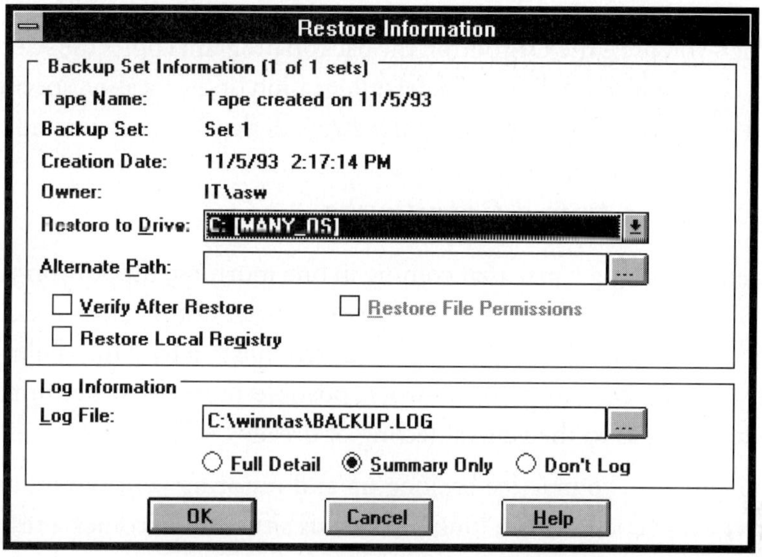

```
┌─────────────────────────────────────────────────────────────┐
│ ─                     Restore Information                     │
│  ┌─ Backup Set Information (1 of 1 sets) ──────────────────┐  │
│  │  Tape Name:      Tape created on 11/5/93                │  │
│  │  Backup Set:     Set 1                                  │  │
│  │  Creation Date:  11/5/93  2:17:14 PM                    │  │
│  │  Owner:          IT\asw                                 │  │
│  │  Restore to Drive: [ C: [MANY_OS]            ]  ▼       │  │
│  │  Alternate Path:   [                         ]  [...]   │  │
│  │    □ Verify After Restore      □ Restore File Permissions│ │
│  │    □ Restore Local Registry                             │  │
│  └─────────────────────────────────────────────────────────┘ │
│  ┌─ Log Information ───────────────────────────────────────┐  │
│  │  Log File:    [ C:\winntas\BACKUP.LOG        ]  [...]   │  │
│  │         ○ Full Detail   ◉ Summary Only   ○ Don't Log   │  │
│  └─────────────────────────────────────────────────────────┘ │
│        [   OK   ]        [  Cancel  ]        [  Help  ]        │
└───────────────────────────────────────────────────────────────┘
```

Figure 4.10
The Restore dialog.

In the Restore dialog you can select the drive on which to restore, as well as an alternate path. Normally the **Restore** option restores files to the directories they came from, creating those directories as necessary. The **Alternate Path** option is useful when you want to use a tape like a large floppy disk and need to restore information from the tape to an arbitrary directory on an arbitrary disk. When you select an alternate path, the **Restore File Permissions** option is available. If selected, the file permissions associated with the original files when they were stored to tape will be copied onto your hard disk. Otherwise the permissions of the alternate directory are inherited by each file as it is restored.

You may also select the **Verification** option, which restores all information from the tape and then rewinds it to compare the tape and hard disk images byte-by-byte.

The **Restore Local Registry** option allows you to recover any registry information stored on the tape. This information gets stored by setting the **Backup Registry** check box when creating a tape.

The **Logging** section lets you record information about the restoration in a log file. The **Full Detail** option stores a complete log to disk. All file names restored from the tape end up in the log. The **Summary Only** options store only major operations, such as starting the restoration and file failures, to the log file. The **Don't Log** option eliminates the log file.

When you press the **OK** button the backup program copies the selected files from the tape to the hard disk at the default location or the location specified. You will see a progress dialog that reports any errors as they are encountered.

4.4 Recovering from a Catastrophe

There is nothing worse that coming in one morning, flipping on your machine, and having it stare at you blankly or emit an obtuse error message that means the rest of your day is going to be wasted due to a hard disk failure. Hard drives somehow seem to pick the worst possible moment to terminate their lives, and that adds to the general feeling of dread.

You will want to practice backing up and restoring your system using the NT emergency repair facility long before this situation becomes a reality. You can document recovery procedures in a panic-free environment this way, and see what works and doesn't. It is also highly recommended that you try to simulate a crash and restore cycle before you have loaded half a Gig of critical data onto your system. Once you have practiced recovery, and as long as you have a backup tape, there is little to worry about following a disk crash. In a worst case situation you will have to reinstall NT from scratch and then recover all the other files and directories around it from the tape.

! Administrative Strategy

Have a few fire drills so you are ready for the real thing.
    You should simulate a disk disaster several times so that you are ready and relaxed for the real thing. Load NT, some applications, and some data onto a disk, back it up, and then simulate a disk crash by reformatting the disk. Practice recovering. **Write down the exact steps you take and save that sheet of paper in a safe place.** When the time comes, you'll be glad you have it.

A total failure or loss of a machine that has a large number of drives can be especially traumatic. It is important to create not only backup tapes of the data on such a machine, but to also create an image of the partition map. The Disk Manager (Chapter 6) can create this image, and you should place it on your emergency repair diskette. If you replace the machine with identical equipment, the Disk Manager can reload the image and re-create your previous system's partition map instantly.

Let's say you do walk in one day to find that your machine will not boot Windows NT because of a fatal hard disk problem. For example, your machine might display a message "No boot device found," meaning that it cannot see the hard disk. If that message is combined with an unusual noise it is a bad sign. If not, it could be something else. Here are the steps you should take:

- With a machine having a non-functional hard disk, the problem can lie in many different places. It could be the drive, the cables to the drive, the interface to the cables, etc. Try turning the machine off and on again to see what happens. If you are so inclined, open up the computer and try reseating the cables. If you are in an organization blessed with a hardware services department, call up the appropriate person.
- If the drive truly is dead, then replace it.
- Reinstall Windows NT on the new disk. You have to do this so that you can get back to a point where you can use the Tape Backup program.
- Use your backup tape and restore your directories. Also restore the `c:\winnt\system32\config` directory to recover your account list, user profiles, and so on. The **Backup Registry** option saves this information, or you can save it explicitly yourself.

There are several other ways, besides a dead hard drive, to make an NT machine totally unusable. For example, you might accidentally erase or corrupt a file that NT needs in order to boot properly, or you might set file permissions on the `c:\winnt` directory in such a way that the operating system directory cannot be used (e.g., by setting No Access permissions for the group Everyone), or you might forget your administrator password and find yourself unable to log on.

To solve these problems, get out the setup disks and the emergency repair disk you created when you installed NT. See Appendix B. Take the following steps:

- Restart the machine with the first setup disk. On PC-based machines, reboot the machine with setup disk 1 in Drive A:. On other platforms, read and follow the manufacturer's instructions.
- On the first screen, type "R" to repair.
- Follow the instructions that you receive. The repair program will look at the situation and advise you depending on what it finds.

If you have forgotten your passwords, you need to reload the user account database that was created during installation. Once you are in the **Repair** section, select the **Inspect configuration registry files** option and then ask the system to replace SAM (the user accounts database). You will lose all of your user accounts on the machine, but you will be able to log on using the original administrator password. If you cannot remember *that* password, then you will need to reinstall NT from scratch.

Installation passwords

When you originally install Windows NT, you might consider using an empty password for the administrator account so that if you forget your passwords you can get back in. This creates a small security hole, but the person will have to have access to your emergency repair disk to use it.

If you modify drivers or system parameters that disable the system, NT will sometimes catch the problem and fix it itself. In other cases it won't. For example, if you load a faulty screen driver, NT will load but you will be unable to see anything. The next time you reboot NT, notice that it has an option that allows you to press the space bar to restore the last known good configuration. You can often use that option to solve a minor driver crisis. Simply reboot NT and press the space bar when the prompt arrives. If you cannot see anything, repeatedly press the space bar as NT is coming up to catch it at the right moment.

4.5 Backing Up with Batch Files

The Tape Backup program has a command line implementation that allows you to create batch files to automate the backup process. For example, if you want to back up certain drives at 3:00 in the morning, you can create a simple batch file and activate it with the `at` command. You can also create multi-drive backup scripts and replay them each day, rather than having to click through all the drives and directories to activate their check boxes.

The command-line version of the Tape Backup software is named `ntbackup`, and is described in the Help file for the Tape Backup program (look under the subject "Batch files"). This version of the program duplicates

almost all of the functionality of the graphical version, and in fact brings up the
graphical version as it runs. The following command demonstrates the process:

```
ntbackup backup c:\users /a /v /t normal
```

This command tells the program to backup `c:\users`, to append the
backup onto the end of the current tape, to verify it, and to do a "normal" backup (as opposed to incremental, differential, etc.). See the Help file for more information on the command line options.

In our office we use a batch file to backup our network at 3:00 a.m. every
day. The batch file looks like this:

```
net use s: \\five\c
net use k: \\two\c
net use l: \\four\c
ntbackup backup c: k: l: s: /t normal /d full
```

The first three lines guarantee that the network drives are connected properly. If the drives are already connected using the File Manager then these lines
will be ignored and are therefore harmless. The last line backs up the four
drives. If for some reason NT was unable to connect to one of the remote
drives, it is also harmless. The backup command will simply ignore that drive
and leave an error message behind in the log.

To run the batch file at 3:00 a.m., do the following:

- Go into the Services applet and make sure that the Schedule service is running in AUTOMATIC STARTUP mode. See Section 7.1.6 for details.
- In an MS-DOS window type:

```
at 3:00 /every M,T,W,Th,F nghtback
```

where "nghtback" is the name of the batch file. See the MS-DOS Help
file for details on the `at` command. Once you set an `at` command, the
system will remember it even if you reboot the machine. It is persistent
until you specifically delete it.

Once you have this mechanism in place, backups are automatic. All that
you have to do each morning is remember to look at the log file to make sure
nothing went wrong, and then change the tape.

4.6 Designing a Backup Strategy

If you are backing up a single machine of your own, then you can judge the
importance of your data and decide on a daily or weekly routine that protects the

Administrative Strategy

Alternate backup program

NT also provides a second backup command, named **backup**, that copies files to diskettes. If you have a few files that need to span several diskettes because of their size, this command is useful. It would be extremely painful to back up an entire NT machine this way, however. See the Help file for the MS-DOS prompt (double click on the Help icon in the Main group of the Program Manager) for more information. You can later restore the data with the **restore** command.

information you create. Backing up less than once a week is dangerous because you can lose quite a bit of data. Given the speed of current DAT drives and the low cost of tapes, backing up your work every night is a good habit to get into.

When you begin acting as the administrator for a network, small or large, the importance of accurate and timely backup tapes grows. In a small business it is often not an exaggeration to say that the company's future lies in the data on the network. The critical nature of a network's data makes it important to plan a complete backup strategy that ensures that all user data is secure. When designing a backup strategy, keep the following goals in mind:

- You want the backup schedule to bother users as little as possible. For example, if you back up in the middle of the day each user will feel the effects of the backup in the form of high disk utilization, and this can make other programs seem sluggish while the backup is taking place. Attempting to backup files while they are in use will also result in locked file conflicts that waste your time.

- You want your strategy to prevent the loss of any data. Although this is not ever completely possible, it is a good goal to strive for. A daily backup schedule minimizes data loss.

- You want your strategy to guard against catastrophes such as fire or theft that cause all on-site backups to disappear.

- You want your strategy to be simple and automatic enough so that you actually stick to it and perform the necessary backups on schedule.

In order to satisfy the first goal, you generally have to perform backups at night or early in the morning. Since this means you can perform backups once a day at most, it is difficult to design a strategy with less than a 24-hour lag time. Consequently, at the moment of any given disk failure, users can lose up to a full day's work. You should make your users aware of this situation and encourage them to keep their own backups of their daily work.

To meet the third goal, you should keep duplicate copies of backup tapes off-site. As mentioned earlier, some off-site tapes should be within relatively easy reach, while others should be hundreds of miles away in case of a natural disaster.

Sit down and work out a complete schedule for your backups. For example, you might come up with the following:

- Sunday morning: Make three complete backup tapes of the network. The first is done in COPY mode and kept on-site. The second is also done in COPY mode and is kept off-site locally (within the same town). The third is done in NORMAL mode so that it clears all of the archive bits, and this tape should be mailed somewhere that is a good distance away. Off-site tapes should be held in a secure manner by a trusted party.

- Each weeknight: Perform two incremental backups. An incremental backup saves only those files whose archive bits are set (the archive bit is set whenever data is written to a file). The first incremental backup should be done in DIFFERENTIAL mode, and this tape can remain on-site. Because it is on-site you can append a week's worth of incrementals onto a single tape. The second tape should be made in INCREMENTAL mode so that it clears all archive bits. Send this tape to the local off-site archive.

Given this strategy, no user can lose more than a day's worth of work unless the entire city is destroyed. In that case, the maximum data loss is one week. If a third incremental backup were created each night and mailed to the distant remote site, it would take a fairly overwhelming national disaster to cause more than a day's data loss.

In order for all of this to work, you have to actually implement the schedule every day. You also need to make users aware of archive bits. For example, if a user clears any archive bits, then the affected files will not get backed up daily. The user might do this inadvertently by running the **backup** command to form personal archives. Make sure users know what an archive bit is, and show them how to use software so that the archive bits never get modified accidentally.

4.7 Examples

Let's say that you are administrating a single, isolated machine that is used by five different people. You need to design a backup strategy for that machine that prevents data loss for those users. But, since you will be the one walking into the room each day to do the backup, you also want to minimize your time.

One approach is to come in Sunday night or early Monday morning and do a complete backup of the entire hard disk. This might take an hour or more for a large disk. Then you might come in early every morning, or during lunch, and perform a much shorter incremental backup. Another strategy to shorten the amount of time you spend in the lab, and the downtime for the users while you are making the tapes, is to place all the user's home directories in one place (e.g., `c:\users`) and then back up only that directory. You can do this on the assumption that hard disk failures are rare, and if one does occur you can simply reinstall NT and all applications from their installation disks. Also, be sure to save the information in `c:\winnt\system32\config` onto your tapes to preserve user account and profile information, or choose the **Backup Registry** option when creating the backup.

If going to the lab each day becomes a problem, you may want to teach one of the users how to use the Tape Backup program and then put that user in charge of daily backups. Simply make that user a member of the Backup Operators group.

If all of the data on the system fits onto one tape, you might want to create a batch file as described in Section 4.5 and let the machine automatically back itself up every night using the `at` command. Each day as you leave the office you can stop by the lab and insert a tape. The next morning your can retrieve the tape when you come in.

If the hard disk crashes, simply replace the hard disk, reinstall Windows NT, and then restore the tape. Restore local registry information as well and you are back in business. See Section 4.5 for details.

4.8 Conclusion

Backup practices and strategies are clearly an administrative task. No user wants to worry about backing up his or her machine every day. Users especially do not want to have to worry about storing multiple copies at several different remote sites. Yet that is what must happen if the user's data is going to be secure.

If you are managing a single machine on your desk, you should create a back-up strategy of your own to protect yourself from loss. If you are administrating a network for your company, it is extremely important that your backup practices protect all of the users on the net from unforeseen problems. There is no easier way to become the enemy of your users than to lose their data. This fact makes backing up user data one of the most important functions of the administrator.

U̲NINTERRUPTABLE POWER SUPPLIES 5

Power failures are one of the most common causes of data loss in any computer system. All information loaded into the computer's memory but not yet saved to disk disappears completely when a power failure occurs. If the system is in the middle of a disk write at the moment of the power failure, then the probability of media damage or disk errors is also very high. A UPS prevents power failures and therefore increases the overall reliability and stability of your machine tremendously. This chapter shows you how to hook a standard UPS to your NT machine, and how to make NT aware of its status.

5.1 Overview

A UPS generally consists of a battery, a charger for the battery, and an inverter of some sort. The inverter converts the battery's power into normal 110 volt wall current. Either the inverter is always on, or the UPS detects a power failure and activates the inverter in a matter of milliseconds.

Most modern UPSs contain a serial communications interface. If you connect a serial cable between a UPS and the computer, the UPS can tell the computer when a power failure occurs, and can also tell the computer that it has only a few minutes of power left. With some UPSs, the computer can also send back a signal telling the UPS to shut down. This has the advantage of letting the computer turn off the UPS before it is completely drained, so that it recharges more quickly. Since power failures often come in clusters, this improves reliability.

When you purchase a UPS, you should make sure that its serial interface conforms to the Windows standard for serial communications. If it does not it may perform erratically or not at all when trying to communicate with NT.

Installation of a UPS is easy. Plug it into the wall, and then plug the computer, the monitor, and any peripherals like external hard disks into the UPS. Your goal is to plug as few things as possible into the UPS to conserve its power, but to make sure that you plug in everything needed when the power fails. For example, if you have a machine consisting of the CPU unit, the monitor, an external tape drive, an external SCSI CD-ROM drive, and external SCSI hard drive, you will probably want to plug the CPU, monitor, and external hard drive into the UPS. The CD-ROM drive and tape drive are unneeded during a power failure. One thing you do not want to plug into the UPS is your printer, because printers use a lot of power and are generally not needed during a power failure. Connect the serial cable from the UPS to a serial port on your computer, and the installation is complete.

5.2 Configuring NT for the UPS

Once you have installed the UPS, you must set up NT to recognize communication signals from the UPS. Log on as the administrator and start the Control Panel application by double clicking on it in the Main group of the Program Manager. Find the UPS applet in the Control Panel and double click on it. You should see a dialog similar to the one shown in Figure 5.1.

Click on the check box in the upper left hand corner so that NT knows a UPS is available. In the combo box to the right of the check box indicate the serial port that you have used for the UPS. Now, get out the documentation that came with the UPS and use it to set the check boxes in the **UPS configuration** section.

The standard interface for a UPS uses three lines on a serial port for communication with the host system. The names for these lines will sound a little foreign to you if you are not familiar with the lingo of RS-232 communications protocols, but they are standard lines used for modem and terminal connections over an RS-232 line. When the power fails, the UPS tells the host about the problem by sending a signal on the Clear To Send (CTS) line. When the UPS feels that its batteries are drained to the point that failure is imminent within two minutes, it can send another signal on the Data Carrier Detect

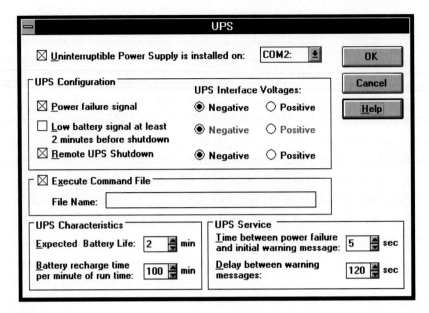

Figure 5.1
The UPS dialog.

(DCD) line. Finally, the computer can tell the UPS to shut down using the Data Terminal Ready (DTR) line. The UPS documentation will tell you which lines the UPS supports, and whether it supports positive or negative signaling on each line. Set the configuration check boxes appropriately.

You can also cause NT to execute a program or batch file when the power fails. Select the **Execute Command File** check box and type the name of the command or batch file in the **File Name** edit area. You might have the batch file shut down all network connections and broadcast a message with the `netsend` command when the power fails. See Section 7.1.6 for more details on broadcasting messages. This batch program must be able to complete execution within 30 seconds in a worst case scenario. Test it to make sure. Place the file in the `c:\winnt\system32\repl\import\scripts` directory with your other scripts.

In the **UPS Characteristics** section, describe the behavior of the battery. This section will be available only if the UPS does not have low battery signaling capabilities. In this section you describe the expected battery life of the UPS as well as the recharge time. NT uses this information to estimate how long the battery will last, and also to determine how much the battery has recovered if two power failures occur in rapid succession. The best way to determine discharge and recharge information is through testing with your specific configuration. You may wish to fudge on the expected battery life information if you want NT to turn off the UPS before it drains the battery completely.

Finally, the **UPS Service** section lets you customize the warning messages that NT sends to your machine when a power failure occurs. You determine the time before the first message appears, as well as the interval between subsequent messages.

Check the configuration information that you have entered and, when it is correct, click the **OK** button. Now double click on the Services applet in the Control Panel. In order for the UPS to signal you properly the Alerter, Messenger, and UPS services must all be on, and they must be set to start automatically. See Section 7.1.6 for more information on activating services.

5.3 Testing

Once you have plugged in and configured the UPS properly in NT, let it charge completely. Then test it. Before performing the test you should back up the system in case something goes wrong (see Chapter 4), and you should also make sure that no important programs, especially programs that are highly disk intensive, are running. Have a stop watch or clock available during the test so you can find out the actual life of the UPS with your configuration.

Testing is simple: Pull the plug on the UPS and it will think that a power failure has occurred. Start your stopwatch. When the UPS detects the power failure, NT should present a dialog that warns you of the situation. If you see no dialog, either you have cabled the UPS improperly, or you have set the configuration information for the UPS incorrectly in the UPS applet. Plug the UPS back in, check your configuration, and try again.

When NT feels that the UPS is drained, either because of the time estimate you gave it, or because the UPS signals its condition, you should see your batch file execute. NT then will shut itself down. The UPS should eventually fail and cut off the machine. Stop the stop watch. Now note the time. Most UPSs have LED indicators that let you see when they have reached full readiness again. Watch the UPS over the next couple of hours to see how long it takes to recharge. Use the length of time the UPS lasted, as well as the recharge time (in minutes) divided by that time, to properly set the UPS characteristics. Retest to make sure that the settings are accurate.

5.4 Example

Let's say you are working on your NT machine and the power fails. You will see the UPS dialog appear. Probably the best thing for you to do is to quickly bring your work to closure, shut down the machine yourself, and then turn it off. Or, if the machine is expected to be on 24 hours a day, you may want to leave it on (after you have closed your work) and let the UPS drain down so that the machine comes back to life when the power is restored.

Managing Disks

6

The Disk Administrator manages the hard disks that are physically attached to your NT machine. You will use it whenever you add a new hard disk to your machine, or when you want to reconfigure your drives. It has a number of interesting capabilities, including disk striping and multi-disk volumes, that can be quite useful if you have multiple hard disks available. However, if you never actually install a new disk drive then you may never need to use the Disk Administrator.

In this chapter you will learn about partitions, and you will discover how the Disk Manager lets you manipulate these partitions to better meet your storage requirements.

6.1 Overview

Before you get started, heed this important message about the Disk Administrator: *The Disk Administrator makes it extremely easy to destroy vast quantities of data*. You can click on a couple of selections and delete 4 Gigabytes of data without even realizing it. Be cautious and slow when you use this tool.

The Disk Administrator works with hard disks. You can think of a hard disk as a black box capable of storing so many bytes of file information. That is how the Disk Administrator presents it to you. Alternatively, you can think of it as a set of rotating disks divided into concentric tracks, each of which contains a number of pie-wedge-shaped sectors capable of storing a fixed number of bytes. The black box representation is generally easier to understand. However, it is helpful to know about sectors as well. For example, the system stores the partition table in sector 0 of each hard disk.

The Disk Administrator has two jobs. First, it lets you break a hard disk up into partitions. A partition lets the operating system perceive a single physical hard disk as several individual drives. Generally you do this so you can support more than one file system on a single drive. For example, if you own an NT machine that has one hard disk, and you want to support both the FAT file system and NTFS on the same drive, you have to partition the drive. The second job for the Disk Administrator is to combine partitions on separate hard drives into what appear to be single drives. You do this to create huge disks under a single drive letter, or to improve performance. As you can see, the Disk Administrator both divides and combines hard disks in ways that help you to use your disk drives more efficiently.

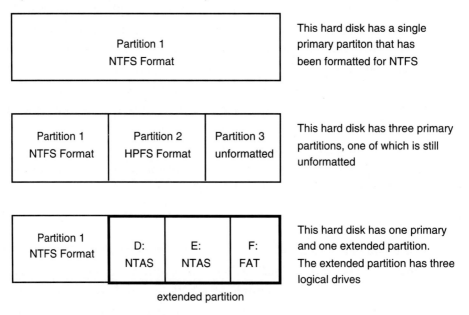

Figure 6.1
Three different ways of partitioning a hard disk.

In order to understand the Disk Administrator, you have to feel comfortable with the concept of a disk *partition.* Much of the terminology and vocabulary of partitions in NT comes from MS-DOS, and it may seem to you at times a bit unorthodox because of that. At its most basic, however, partitions are simply a way of fooling the operating system into seeing more than one hard disk. It is a completely arbitrary notion, an illusion supported by a low-level portion of the system to solve certain problems that confront administrators.

The physical basis of partitions is easy to understand. The first sector of the hard disk contains a *partition table*. This table holds the starting and ending sector numbers for each partition. When the computer system first looks at the hard disk at boot time, it reads the partition table and uses that information to guide how it perceives the hard disk. If the partition table indicates that the disk is to be perceived as a single disk, then the system perceives it that way. If, on the other hand, the partition table specifies three separate partitions, the system will think of the one hard disk as three separate drives of the sizes indicated in the table. If one of the partitions is marked as *active*, then the system uses that partition to retrieve its boot instructions. Therefore, it is possible to create three separate partitions on a hard disk, load three separate operating systems onto the different partitions (e.g., DOS, NT, and UNIX), and then boot into the different operating systems by changing the active partition in the partition table.

The Disk Administrator's job is to manipulate the partition table. A partition table has a maximum of four entries, so you can create up to four partitions on any hard disk using the Disk Administrator. NT supports two different types of partitions:

- Primary partitions: A primary partition is a partition that you can mark as active. You cannot subdivide a primary partition in any way. Each primary partition can have its own drive letter, or you can combine partitions together into *volume sets* under a single drive letter. You can create up to four primary partitions on a drive, or you can create three primary partitions and one extended partition.

- Extended partitions: An extended partition is a partition that you later subdivide further into *logical drives*. Each logical drive has a drive letter. You can create only one extended partition on a drive, but it can hold up to 23 logical drives. The 23 drive limitation exists because there are only 26 letters in the alphabet. The letters A and B are reserved for the two floppy drives. Some other letter must designate the primary partition that holds NT itself. That leaves 23 unused drive letters on any NT machine.

Extended partitions and logical drives are residue from DOS. Why would you want to take a big hard disk and chop it up into a bunch of little pieces? In old DOS machines you had to do this because DOS limited hard disks to 32 MB. You would chop up a big disk into a set of logical drives each smaller than 32 MB. NT has no such size restrictions. If you are running a strictly-NT machine you will probably use only primary partitions, unless you have a special need for a disk to have more than four sections.

Creating DOS-compatible partitions

One reason to create an extended partition in NT is because you have a dual-boot machine and you want DOS and NT both to be able to access the hard disk. If you do need to be compatible with DOS, then any disk drive that you partition with the Disk Administrator should contain *only one primary partition, and one extended partition.* DOS will be able to see those two partitions, and any logical drives that you create in the extended partition, if you format them with the FAT file system. Do not try to create any other configuration if you want DOS to be able to access the drive.

Once you create a partition or a logical drive, it is unusable until you format it. Formatting writes data structures onto the partition so that a file system can use it. The data structures have slots for file information such as the file name, creation date, and so on, as well as for the file data itself, and these data structures are different depending on the file system. NT currently allows you to format drives with three different file systems: NTFS, FAT, and the High Performance File System (HPFS) used by OS/2. The act of formatting is done outside of the Disk Administrator using the `format` command in the MS-DOS window, and really has nothing to do with the Disk Administrator. However, you cannot use the partitions and logical drives you create until you format them.

If this is your first venture into disk management then the above may seem confusing initially. That is normal. You are probably wondering when you will actually use this tool. At the minimum, you need to use it whenever you add a new drive to your machine. A new drive is nothing but raw space, so you will need to run the Disk Administrator to create at least one partition out of that raw space. This step initializes the partition table. Once you have created the partition, you can then format and use it.

If you have several drives on your machine, you can use the Disk Administrator to create two other structures on your hard disk:

- Volume sets: A volume set lets you combine partitions from several hard disks into a single volume under a single drive letter. For example, if you have four 2 Gigabyte SCSI drives and you want to perceive them as a single 8 Gigabyte drive under a single drive letter, you use volume sets to do that. Volume sets have an interesting feature: If you later add a fifth drive, you can extend the volume set by adding that new drive to the end of it. NT will enlarge the volume automatically when the system restarts, without losing any data. Up to 32 partitions can combine to form a volume set. Note that volume sets are extensible only if they are formatted with NTFS.

- Stripe sets: A stripe set, like a volume set, lets you combine sections from multiple drives into a single drive. However, a stripe sets stores data across all of the drives simultaneously, whereas a volume set stores it sequentially. That is, while a volume sets fills up the first drive in the set, then the second, then the third, and so on sequentially, a stripe set stores the first sector on the first drive, the second sector on the second drive, and so on. In a stripe set, all of the drives fill equally and simultaneously.

The advantage of a volume set is extensibility. You can keep appending drives over time, and you do not need to do any reformatting to make the additions. On the other hand, the theoretical advantage of stripe sets is performance. With multiple drives seeking and acquiring data at the same time, a stripe set should give faster disk access. You will want to test stripe sets on your own drives and make sure that there really is a performance boost before you commit your drives to this format. If you find that there is no performance boost, then a volume set is preferred because of its extensibility.

The following list reviews the new vocabulary introduced in the preceding paragraphs.

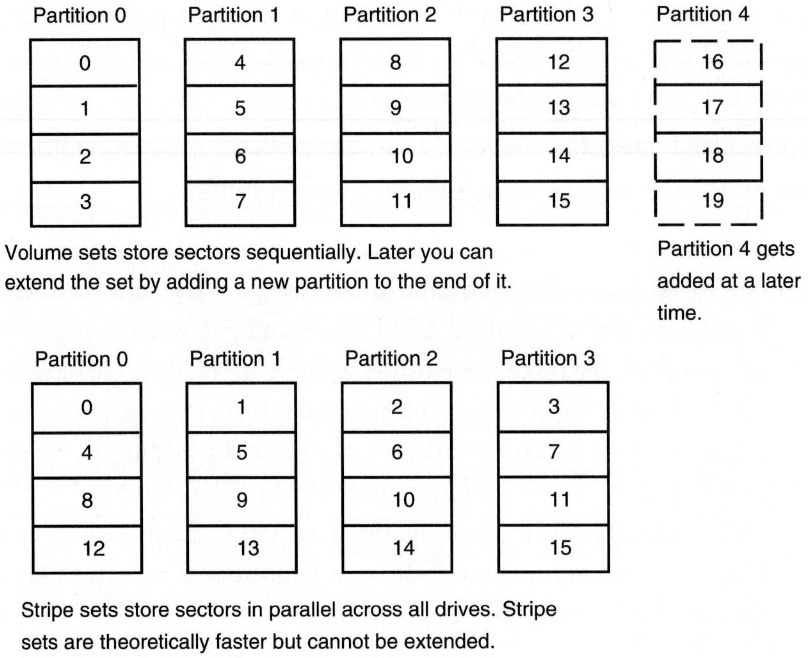

Partition 0	Partition 1	Partition 2	Partition 3	Partition 4
0	4	8	12	16
1	5	9	13	17
2	6	10	14	18
3	7	11	15	19

Volume sets store sectors sequentially. Later you can extend the set by adding a new partition to the end of it.

Partition 4 gets added at a later time.

Partition 0	Partition 1	Partition 2	Partition 3
0	1	2	3
4	5	6	7
8	9	10	11
12	13	14	15

Stripe sets store sectors in parallel across all drives. Stripe sets are theoretically faster but cannot be extended.

Figure 6.2
The differences between volume sets and stripe sets.

- partition: An abstraction that allows you to subdivide a hard disk into what appears to be a set of smaller hard disks. Each partition can receive its own drive letter, and you can format it with any file system.

- partition table: Partition information for each drive stored by the Disk Manager at the front of the drive.

- active partition: The partition from which the computer loads its boot information.

- extended partition: A special type of partition that you can subdivide into one or more *logical drives.*

- logical drive: Part of an extended partition. It has its own drive letter, and you can format it separately with any file system.

- volume set: A sequential combination of same-format partitions that have a single drive letter. If NTFS is used, you can extend a volume set with additional partitions on the fly, up to a maximum of 32 partitions.

- stripe set: A parallel combination of same-format partitions that have a single drive letter. You must use NTFS.

The sections below show you how to use all of these different capabilities to effectively manage your available disk space.

6.2 Getting Started

Log on as the administrator and start the Disk Administrator by double clicking on its icon in the Administrative Tools group in the Program Manager. Once the Disk Administrator appears on the screen you will see a window describing your disk configuration. The configuration is unique to your machine. Figure 6.3 shows a typical display from a machine having a 200 MB and an 80 MB SCSI hard disk shortly after installing NT.

Figure 6.3
The Disk Administrator.

In Figure 6.3, the two drives are labeled 0 and 1. Drive 0 has one primary partition of 120 MB, with 82 MB of *free space*. Free space is space on the drive that has not yet been allocated to a partition. Drive 1 has not yet been partitioned at all, so all of its space is free. Note that you cannot ever modify the NT system partition using the Disk Administrator. In the case seen in Figure 6.3, the partition on Drive 0 holds NT. You would have to delete the NT partition to modify it, and the Disk Administrator is smart enough to prevent that. Partitioning Drive 0 therefore requires special tools, as discussed in Section 6.10. You can manipulate all other drives and partitions freely using the Disk Administrator.

If your machine has just one drive containing one partition and no free space, then there is not much that you can do with the Disk Administrator. The **Options** menu will let you adjust how the screen displays drive information. You can enable and disable the status bar and the "legend" at the bottom of the screen. You can also change the colors and the patterns used to represent different types of partitions, as well as the way that the program displays regions.

You can change the drive letter used for any partition. Select the partition by clicking on it, and then choose the **Drive Letter** option in the **Partition** menu. Change the drive letter to one that you find more suitable using the combo box. Changing the NT system partition to something other than Drive C: is not recommended, however, because many programs wrongly assume that Drive C: holds the system information.

6.3 Creating and Formatting Primary Partitions

If your Drive 0 has two or more partitions, or if you add a new hard disk to your machine, then you will use the Disk Administrator to create partitions. You can create any of four different entities from the free space:

- One or more primary partitions
- One extended partition with one or more logical drives
- A volume set, provided that you have two or more free partitions
- A stripe set, provided you have two or more free partitions on separate drives

The easiest thing to do is to create a primary partition. To create a primary partition, select the free space that will contain the partition by clicking on it. For example, in Figure 6.3 you can click on either of the two blocks marked "free space." In the **Partition** menu, select the **Create** option. You may see a dialog like the one shown in Figure 6.4 if you are working on a dual-boot machine that runs both DOS and NT. DOS recognizes only one extended and one primary partition, so extra primary partitions that you create with the Disk Administrator in NT are invisible when you reboot to DOS. Figure 6.4 is warning you about this problem. If you are concerned about it, create an extended partition instead of a second primary partition. See Section 6.4. If your machine runs NT only, do not worry about it.

You will next see a dialog like the one shown in Figure 6.5. It lets you choose the size of the new primary partition. You can use all of the free space available,

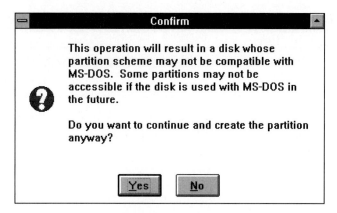

Figure 6.4
The Confirm dialog. If you are working on a pure NT machine, you will not see this dialog.

or any part of it. It will receive the next available drive letter as its designation. Figure 6.6 shows a new 40 MB primary partition on Drive 0 that has received the Drive letter D:. If you want to change the drive letter, select the new partition by clicking on it and use the **Drive Letter** option in the **Partition** menu.

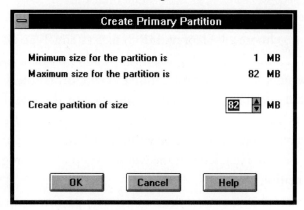

Figure 6.5
The Create Primary Partition dialog.

In order to use the new partition, you must exit the Disk Administrator. When you do this, it will ask you if you want to save the changes. If you choose to save the changes, the system will write the new configuration to the partition table and then shut down and restart NT.

Figure 6.6
The newly created partition.

Once NT restarts, you need to format the new space in order to use it. Log back in as the administrator and start up an MS-DOS command window. To format a new Drive D: with NTFS, type:

```
format d: /fs:ntfs
```

You can also choose a FAT or an HPFS file system: Type `format /?` for more information. See Section 6.7 for information on choosing between the different file systems. The `format` command will format the disk and ask for a volume label. This label is a name for the drive. In the FAT file system the volume label has an 11 character limit, while in NTFS it can be much longer. You can later change the volume name with the `label` command in the MS-DOS prompt. See the Help icon in the Main Group of the Program Manager for more information.

Once formatted, you can use the new primary partition just like any other disk drive. It will appear in the File Manager with its own drive letter.

6.4 Creating Extended Partitions and Logical Drives

If you need to create a partition that is visible to DOS on dual-boot machines, or if you want to create a large number (more than four) of small drives from a single disk, you should create an extended partition. Each disk can have one extended partition, and that partition can contain up to 23 different logical drives. An entire system cannot have any more than 26 individual drive letters, nor can it have less than three since A and B are reserved for floppy drives and the NT partition takes up one more letter.

To create a new extended partition, select the free space for the new partition by clicking on it. For example, in Figure 6.3 you can click on either of the 2 blocks marked "free space." Select the **Create Extended** option in the **Partition** menu. You will see a dialog similar to the one shown in Figure 6.5 that lets you set the size for the extended partition. After you create the extended partition and return to the Disk Administrator window, it will be very hard to tell that anything at all happened. The Extended partition is marked only by a different hatching pattern as shown in Figure 6.7. If you click on an extended partition to select it, the label in the status bar reads "Empty Extended Partition."

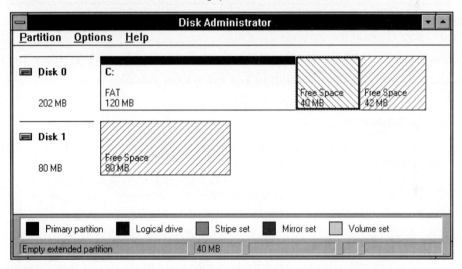

Figure 6.7
The new extended partition is selected. Note the different hatching pattern.

Now you can create one or more logical drives in the extended partition. Select the extended partition, and then choose the **Create** option in the **Partition** menu. You will see a dialog that lets you choose the size of the logical drive. The logical drive can fill the extended partition, or any part of it. Figure 6.8 shows a 40 MB extended partition split into two 20 Meg logical drives.

Once you have created the logical drives, *exit the Disk Administrator* and let the system restart. Format the new drives as described in Section 6.3. If you

Figure 6.8
Two logical drives in the extended partition.

want the drives to be visible in DOS, format them with the FAT file system. Otherwise you can format them in any file system you like.

*Administrative
Strategy*

Disk quotas

   Version 3.1 of Windows NT does not support any sort of disk quota system. In UNIX, the quota system lets the administrator determine each user's maximum disk space usage. When users run over their limit, the system gives them several warnings and then prevents them from logging in.

   One crude way to simulate a quota system on an NT machine is to assign logical drives of a fixed size to each user as their home directories. Users then will be unable to store more information than will fit in the logical drive they can access.

6.5 Creating and Extending Volume Sets

   If you want to create a single drive letter that spans several physical drives or partitions, then you can use a volume set to do it. If you format the volume set with NTFS, one of its key advantages is that you can later add an additional partition to the set to enlarge it without reformatting. When you add the new partition, NT recognizes the change and formats the addition at system start-up. NT preserves all of the existing data.

To create a volume set you need free space on two or more drives, or you need discontiguous free space on a single drive. Click on the first block of free space, and then Ctrl-click on the other blocks of free space. You can select up to 32 blocks for a volume set. Select the **Create Volume Set** option in the **Partition** menu to create the volume set. You will see a dialog like the one shown in Figure 6.9. If you select all of the space available, NT will use it. If you select a smaller amount than the total free space, NT will divide the free space across volumes, evenly splitting the space as best it can.

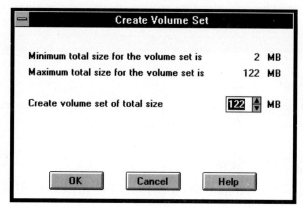

Figure 6.9
The Create Volume Set dialog.

Once you have created the volume set, *exit the Disk Administrator.* It will save the new partition table and restart the system. Once the system restarts, log on again as the administrator and format the new volume set with NTFS as described in Section 6.3. Figure 6.10 shows what a volume set looks like after formatting.

If you add a new disk drive and wish to add its free space to an existing volume set, start the Disk Administrator. Click on the existing volume set. Ctrl-click on the free space in the new drive. Select the **Extend Volume Set** option in the **Partition** menu. You will see a dialog similar to the one shown in Figure 6.5 that asks you to specify the size for the extended volume set. After you choose the size, *exit the Disk Administrator* to save the changes to the partition tables of the affected disks. As the system restarts, the extension to the

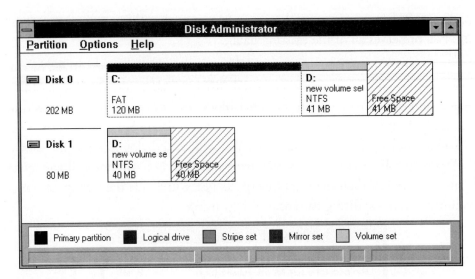

Figure 6.10
The new volume set.

volume set will be checked and formatted, and the volume set will acquire the new space. The existing data on the partition remains intact.

6.6 Creating Stripe Sets

A stripe set, like a volume set, spans multiple drives. A stripe set, however, is designed to improve system performance by causing multiple disk drives to work simultaneously. In a volume set, different partitions are arranged sequentially. The first partition fills, then the second, and so on. In a stripe set, sectors are interleaved across all of the drives in the set, so that all of the drives work in parallel. Ideally this parallelism creates a performance increase. Before you commit to striping however, you should test and make sure that there is a tangible benefit. If not, use a volume set instead for its extensibility. Or switch to the Advanced Server (Chapter 13), which supports striping much more completely.

You create a stripe set just as you do a volume set: Click on the first piece of free disk space to select it, and then Shift-click on the other free spaces on other drives (while in a volume set different pieces of the set can exist on the same drive, all parts of a stripe set must be on different drives). In general, it is a good idea to choose sections of equal size, because NT will base the maximum size of the stripe set drive on the smallest of the chosen pieces. Once you have selected all of the pieces, choose the **Create Stripe Set** option in the **Partition** menu. Choose the size for the new set. NT will divide the amount of space you chose evenly across all of the free space available.

Exit the Disk Administrator so that it can update the partition tables and restart the system. Then format the new stripe set with NTFS.

Administrative Strategy

Creating stripe sets

It is best to create a stripe set on a collection of identical, blank drives. This arrangement ensures that the drives have equal capabilities, and tends to enhance performance. If you wish to test the performance of the set you have created, copy a directory containing 50–100 MB of information to the stripe set and time how long it takes to complete the operation. Then delete the stripe set, create an identically sized volume set in its place, and try the copy again. If the times are not significantly different, use a volume set for its extensibility.

6.7 Choosing a File System

After you create any kind of partition or logical drive using the Disk Administrator, you must *format* that partition with one of the three file systems listed below:

- NTFS: The NT File System is fault tolerant, almost infinitely extensible, and secure.
- HPFS: The High Performance File System is compatible with OS/2.
- FAT: The File Allocation Table File System is compatible with DOS.

In almost every case, you should use NTFS when you format a drive. This is the file system that NT is designed to work with. NTFS is an advanced, robust, and secure file system.

The only reason to ever choose the FAT File System for a partition is because you have a dual boot machine running DOS. DOS needs to live in a FAT partition. You can create a second NTFS partition on that same machine, however, to hold NT. The only reason to create an HPFS partition is because you have a dual-boot machine running OS/2.

To format a partition, use the `format` command in the MS-DOS command window. For example, if you have created a new partition on the hard disk and assigned it drive letter G, you can format it with NTFS by typing the following command:

```
format g: /fs: NTFS
```

See the Help file in the Main Group of the Program Manager for more information on the `format` command.

You can later convert FAT and HPFS partitions to NTFS partitions using the `convert` command in the MS-DOS command window.

6.8 Deleting Partitions

Whenever you delete a partition, you lose all of its data. Deleting a partition is an extremely easy way to lose many megabytes of information, so be careful with this menu option. You can delete any partition except the one that holds the NT system files.

To delete a primary partition, a stripe set, or a volume set, select the partition and then choose the **Delete** option in the **Partition** menu. You get one warning, and then the partition and all of its data are gone forever once you exit the Disk Administrator.

To delete an extended partition, you must first delete each of its logical drives. Once they have been deleted, you can delete the extended partition itself by selecting its free space and choosing the **Delete** option. The only way to detect the extended partition's free space is by noticing its different hatch pattern.

6.9 Saving Configuration Information

Whenever you change the partition configuration of your disks, you should save the new configuration to a blank floppy disk or to your emergency repair disk. If a disk drive crashes you can replace it and then restore the partition configuration from diskette.

To save configuration information, choose the **Save** option in the **Configuration** option of the **Partition** menu. To restore the information, use the **Restore** option. See Section 4.3 for more information.

6.10 Partitioning Your Drive 0 Disk Before Installation

The vast majority of NT machines have just one hard disk drive installed. It is called Drive 0. If that drive has just one partition on it when you install NT, then it is impossible to re-partition it because NT will forbid the deletion of its own partition. You therefore have to re-partition the drive prior to installation. On DOS machines, you re-partition using a command named `fdisk`. On Reduced Instruction Set Computer (RISC) machines, you use the manufacturer's supplied partitioning utility. Your NT installation program may also allow you to partition your drive just prior to installation.

If you have a dual boot PC that you switch between DOS and NT, then there are several reasons to create multiple partitions on your hard disk. For example, you may wish to experiment with NTFS. While the DOS portion of the hard disk must be in the FAT file system in order for DOS to see it, other partitions can use other file systems. On RISC machines, NT requires a 2 MB FAT partition for system files, and then any number of other partitions are allowed to have any format you like. Note that on RISC machines, the Disk Manager contains a menu option in the **Partition** menu called **Secure System Partition** that secures this FAT partition so that only the administrator can access it.

If you have a pure NT machine you can get by with a single partition in Drive 0. There is a good reason for you to consider dividing your Drive 0 into two partitions however: It allows you to create a single large volume set from the free space on Drive 0 as well as any other drives that you add. You can place the NT system and its paging file and temp space in the first partition on Drive 0, and then you can place the remainder of the space in a second partition to maximize the size of the volume set. The NT system files cannot exist in a volume set or stripe set, so you will always have one primary partition and then other partitions as needed.

Partitioning Drive 0 requires a bit of patience and experimentation. It is hard to pick a good size for the NT system partition the first time you install it, and changing the partition size requires you to reload everything from scratch. A partition size of 150–200 MB is probably more than adequate for the system (60–70 MB), the paging file (50 MB), and temp space (the remainder) on PC class machines. If you want to place application code in this same partition, consider it also when sizing the NT partition. Keeping all of the system files on one partition makes backing up your drives much easier.

You cannot use the Disk Administrator to divide Drive 0 into partitions because that would require you to delete the NT system partition. You must therefore do the partitioning before you install NT on the drive, either in the installation program itself or prior to running the installation program. On

DOS machines, you can load DOS from a floppy disk containing the `fdisk` utility and partition the drive with `fdisk`. Create a single Primary partition of the size required for NT and leave it at that. You can later specify how to use the remaining free space on the drive in the Disk Administrator. On RISC machines, the manufacturer will ship a partitioning utility with the machine and you should use it before installation.

The installation program also contains the ability to partition drives. You will come to a point during the installation process where you are asked which of the existing partitions that you wish to install NT into. At this point, you can press P to create and delete partitions. *If you have existing data on the drive, do not delete the partition.* The only way to split a partition into two is to delete the original partition, and that will destroy all of its data.

Once you have partitioned the drive, load NT onto the primary partition. After installation you can use the Disk Administrator to partition the available free space remaining on the drive.

6.11 Examples

Let's say you are administering an NT machine and you run out of disk space. You purchase a second drive and install it in your system. You need to use the Disk Administrator to initialize the drive. When you start the Disk Administrator, you can select the free space on the new drive and either: 1) create a new primary partition, 2) create an extended partition and then create logical drives in that partition, or 3) add the free space to the end of an existing volume set. The new partition can use all of the available free space on the new drive, or just a part of it.

At some later time you may discover that you need to use that NT machine as the server for a 6 Gigabyte database. You purchase three new 2 Gigabyte drives and install them on the machine. You can bind those drives together under a single drive letter by using either a volume set or a stripe set. If you know that you will need to extend the drive in the future by adding additional partitions, choose a volume set. If you don't expect extensions and performance is important, test the drives with a stripe set and see if it gives you a performance boost.

Say that a new NT machine arrives and you need to decide how to partition the hard disk before installing NT. Here are some questions to ask yourself:

- Is there any need, because the machine will dual-boot into DOS or OS/2 as well, to have a FAT or HPFS partition on the machine? If not, plan on using NTFS partitions exclusively.

- Will you need to add additional drives to the machine in the future? If you expect to, you may want to partition Drive 0 initially into one partition big enough to hold the NT files, and then a second partition for data. You will later be able to make the second partition part of a larger volume set under a single drive letter as you add new drives.

- Is there any need to subdivide the available space into a number of smaller spaces? If there is, then create a partition for NT and then a second extended partition containing several logical drives.

- If you are running a dual-boot machine with DOS as the second operating system, you can either create a single partition on the drive to hold both, or you can split the drive into a FAT partition for DOS and an NTFS partition for NT. The advantage of the former configuration is that in DOS mode you can see all of the files on the system. On the other hand, you have no security.

- If you are adding multiple drives and if you find that there is a performance boost from using a stripe set, is speed or extensibility in the future more important? It is somewhat more difficult to enlarge a stripe set than it is to enlarge a volume set. In the case of a stripe set you must back up the whole thing, delete it, recreate it with the new larger size, and then restore the data. With a volume set you simply add the new partition to the set in the Disk Administrator and NT takes care of the rest.

ADVANCED FEATURES AND SYSTEM TUNING

7

The Administrative Tools group in the Program Manager contains the five tools most commonly used by the administrator. However, there are a number of tools and capabilities available to the administrator that are hidden throughout the system. Many of these tools are essential to the proper administration and use of the system.

For example, the `at` command lets you and other users schedule commands for execution at a preset time in the future. However, you cannot use this command until you start the Schedule service using the Services applet of the Control Panel. See Section 7.1.6. Only the administrator (or a power user in this particular case) can start the Schedule service. If you want to be able to use the `at` command, it is up to you as the administrator to make sure that this service starts automatically each time the system boots.

The purpose of this chapter is to make you aware of all of the hidden capabilities and advanced features available to the administrator of an NT system. You will learn about a variety of tools in the Control Panel, and you will also learn about modifying the system configuration and common program groups.

7.1 The Control Panel

Many different parts of the Control Panel are available only to administrators or power users. For example, a normal user cannot change the time and date. In this section, we review each of the Control Panel facilities that requires administrator or power user rights.

7.1.1   The System Applet

The System applet lets you change *environment variables*, and also contains a **Virtual Memory** button that invokes the dialog shown in Figure 7.1. This dialog lets you configure the virtual memory file for Windows NT. Although anyone can view the current settings, only the administrator or a power user can modify the virtual memory characteristics of an NT workstation.

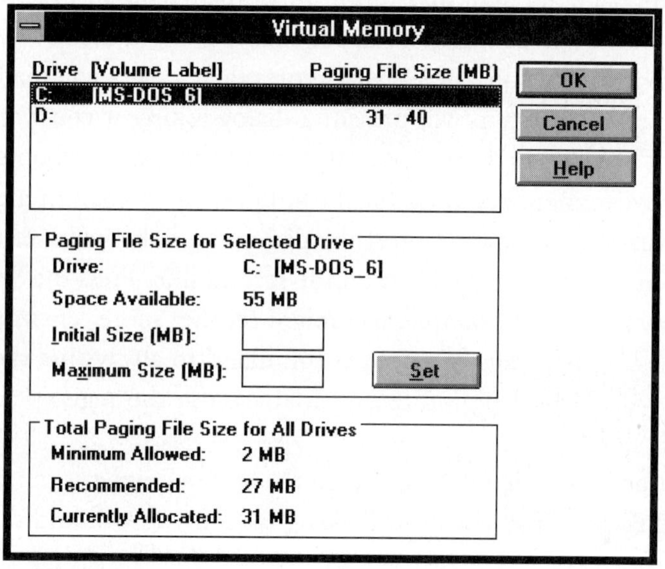

```
┌──────────────────────────────────────────────────────────────┐
│ ▬                        Virtual Memory                        │
├──────────────────────────────────────────────────────────────┤
│  Drive  [Volume Label]        Paging File Size (MB)  ┌────────┐│
│  C:     MS-DOS_6                                     │   OK   ││
│  D:                                  31 - 40         └────────┘│
│                                                      ┌────────┐│
│                                                      │ Cancel ││
│                                                      └────────┘│
│                                                      ┌────────┐│
│                                                      │  Help  ││
│                                                      └────────┘│
│  ┌─ Paging File Size for Selected Drive ─────────────────────┐ │
│  │  Drive:              C: [MS-DOS_6]                        │ │
│  │  Space Available:    55 MB                                │ │
│  │  Initial Size (MB):  [        ]                           │ │
│  │  Maximum Size (MB):  [        ]      [  Set  ]            │ │
│  └───────────────────────────────────────────────────────────┘ │
│  ┌─ Total Paging File Size for All Drives ───────────────────┐ │
│  │  Minimum Allowed:    2 MB                                 │ │
│  │  Recommended:        27 MB                                │ │
│  │  Currently Allocated: 31 MB                               │ │
│  └───────────────────────────────────────────────────────────┘ │
└──────────────────────────────────────────────────────────────┘
```

Figure 7.1
The Virtual Memory dialog.

Virtual memory is a system that allows NT to temporarily save unneeded executable code and data out of RAM and onto the hard disk. By saving and restoring things in an organized way, NT can store in RAM only those pieces of code and data that are actually needed at any given moment. The virtual memory system lets NT believe that it has more memory than it actually does, and therefore allows you to run more or larger applications. The virtual memory file, or *paging file*, holds the RAM image. You can control the maximum and minimum size of the paging file, as well as the drive that holds the paging file, from within the Virtual Memory dialog. NT supports multi-drive paging files.

Consider 25–30 MB to be the lower limit on the size of your virtual memory file. You should set the maximum size in accordance with your available disk space and your expected uses of NT. If NT runs out of virtual memory space while starting or running an application, it will enlarge the paging file up to the maximum setting that you have entered in the dialog. Any memory requirements beyond that cause the system to warn you with a dialog box. For example, if you have three large applications running and a fourth is unable to start because of insufficient memory, you will see a dialog. This is your signal to change the page file specification.

To change the initial or maximum size of the paging file, fill in the appropriate fields in the Virtual Memory dialog box. *Then press the Set button.* If you fail to press the **Set** button, the system ignores the changes you made. Press the **OK** button and the system will present a dialog asking if you want to restart the system. The changes do not take effect until the system reboots.

User environment variables for the administrator account are also set in the system dialog. At the bottom of the dialog, type the name of the variable on the first line and the value for it on the second line. Press the **Set** button to store the new value. For example, you might set the "more" environment variable to "/e." This will cause the `more` command to always use the /e option. To set the system-wide environment variables, use the registry editor as described in Appendix C.

One other thing that you can set in the System applet is the treatment of background tasks. If you click the **Tasking** button you will find that you have three options:

- Best Foreground Application Response Time
- Foreground Application More Responsive Than Background
- Foreground and Background Applications Equally Responsive

Choose whichever option makes you the most comfortable when you are using the machine.

7.1.2   The Date/Time Applet

The Date/Time applet lets you set the current date and time, as well as the time zone and daylight savings time behavior of the system. Only an administrator, power user, or a member of a group with the **Set Time and Date** privilege (see Section 2.1) can use this applet. Figure 7.2 shows the Date/Time window.

Setting the date and time is straightforward. Just click on a value and type a new value, or use the arrow buttons. You can also set the time zone for your location. The GMT zone is useful for testing.

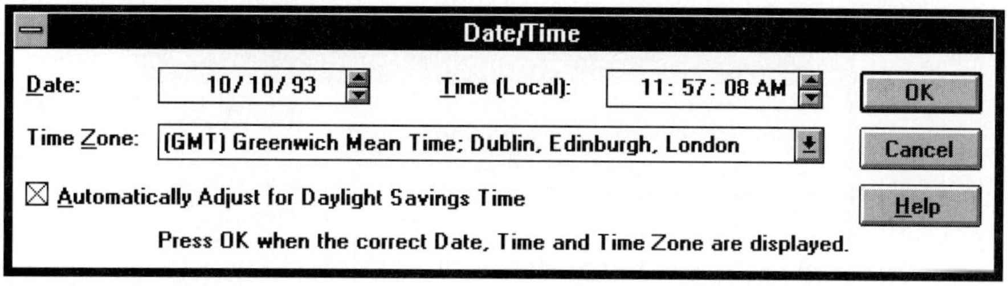

```
┌────────────────────────────────────────────────────────────────┐
│ ⊟                          Date/Time                             │
├────────────────────────────────────────────────────────────────┤
│  Date:        [  10/10/93  ▲▼]    Time (Local):  [ 11:57:08 AM ▲▼]   ┌─────────┐  │
│                                                                    │   OK    │  │
│  Time Zone:  [(GMT) Greenwich Mean Time; Dublin, Edinburgh, London ▼]   └─────────┘  │
│                                                                    ┌─────────┐  │
│  ☒ Automatically Adjust for Daylight Savings Time                 │ Cancel  │  │
│                                                                    └─────────┘  │
│           Press OK when the correct Date, Time and Time Zone are displayed.  ┌─────────┐  │
│                                                                    │  Help   │  │
│                                                                    └─────────┘  │
└────────────────────────────────────────────────────────────────┘
```

Figure 7.2
The Date/Time window.

7.1.3   The Drivers Applet

Device drivers let NT talk to different hardware devices. Drivers are loaded and configured in one of four different places in NT:

- The Print Manager handles printer device drivers.
- The Windows NT Setup application (see Section 7.2) manages the drivers for the screen, the keyboard, the mouse, the tape drives, and any SCSI devices.
- The Network applet (see Chapter 10) handles the network card.
- The Drivers applet handles all other device drivers for add-on hardware such as sound cards. You can add, remove, or modify certain driver settings in the applet.

Only the administrator can use the Drivers applet.

Figure 7.3 shows a screen dump of the applet. When you purchase a device, the hardware manufacturer will generally supply a diskette containing the appropriate driver. NT also provides a number of drivers for standard devices on the installation disks, so if there is no supplied driver you may find one there. To add the device driver, click on the **Add** button. If the driver is native to NT, click on the device in the list. When the system asks you for the source drive, point it to the correct directory for the CD-ROM drive, or specify Drive A: or B: if you installed NT from diskettes. It will ask you for the appropriate diskette. If you do not find the device name in the list, choose the "Unlisted or Updated Driver" selection at the top of the list, and load the manufacturer-supplied driver from a diskette.

To remove the driver and disable the device, select the device in the list and click the **Remove** button. If you want to update configuration information, choose the driver and click the **Setup** button. Some drivers are configurable, while others are not.

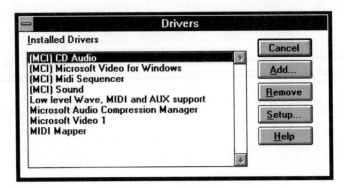

Figure 7.3
The Drivers Applet.

7.1.4   The Network Applet

The Network applet lets you configure your network card, as well as the protocols used by your machine. It is discussed in detail in Chapter 10.

7.1.5   The Server Applet

As described in Part 2 of this book, other users can connect to your machine to use its drives and printers. This makes every NT machine a server. The Server applet displays information about the use of your machine as a server. For example, it can track the number of people currently sharing a certain drive on your machine. It can also show you every resource that a certain person is using. Figure 7.4 shows a screen dump of the Server applet.

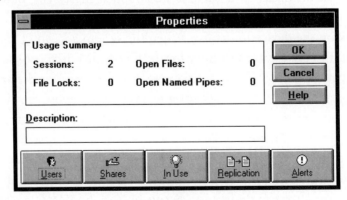

Figure 7.4
The Server applet.

The main screen presents summary information about four pieces of data:

- Sessions: Indicates the number of users connected to your machine.
- Open files: Indicates the number of files open on your computer.
- File locks: Indicates the number of locks in place. A program will lock a file or a record in a file to enforce exclusive access to it.
- Open named pipes: A named pipe allows inter-process communication to take place locally or over the network. A pipe is opened when two machines need to transfer data between one another.

Hidden in the middle of the applet is the field that lets you change the description of the machine that other users see when they are browsing the network. The applet also holds five buttons along the bottom.

The dialog for the **Users** button is shown in Figure 7.5. This dialog displays a list of users and the resources they have allocated. You use the dialog to disconnect users entirely, or to disconnect them from a specific resource. You might do this because you plan to shut down your machine (although the shut down procedure will do it automatically, you may want to do it manually for the satisfaction that it brings), or because someone is in an area where they do not belong.

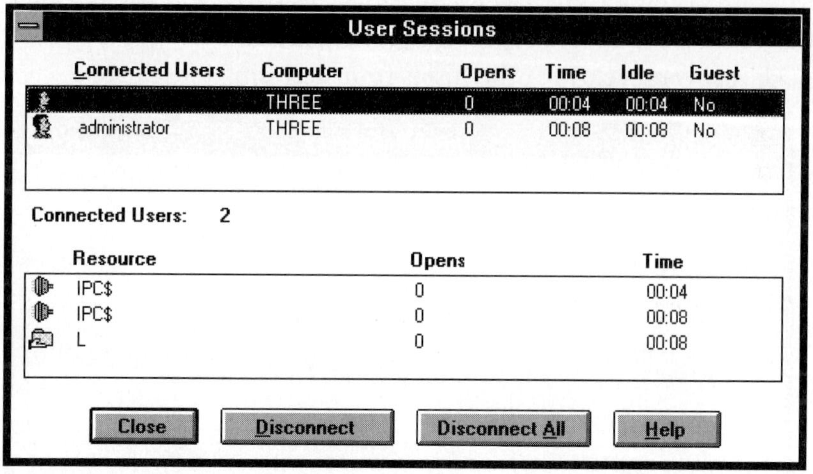

User Sessions						
Connected Users	Computer	Opens	Time	Idle	Guest	
	THREE	0	00:04	00:04	No	
administrator	THREE	0	00:08	00:08	No	

Connected Users: 2

Resource	Opens	Time
IPC$	0	00:04
IPC$	0	00:08
L	0	00:08

Close	Disconnect	Disconnect All	Help

Figure 7.5
The User Sessions dialog.

The dialog for the **Shares** button is shown in Figure 7.6. It is the complementof the previous dialog, and shows which users are using which resources on your machine. It also allows you to disconnect specific users, or all users, from a resource. You might do this prior to changing the disk in a CD-ROM or cartridge drive.

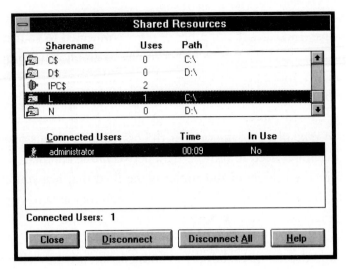

Figure 7.6
The Shared Resources dialog.

Figure 7.7 shows the dialog for the **In Use** button. This dialog displays all of the resources and file locks allocated to specific users, and allows you to close the individual connections as you see fit. You might use this dialog to remove a file lock that is preventing other users from accessing a resource.

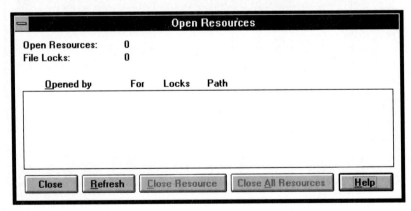

Figure 7.7
The Open Resources dialog.

The replication dialog, in conjunction with an NT Advanced Server acting as a replication exporter, enables file and directory replication. Figure 7.8 shows its dialog. See Section 13.6 for more information.

Figure 7.8
The Directory Replication dialog.

The **Alerts** button displays the dialog shown in Figure 7.9. This dialog allows you to cause duplicates of important alert dialogs to display themselves on other machines. For example, if the UPS detects a power failure, it will generate a dialog box. You can cause the machine to send that dialog to the central administrative machine in your office as well as to the local machine. Type the computer name or user name into the edit area and add it to the list of recipients with the **Add** button.

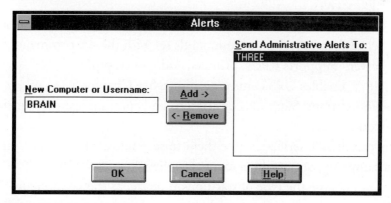

Figure 7.9
The Alerts dialog.

7.1.6   The Services Applet

Services are tasks that execute in the background to enable certain NT commands or capabilities. For example, the `at` command requires that the Schedule service be active. This service runs in the background triggering commands at the appropriate moment. Unless you, as the administrator, start the Schedule service, no one is able to use the `at` command. Whenever anyone tries to use it they get a "Service has not been started" message. Figure 7.10 shows the Services applet in use. The list below describes several of the common services:

- Alerter: Enables administrative alerts.
- Clipbook Server: Makes remote clipbook pages available on the net.
- Computer Browser: Monitors computers available on the network and makes a list of them available to applications.
- Directory Replicator: Maintains replicas of files and directories on other computers. See Figure 7.8 also.
- Event Log: Enables event logging. See Chapter 8.
- Messenger: Sends and receives messages and alerts over the network or on this machine.
- Net Logon: Authenticates users.
- Network Dynamic Data Exchange (DDE), DSDM: Handles DDE conversations over the network.
- Remote Procedure Call (RPC) Locator: Provides name services for RPC servers.
- RPC: Handles network communications for RPC clients and servers.
- Schedule: Activates the commands set with the `at` command.
- Server: Supports RPCs, printers, and named pipes.
- UPS: Enables UPS communications. See Chapter 5.
- Workstation: Supports connections and communication over the network.

You can disable services, cause them to start automatically every time the machine comes up, or start them manually when you need them. Use the **Start-up** button to choose the type of startup you desire, as shown in Figure 7.11.

All services must log on when they start. Most log on to a generic system account, but it is also possible to create specific accounts in the User Manager for certain services. The Schedule and Directory Replicator services allow this sort of logon. For example, you may want commands executed under the

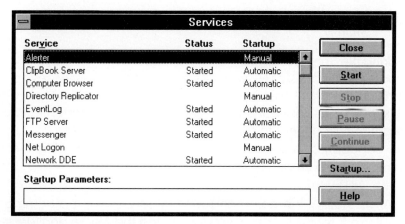

Figure 7.10
The Services dialog.

scheduler to read and write from a specific, restricted directory. By creating an account in the User Manager for the Schedule service and causing it to log on under that account, you can give it access to the desired directory.

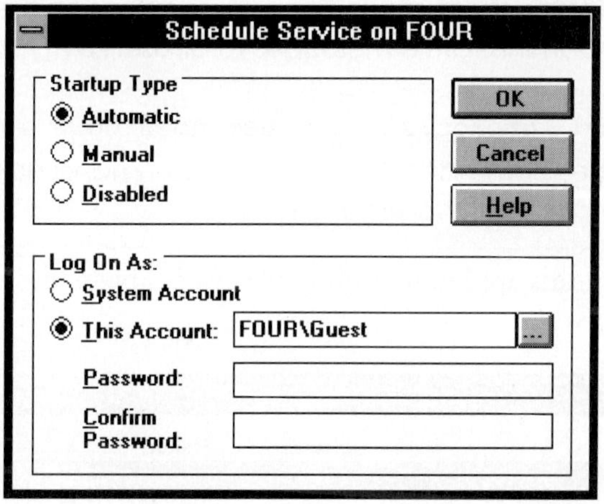

Figure 7.11
The Startup dialog.

You can start or stop a service with the corresponding button. Certain services also allow pausing using the **Pause** button seen in Figure 7.10.

7.1.7   The Devices Applet

The Devices applet is shown in Figure 7.12. It allows you to start and stop devices available on your machine. You will find entries for many different

Checking the Services applet

When you first install NT, you will want to check the Services applet and make sure that the Alerter, Messenger, and Schedule services have started. After installation they are set for manual startup, and you will want to switch them to automatic startup if you want to use any of these capabilities. You can test the Schedule service using the `at` command. For example, type something like this:

```
at 0815 "dir"
```

At 8:15 a.m. (this command uses military time), the command `dir` will execute in a separate window. To test the Alerter and Messenger services, type the following command:

```
net send xxx "hello"
```

Where xxx is the name of a machine on the network. First send a message to your own machine (use the Network applet to find your machine name if you don't know it), then send one to another machine. If you enable these services on all machines on the net, you can also send out administrative messages to all users by typing something like this:

```
net send /broadcast "the net goes down in 5 minutes"
```

See the net command in the on-line command Help file for more information on network commands.

types of devices in this applet, including the system beep, the floppy drives, and the parallel port.

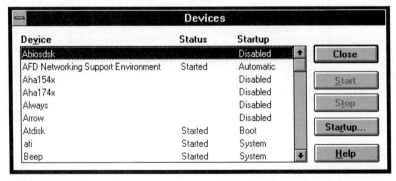

Figure 7.12
The Devices applet.

Administrative Strategy

Disabling floppy drives

If you want to disable the floppy drives so that no one can use them, use the Devices applet, select the Floppy device, click the **Start-up** button, and disable the device. Restart the machine and it will have no floppy drives. This simple operation will prevent someone from copying information on or off diskettes, but there is nothing to prevent a user of a PC-class machine from resetting the machine and then re-booting with a different operating system such as DOS. The only way to truly disable floppy drives is to remove them. See Appendix G.

7.1.8   The UPS Applet

The UPS applet lets you configure NT to communicate with a UPS. See Chapter 5 for more information.

7.1.9   The File Transfer Protocol (FTP) Applet

The FTP applet lets you see and disconnect users connected to the FTP server on your machine. See Section 14.4 for details on the FTP server.

7.2 Windows NT Setup

The Windows NT Setup Program is located in the Main group in the Program Manager. It lets you configure all of the primary device drivers used in your system, including the drivers for the screen, keyboard, mouse, SCSI adapter, and tape drive. It also contains facilities for adding application icons to the Program Manager, managing Windows components, and deleting user profiles in the registry.

To use the Windows NT Setup application, double click on its icon in the Main group of the Program Manager. You will see a window similar to the one shown in Figure 7.13. This window shows you the currently selected display, keyboard, and mouse drivers. To change any of these drivers, select the **Change System Settings** option in the **Options** menu. You will see a dialog containing a combo box for each of the three devices. Choose a new driver from the available options. If the device is not listed and you have a driver on diskette from the manufacturer, then find the **Other** option at the bottom of the list and select it. The system will prompt you for the diskette and load the driver from there.

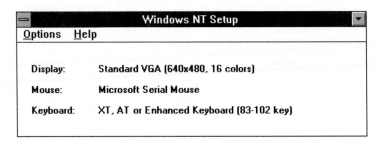

Figure 7.13
The Windows NT Setup Program.

Follow the same sort of procedure to change SCSI adapter drivers or tape drive drivers. For example, to change the SCSI card driver choose the **Add/Remove SCSI Adapters** option in the **Options** menu. You will see a dialog that shows you the currently selected driver. Select the driver and click on the **Remove** button to remove it. Then click on the **Add** button to see a list of available drivers, or click the **Other** option to load a driver from a diskette.

The **Set Up Applications** option allows you to search your hard disks for application executables and add their icons to the Program Manager automatically. After you select the menu option you will see a dialog that asks you to choose which drive you want to search for applications. Optionally you can direct the program to search only those directories in your current path. After you press the **OK** button, the search begins. You will eventually see a dialog similar to the one shown in Figure 7.14. You can select individual programs that you want to add to the Program Manager, or you can select all. The icons that get added will be placed in a group named "Applications," and you can copy or move the icons from there.

The **Add/Remove Windows Components** option in the **Option** menu lets you tell the system to add and remove categories of Windows NT files, as shown in Figure 7.15. NT inherits this capability from Windows 3.1. It is sometimes useful in installations where disk space is extremely tight. For example, you might choose to remove all of the games. For most people running NT, a savings of 300K bytes of disk space is fairly meaningless. The capability is there, however, and you can easily add components again later using the same tool.

The **Delete User Profiles** selection lets you delete extra user profiles from your system. A profile contains information about the user's Program Manager configuration, screen colors, and so on. When attached to an NT Advanced

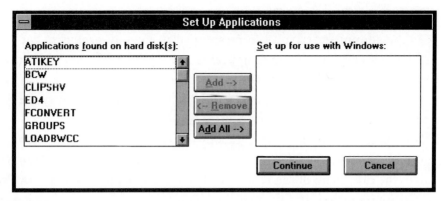

Figure 7.14
The Set Up Applications dialog.

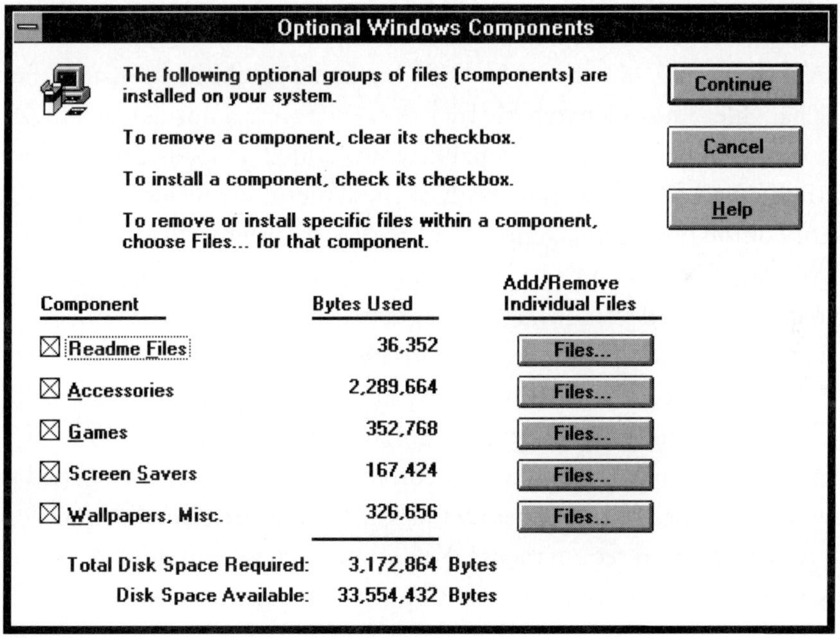

Figure 7.15
The Optional Windows Components dialog.

Server, an individual machine will load a copy of a user's profile whenever a logon from the server takes place. This menu option gives you an easy way to delete the extra copies.

7.3 Common Program Groups

As the administrator you can create special program groups in the Program Manager and cause them to appear in the Program Manager window of all users on the system. You might do this after adding an application to the system, so that the application's group and icons are available to everyone who uses the system.

You create a common group in exactly the same way that you create a normal group in the Program Manager. Logon as the administrator. Select the **New** option in the **File** menu of the Program Manager. Click on the **Common Program Group** radio box, and then click the **OK** button. The Program Manager will create a new group. Now fill it with any icons that you desire. All users will see this group in the Program Manager the next time they log on.

7.4 Autoexec Files

As far back as 1983 or so, MS-DOS has had a capability known as the "autoexec.bat" file. This is a batch file that runs each time a normal MS-DOS system boots. Later a "config.sys" capability was added. It loads device drivers at boot time. On a DOS machine, both of these files must be located in the root directory of the boot drive, generally Drive C:, in order to load properly.

Windows NT, in order to maintain backward compatibility when running older DOS and Windows 3.1 programs, supports the `autoexec.bat` and `config.sys` capabilities. NT adds two files called `autoexec.nt` and `config.nt` that are loaded whenever any 16-bit application executes. You will find, as the administrator, that you may need to adjust these files in order for certain 16-bit applications to run correctly. Simply place the needed statements into the file. See the documentation for the programs in question for more information on requirements. You can also create different autoexec and config files for specific applications using the PIF editor.

7.5 Bequeathing Your Administrative Powers

One thing you might have noticed in this and previous chapters is that there are a huge number of system details controlled by the administrator. If you choose to, you can lock down a system so that only you, as the administrator, can configure the printer, use the tape drive, change the time and date of the machine, and so on.

However, there are many situations where you want to give a knowledgeable user control of his or her machine. You can do this in either of two ways. You can give the user total control of the machine by making the user's account a member of the Administrators group. In general this is a bad idea, because it gives the user too much control and adversely affects the security of your network. As a member of the Administrators group, a user can do anything that the actual administrator can. You can give the user slightly less control of a machine by making his or her account a member of the Power Users group. A good description of a power user is someone who is allowed to use the machine as though he or she owned it. A normal user, for example, cannot change the system time, but a power user can. A power user has many administrative privileges, although security-sensitive areas still remain off limits.

You can also give certain users access to certain devices. For example, you can give a user varying levels of access to certain printers in the Print Manager. See Chapter 3. You can give someone the ability to back up the system by adding them to the Backup Operators group. By taking advantage of these various levels of access to the system, you can allow certain trusted people more access to their machines, while at the same time maintaining the security of the system and the network.

7.6 Examples

Let's say that you are administrating an NT machine and you want to add a new SCSI controller card and a new SCSI tape drive to it. Find the Windows NT Setup icon in the Main Group of the Program Manager. Double click on it and then choose the **Add/Remove SCSI devices** option in the **Options** menu. Click on the **Add** button, and then choose the new driver from the available list. If the manufacturer of the board supplied their own driver, then choose the **Other** option at the bottom of the list. You will be asked to specify the diskette or CD-ROM drive holding the driver. Follow the same procedure for the **Add/Remove Tape Devices** option in the **Options** menu.

One day a user walks into your office and asks why the `at` command does not work on her NT machine. She wants to schedule a batch file to run late at night. On her machine, you open the Control Panel and then the Services applet. You set the Schedule service to automatic startup. Now the `at` command works correctly.

Say you have three users sharing an NT machine in a lab, and they are each having to use the same set of applications in their work. You might create a common program group in the Program Manager and place into it the icons for these applications. When these users log on they will all see this same group.

A user stops you in the hall one day to ask why he is unable to calculate through a monster spreadsheet he is using. He keeps getting a dialog warning him about insufficient memory. You use the System applet in the Control Panel to change the maximum size of his virtual memory file so that he no longer has this problem. Unfortunately, a week later he's back because he is out of disk space. You decide to add a 2 Gigabyte SCSI hard disk to his machine to supplement his two IDE drives. You add the SCSI controller in the manner described above, and then use the Disk Administrator in Chapter 6 to create a new primary partition from its free space. Then, using the System applet in the Control Panel again, you move the paging file to the new SCSI drive.

EVENT MONITORING

Windows NT has a complete Event logging facility built in to the operating system. This facility centrally records all system events, security events, and application events, and presents them through the Event Viewer in a standard format for easy reading. In this chapter you will learn how to use the Event Viewer to track system and security problems.

8.1 Overview of System Events

The Event log stores *events* and lets you view them at any time using the Event Viewer. Critical events, such as an overflowing disk drive, appear in a dialog on the screen as well as in the Event log. All non-critical events appear in the log without fanfare. Events can be quite useful when troubleshooting problems or when trying to track down security violations. For example, if a system service has trouble starting or fails midway through a session, it will record the problem in the Event log. You can also use the Event Viewer to track a wide range of security-related events such as failed logon attempts. See Sections 2.8 and 3.5 for information on starting the Security logging facilities of the User Manager and Print Manager.

Start the Event Viewer by logging on as the administrator and double clicking on the Event Viewer icon in the Administrative Tools group of the Program Manager. The Event log records events from three separate sources in three separate logs:

- *System events* are events generated by any part of the NT operating system.

129

- *Security events* are events generated in response to security checks specified in the User Manager, Print Manager, File Manager, and Registry Editor.
- *Application events* are errors and other items of interest generated by applications running on your machine.

You can switch between the different logs using the first three options in the **Log** menu. Figure 8.1 demonstrates a typical system log.

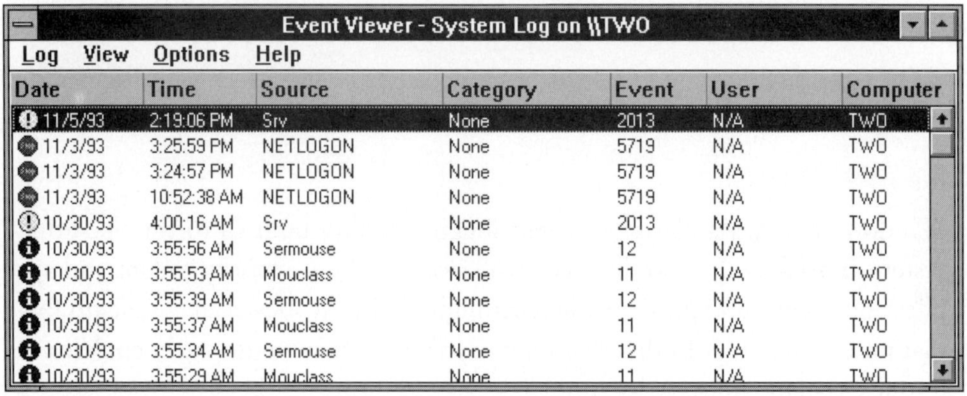

Date	Time	Source	Category	Event	User	Computer
11/5/93	2:19:06 PM	Srv	None	2013	N/A	TWO
11/3/93	3:25:59 PM	NETLOGON	None	5719	N/A	TWO
11/3/93	3:24:57 PM	NETLOGON	None	5719	N/A	TWO
11/3/93	10:52:38 AM	NETLOGON	None	5719	N/A	TWO
10/30/93	4:00:16 AM	Srv	None	2013	N/A	TWO
10/30/93	3:55:56 AM	Sermouse	None	12	N/A	TWO
10/30/93	3:55:53 AM	Mouclass	None	11	N/A	TWO
10/30/93	3:55:39 AM	Sermouse	None	12	N/A	TWO
10/30/93	3:55:37 AM	Mouclass	None	11	N/A	TWO
10/30/93	3:55:34 AM	Sermouse	None	12	N/A	TWO
10/30/93	3:55:29 AM	Mouclass	None	11	N/A	TWO

Event Viewer - System Log on \\TWO — Log View Options Help

Figure 8.1
A typical System Log.

The different data fields that you see in Figure 8.1 are described below:
- Date and time: The date and time at which the event occurred.
- Source: The program or system that detected the event.
- Category: A categorization for the event chosen by the source.
- Event: An integer ID for the event.
- User: The user who was logged in when the event occurred.
- Computer: The computer on which the event occurred.

Please note that if you see no events, it probably means that the Event log service is turned off. See Section 7.1.6 for information on starting services.

To get more detail on a specific event, you can double click on it. You will see a dialog like the one shown in Figure 8.2.

In the **Event Detail** dialog, you see a detailed description of the event, along with supplemental data.

In order to get any benefit from the system Event log, you have to actually look at it occasionally. You should do this on some regular schedule, like once

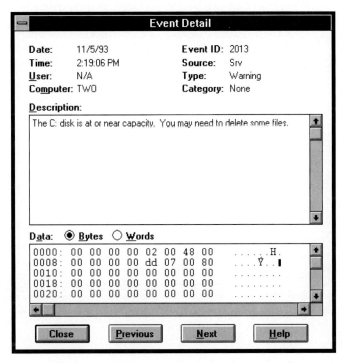

Figure 8.2
A detailed description of an event.

a day or once a week. You should also look at it first whenever any component of the system is not working correctly. Components experiencing problems often write useful data into the Event log that can help to fix the problem.

When a serious event such as a power failure occurs, the system will display a dialog box informing you of the situation (if you have a UPS). In some cases you may redirect those messages to a central machine so that an operator is instantly aware of the problem. See Section 7.1.5 for information on how to route the messages to other machines.

8.2 Customizing the Event Viewer

A number of menu options in the Event Viewer allow you to customize the way that the viewer presents its data. For example, the **View** menu contains a **Filter Events** option, as demonstrated in Figure 8.3. This option lets you specify the events that you want to view. You can select the time range for the events of interest, their type, and any special field values. Any events that match your specifications appear in the Event Viewer list, while all others are omitted.

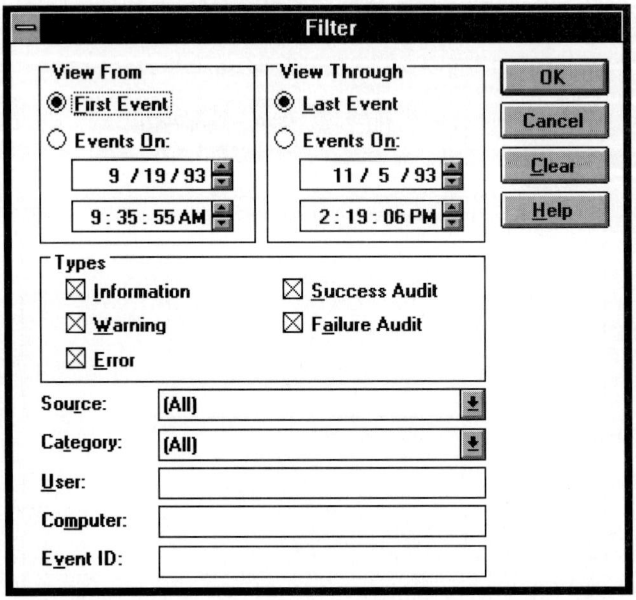

Figure 8.3
The Filter Events dialog.

The **Newest First** and **Oldest First** options in the **View** menu let you change the sort order for the events displayed. The **Find** option lets you find a specific event. A dialog like the one shown in Figure 8.4 appears and lets you select the criteria for the events that you wish to find in a manner similar to the Filter Events dialog shown in Figure 8.3.

The **Detail** option in the **View** menu does the same thing as double clicking on the event. The **Refresh** option adds any new events to the window (the window does not incorporate new events as they occur; you must select the **Refresh** option).

In the **Log** menu, the **Clear All Events** option erases all of the events in the log. Before the events disappear, the system asks if you want to save a copy of the log to disk. See Section 8.4 for details.

If you select the **Log Settings** option you can specify the behavior of the logging file. Figure 8.5 demonstrates this dialog. You can select the log you wish to customize, the maximum size of the log file, and the behavior of the Event Viewer as the file fills. For example, if you select the **Overwrite Events As Needed** option then, when the log file reaches its maximum size, old events are erased to make room for new ones. You can also set a specific limit on the number of days of information retained to keep the log file within an average size range.

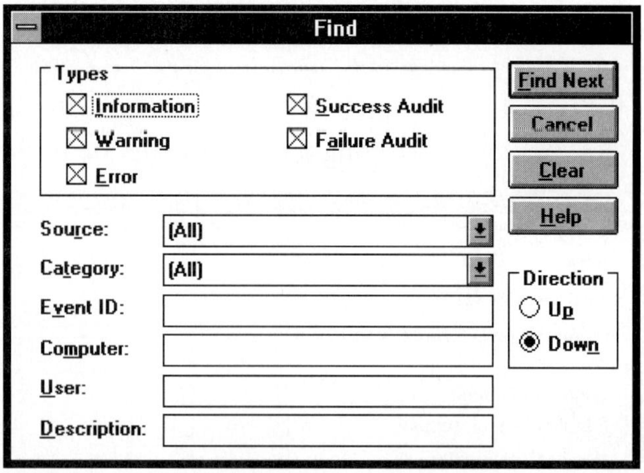

Figure 8.4
The Find Event dialog.

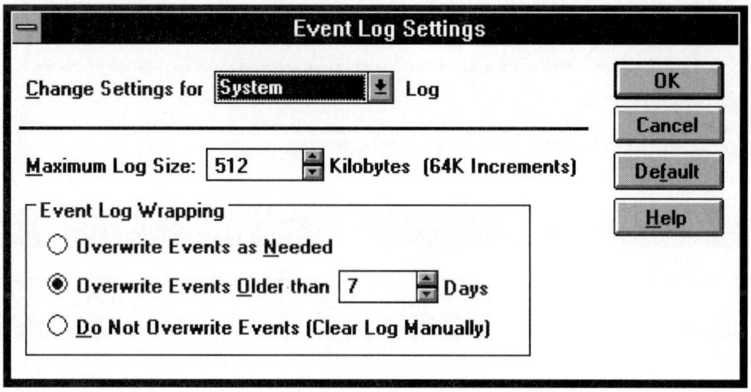

Figure 8.5
The Log Settings dialog.

It is also possible to view the Event log on any computer on the network using the **Select Computer** option. This allows you to view the log files of all machines on your net without leaving your office.

If for any reason you ever want to turn off Event logging, double click on the Control Panel application in the Main group of the Program Manager. Then double click on the Services applet and disable the Event log service. See Chapter 7 for details on services.

8.3 The Security Log

In Chapter 2 you saw that you can set the Audit Policy in the User Manager to log security events. This is done by selecting the **Audit** option in the **Policies** menu and then choosing the security events you wish to monitor. A typical Audit Policy dialog is pictured in Figure 8.6. Figure 8.7 shows a typical Security log. View this log by selecting the **Security** option in the **Log** menu.

Audit Policy
Computer: TWO
OK
Cancel
Help
Do Not Audit
Audit These Events:
Success
Failure
Logon and Logoff
File and Object Access
Use of User Rights
User and Group Management
Security Policy Changes
Restart, Shutdown, and System
Process Tracking

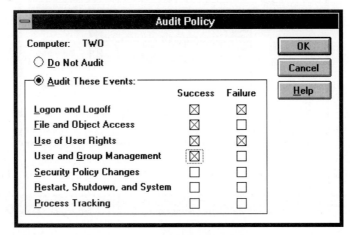

Figure 8.6
The Audit Policy dialog from the User Manager.

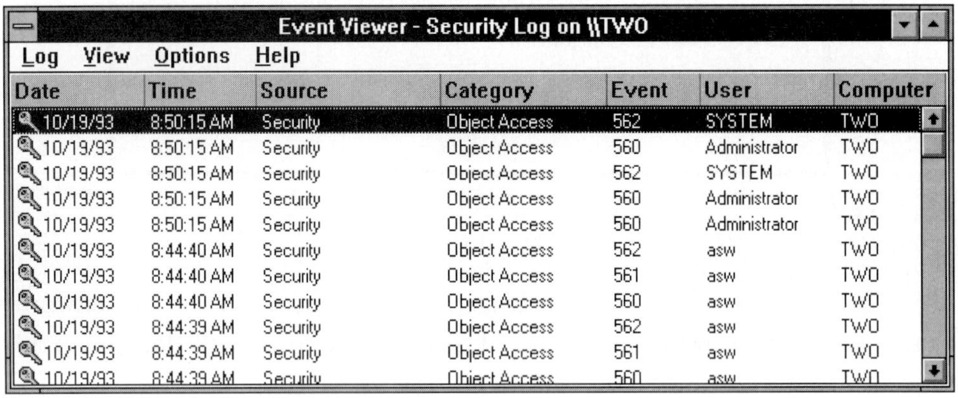

Event Viewer - Security Log on \\TWO
Log View Options Help
Date Time Source Category Event User Computer
10/19/93 8:50:15 AM Security Object Access 562 SYSTEM TWO
10/19/93 8:50:15 AM Security Object Access 560 Administrator TWO
10/19/93 8:50:15 AM Security Object Access 562 SYSTEM TWO
10/19/93 8:50:15 AM Security Object Access 560 Administrator TWO
10/19/93 8:50:15 AM Security Object Access 560 Administrator TWO
10/19/93 8:44:40 AM Security Object Access 562 asw TWO
10/19/93 8:44:40 AM Security Object Access 561 asw TWO
10/19/93 8:44:40 AM Security Object Access 560 asw TWO
10/19/93 8:44:39 AM Security Object Access 562 asw TWO
10/19/93 8:44:39 AM Security Object Access 561 asw TWO
10/19/93 8:44:39 AM Security Object Access 560 asw TWO

Figure 8.7
A typical security log.

You can also audit security events in the Printer Manager, the File Manager, and the Registry Editor.

8.4 Archiving Logs

The Event Viewer provides an extremely easy way to archive logged data to disk for long term storage. You can also use this option to export data to other applications. You can store logs either in their native format, or in one of two different text formats. If stored in their native format, you can reload old log files and review the data they contain, filter them as necessary, find specific events, and so on. If you store the data in a text format, you can load it into other programs to create reports or to look for special events that the Event Viewer itself cannot detect. Text formats are either tab or comma delimited. The order of data in the text file is shown below:

Date, Time, Source, Type, Category, Event, User, Computer, and Domain

Only the events in the currently chosen log section (system, security, or application) are stored, so if you want to store all sections create three separate files.

To save a log file, choose the **Save As** option in the **Log** menu. Select the file type in the **Save File As Type** area of the Save As dialog. To reload a file stored in the Event Viewer's native format (`.evt`), Choose the **Open** option in the **Log** menu. Data saved in the text format cannot be reloaded. All of the Event Viewer services are available on a loaded file except **Refresh** and **Clear All Events** options.

Since you never know when you might need to go back and review data, it is a good idea to get in the habit of saving all log information on either a weekly or monthly schedule. Save the archive files to diskette or tape and store them in a safe place. For example, you might retain security information for a year just in case somebody needs it.

8.5 Examples

One of the most common system dialogs you will get after an NT machine boots up is the "A Service was unable to start" message. When you look in the Event Viewer you will see a line that specifies the Service Control Manager as the source of the error. Double click on that event. In the resulting dialog you might see a message like this:

The Directory Replicator service failed to start due to the following error:
The service did not start due to a logon failure

In the dialog used to start the replicator service, you must specify a special account that it uses. See Section 13.6 or 7.1.5. That dialog will prevent you from entering an invalid account name or password. However, the dialog cannot prevent you from changing the password at a later time in the User Manager, and that will cause the service to fail when it tries to start. Most services that fail to start do so because of a simple problem like this one, or because something like a network card has lost its connection or failed. You use the Event Viewer to get a complete description so that you can fix the problem.

Problems with 32-bit applications are also stored in the Event log. For example, if an application is unable to find a DLL that it needs, or if it has some other problem that it wants to report to the administrator, it will do it in the Event log.

There are many ways that you might use the Security log to monitor user, file, registry, and printer security problems. First, enable the events of interest in the User Manager, File Manager, Registry Editor, or Print Manager (the audit capability must be turned on in the User Manager for it to work at all). For example, you might track failed logon attempts on a machine to see how often they are occurring and whether or not there is any pattern. This might help to track down someone trying to break into the system. You might monitor successful security policy changes to look for another administrator trying to leak information. If you have selected the Shutdown/Reboot audit event, then every time the system boots it will leave a record in the Security log, and that might indicate someone powering down a machine to reboot it under a different operating system.

Look at the Event log every morning and you will often notice new, informative, and unexpected messages. For example:

The C: drive is at or near capacity. You may wish to delete some files

If nothing else, simply look at the log in the morning and then erase it so you see the new items the next day. Archiving the data really is a good idea however. See Section 8.4 for details.

PERFORMANCE MONITORING

9

The Performance Monitor is designed to help you visualize your system's performance characteristics in several different formats. You can, for example, view things like CPU utilization, cache performance, memory usage, and disk throughput. You will use this information either to remove bottlenecks in existing systems, or to help guide you when making new hardware purchases. It is also a fun tool to use simply because it can show you an amazing array of statistics. Anyone who likes box scores will love this tool.

9.1 Overview

The Performance Monitor uses *counters* embedded in the different functional units of the operating system to display performance information about your machine. You can also display the same performance information about other machines on the network for comparison purposes. The counters cover every aspect of the system, including:

- Processor(s)
- Disk drives
- Disk cache
- Memory
- Virtual memory paging file
- Network traffic
- Objects (e.g., the number of semaphores, threads, etc. at any given time)
- Process information
- Thread information

- Server information
- Overall system performance

You can view this information in three different formats: a strip chart, a bar chart, or a spreadsheet-like report. You can also log performance information to disk or use performance characteristics to trigger alerts or batch programs.

Administrative Strategy

Using the Performance Monitor to control disk space

You can create a batch program to compress a certain area of your hard disk, and then cause the Performance Monitor to call that batch file every time available disk space drops below a certain level. Or you might have a batch program automatically copy a certain directory to a server drive or tape drive and then delete it from the local drive each time disk space becomes critical.

As you can see from the variety of information this tool can access, the Performance Monitor is important to the system administrator. You can use it in a variety of ways to monitor and enhance the performance of your machine or your network.

9.2 Viewing Data

One of the more enjoyable ways to use the Performance Monitor is to have it on your screen as a "digital fish tank," displaying a line graph of various statistics simply because they are interesting to watch. Figure 9.1 shows a typical strip chart containing the percentage of the processor time utilized, along with the average number of packets per second that this machine is moving over the network. You can see, from an administrative point of view, that this tool has a number of utilitarian functions. For example, if you have a machine whose CPU utilization is always 100%, then you know that the machine is probably underpowered for its workload and should be upgraded.

You choose the data that you want to view in the chart either by pressing the "+" button that you see in the tool bar of Figure 9.1, or by selecting the **Add to Chart** option in the **Edit** menu. You will see a dialog like the one shown in Figure 9.2.

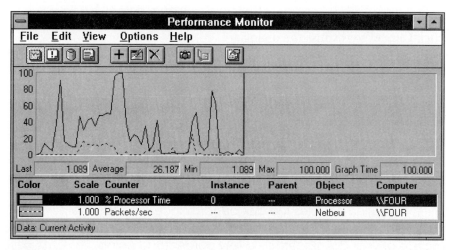

Figure 9.1
The Performance Monitor in strip chart mode.

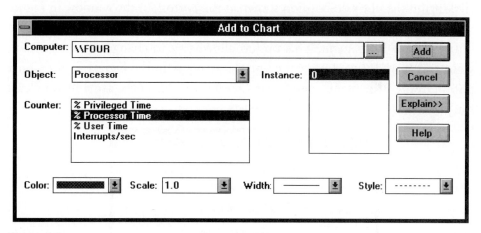

Figure 9.2
The Add to Chart dialog.

The dialog in Figure 9.2 allows you to select the machine that you want to monitor, the counter of interest, and the way that you want to display that information. For example, if you are interested in memory consumption, you can choose the **Memory** option from the **Object** combo box. Over 20 counters are available for this object. If you want to know what the various counters actually mean, click on the **Explain** button and select different counters. You can scale that counter on the graph, and select its color, line width, and style. Click the **Add** button to add the counter to the graph, and then select other counters or click **Cancel** to dismiss the dialog.

Administrative Strategy

Activating disk counters

If you select different disk counters and you find that the Performance Monitor always displays zeros for these counters, then you should open an MS-DOS window and type:

```
diskperf -Y
```

This option enables the disk performance counters the next time you reboot. Be aware that these counters will degrade the performance of your disk access by a few percentage points.

You can edit the lines shown on the graph after creation either by double clicking on the line's description shown at the bottom of the window in Figure 9.1, or by single clicking on the description and choosing the **Edit Chart Line** button in the **Edit** menu. This option allows you to change the line's color, scale, width, and style. Delete the line altogether with the **Delete From Chart** option in the **Edit** menu. The **Clear Display** option in the same menu clears the graph and starts it again from the left.

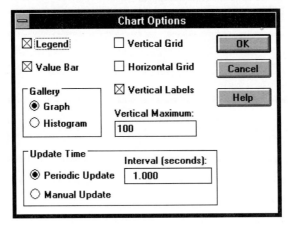

Figure 9.3
The Chart Options dialog.

The **Options** menu contains a **Chart** option that lets you customize the appearance of the chart. Figure 9.3 shows the options that are available. All of them are self-explanatory. The **Options** menu also contains options that let you turn the status bar, tool bar, and menu bar on and off, as well as an **Update Now** option that forces a manual update. The **Always On Top** option forces this window to always remain on top of other windows.

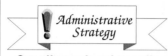

Creating a load monitor

If you turn off the status bar, tool bar, and menu, and in the Chart options dialog turn off the legend and the value bar, you can create a window that contains just the graph, as shown in Figure 9.4. You can make this window always on top, and place it in a corner of your screen to act as a load monitor. Double click on the graph to restore the menu bar.

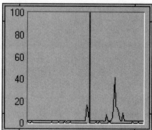

Figure 9.4
A small load monitor created using the Performance Monitor application.

If you create a chart setup that you do not like, or that you want to clear for any other reason, choose the **New Chart** option in the **File** menu. On the other hand, if you create a chart that you would like to reuse again in the future, then select the **Save Chart Settings** or **Save Workspace** option. The former saves the settings for the current chart, while the latter saves the settings for all four components in the application. You can later load a saved configuration using the **Open** option.

While a strip chart is one way to view the data, there are many cases where a numeric display would be more useful or appropriate. To view data numerically, choose the **Report** option in the **View** menu. This option allows you to create a spreadsheet-like report from the different counters. Use the **Add to Report** option in the **Edit** menu to choose the counters of interest. Figure 9.5 shows a typical report. You can customize the update interval in this report using the **Report** option in the **Options** menu.

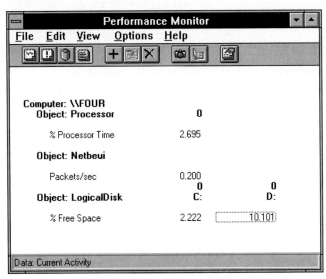

Figure 9.5
A Performance Monitor report.

9.3 Acting on Data

The Performance Monitor has an alert facility that allows you to generate special Performance Monitor alerts. These alerts display themselves in the Log window of the Performance Monitor, but they can also generate dialog boxes on any machine. They can also trigger the execution of a batch file or executable program. These facilities allow you to create very specific responses to certain performance criteria.

For example, say you have had a problem with a machine running out of disk space and dying. This machine might be a data logger that accepts data continuously, or it might be a machine with a large hard disk that you are using as a server on your network. In either case, you might want the machine to send an alert dialog to an operator whenever free disk space falls below a certain level. Or, in the case of the data logger, you might want it to automatically copy compressed data to a floptical disk or tape drive and then send you an alert so that you can come pick up and replace the archiving media. Both of these tasks are easily performed with the Alert facility in the Performance Monitor.

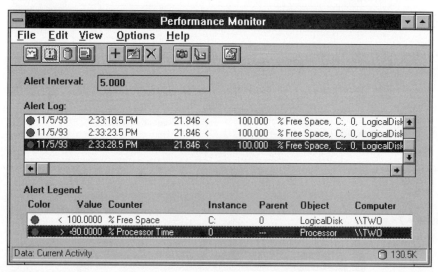

Figure 9.6
The Alert facility.

Switch to the Alert mode by selecting the **Alert** option in the **View** menu. Figure 9.6 shows the Alert facility set up to generate an alert when the number of free megabytes on Drive C: falls below 10, or when the processor load rises above 90%. To add a new alert, choose the **Add to Alert** option in the **Edit** menu. You will see a dialog like the one shown in Figure 9.7. You select the **Computer** field, the **Counter** field, and the **Instance** field in the normal way. You then enter the trigger value for the counter and whether the system should trigger when the counter goes over or under that value. You can also specify that the system run a program or batch file by entering the complete path to the file in the **Run Program On Alert** field. You can cause the system to execute the program on the first instance, or every instance, of the alert using the radio box.

You can further adjust the behavior of the Alert facility using the **Alert** option in the **Options** menu. This option presents a dialog like the one shown in Figure 9.8. In the dialog, the **Switch to Alert View** check box causes the Performance Monitor to switch to the Alert view whenever an alert triggers. The **Network Alert** section allows you to send a dialog box to any machine or user on the network. The **Update** time section lets you specify the time between updates.

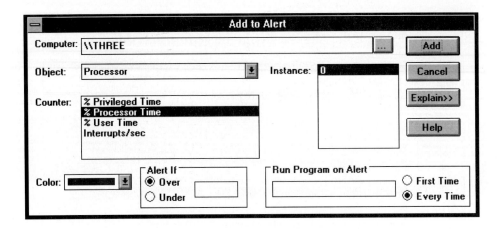

Figure 9.7
The Add to Alert dialog.

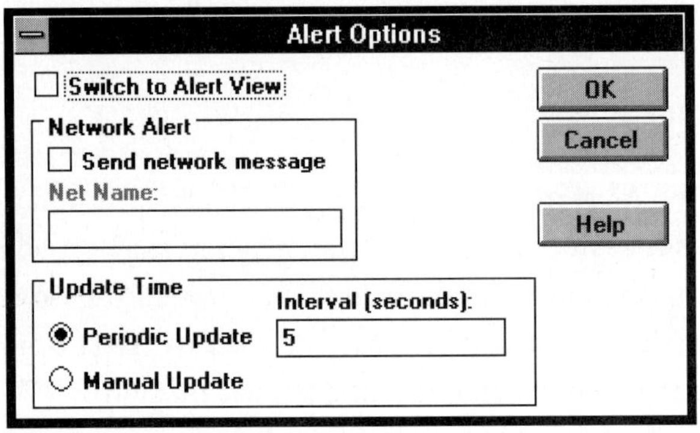

Figure 9.8
The Alert Options dialog.

You will find the Alert section of the Performance Monitor to be one of your most useful administrative tools. It allows you to detect and prevent performance problems on your machine, as well as any machine on the network.

9.4 Logging and Reviewing Data

The Log facility gives you an easy way to save specific data to a log file so that you can review it later. When you reload the data you can view it in any of the different ways seen in previous sections (as a strip chart, as a report, or as alerts). You can also select specific time intervals, or relog the data to see it in "fast motion," so you can see trends and patterns that you might not see otherwise.

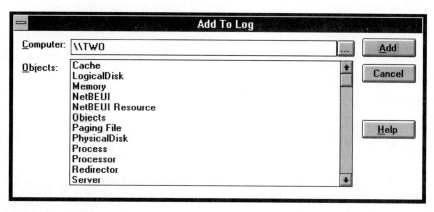

Figure 9.9
The Add to Log dialog.

To create a log file, Select the **Log** option in the **View** menu. Then select the **Add to Log** option in the **Edit** menu. Figure 9.9 shows the dialog that you will see. You add broad categories of counters to the log file. For example, you might be interested in logging information about the processor, memory, disk drives, and the network. Select these different categories from the list, and all of the counters pertaining to those categories will be stored in the log file. The log window will appear as shown in Figure 9.10.

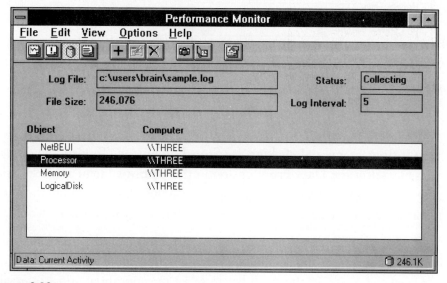

Figure 9.10
The Log display in the Performance Monitor.

To start logging data, select the **Log** option in the **Options** menu. You can select the log file name and the update interval, as shown in Figure 9.11. Log files get large fairly quickly. For example, with the categories selected as shown in Figure 9.10, the file enlarges by about 5,000 bytes at each time interval. Make sure that you have plenty of space on the selected drive. Once you have selected the file name and the interval, be sure to press the **Start Log** button to begin logging. If you select an existing log file, the new data will append to the end of it.

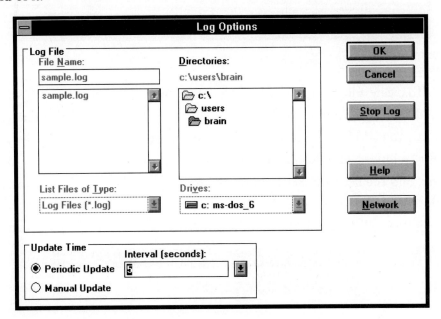

Figure 9.11
The Log Options dialog.

Eventually you will stop the log. Do this by again selecting the **Log** option in the **Options** menu and clicking the **Stop Log** button. To view the data in the log file, select the **Data From** option in the **Options** menu and select the log file name. Choose the strip chart display with the **Chart** option in the **View** menu and select the counters that you want to view as you normally would.

To view specific time intervals, choose the **Time Window** option in the **Edit** menu. You will see a dialog like the one shown in Figure 9.12. Slide the two smaller rectangles seen in the scroll bar to select the appropriate time intervals. Viewing these intervals in the strip chart mode shows you the chart at the selected interval with the counters specified. Selecting the Report mode and picking several counters will show you the averages for the counters specified. Selecting the Alert mode and picking counters will show you all alerts in the interval in question. Finally, you can select the Log mode, select categories from those available in the log file, select a time interval, and then relog the data to a new file.

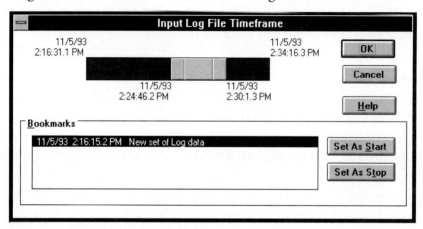

Figure 9.12
The Input Log File Timeframe dialog.

These capabilities help you track down specific bottlenecks, and also let you start logs and then perform specific tests on a single machine or a network of machines. You can then review the results after the test.

9.5 Examples

The following examples show how you can use the Performance Monitor to debug certain system problems and bottlenecks:

1. **Problem: The system seems slow or sluggish.**

    Sluggishness is caused either by a slow CPU, too little memory, or too much disk access. Check the following:

    - Processor: % Processor Time—This counter indicates the percentage of CPU time spent in a non-idle thread, and is an indication of the processor's load. If it is consistently above 80%, it probably means you need a faster processor for the work you are doing.
    - Physical Disk: % Disk Time—If this value is consistently above 75%, especially in combination with a Disk Queue Length greater than twice

the number of drives, it means that your applications are disk bound. Consider getting a faster disk, or separating the paging file to a separate drive.

- Memory: Page Faults/sec—A page fault occurs when processes request memory that is stored on disk in the virtual memory paging file. Excessive page faults are caused by insufficient RAM.

2.   **Problem: The disk light is on all the time.**

If it seems like the disk drive is running constantly, it means either that the paging file is being accessed constantly, or that NT does not have enough RAM for an appropriately sized disk cache, or both. Check the following:

- Memory: Pages/sec—This counter holds the number of disk pages that were demanded to meet virtual memory requests. If its value is greater than 5 or so, then you need to increase the amount of RAM in your system.
- Physical Disk: % Disk Time—If disk utilization is high and you have only one disk drive, then the system is having to wait to load pages off the disk. You might get a second drive and put the paging file on it, or get a drive with better performance. Always increase RAM size before increasing disk speed however.

3.   **Problem: Disk access is sluggish.**

If a disk-intensive application is performing poorly, it could mean that the drive is slow or forced to retry because of errors, that there is not enough RAM so virtual memory accesses are competing detrimentally for the disk, or that the application is poorly designed and accessing the disk too much. Check the following:

- Physical Disk: Average Disk sec/Transfer—This counter indicates the amount of time needed to retrieve a sector from the disk. When this value begins to rise, it may mean that there is a faulty area on the disk that is causing retries. A retry requires the disk to spin one extra revolution, which takes 15 milliseconds or so. This value should be considered a problem if it is greater than 0.2–0.3 seconds.
- Memory: Pages/sec—If this value is greater than 5 or so, the paging activity is competing for the disk drive too much. Increase your system's RAM.
- Physical Disk: Disk Bytes/sec—This value tells you how many bytes per second are moving on and off the disk. If it is low (say 100K) while

the disk is running continuously, then it may mean you need a better interface card or a faster disk.

4. Problem: Numerous "not enough memory" messages.

The "not enough memory" message comes from a lack of virtual memory space on the disk. Increase the virtual memory file's maximum size. You can confirm the problem, if you are curious, by looking at the Paging File: % Usage counter. A high value indicates that more virtual memory space is needed.

You should take time to read the explanations for the many different counters available (check the Add To Chart dialog shown in Figure 9.2 and click the **Explain** button). Many of these counters are quite interesting and, with a little knowledge, you will find your mind putting them together in interesting combinations to answer questions.

PART

II

Part Two introduces you to network administration under Windows NT. This chapter shows how to design and organize your network to best meet the needs of your users. You will learn how to share disks and printers over the network and how to create an e-mail system. You will also learn how to connect to other systems residing on a heterogeneous network.

NETWORK ADMINISTRATION

DESIGNING AND CREATING
A NETWORK

10

In the preceding chapters, you learned how to administrate a lone NT machine. Windows NT is meant to work on a network, however, and doesn't really display its full luster until it is connected to other NT machines. Once you are comfortable with the single-machine administration concepts in the first part of this book, you are ready to begin administering networks.

The purpose of this chapter is to introduce you to network administration under Windows NT. It will help you to familiarize yourself with the vocabulary and issues that arise when working with networked machines. Once you finish with this chapter, you should be able to examine your own computing requirements and design a Windows NT network that meets your needs now and in the future.

10.1 Basic Network Concepts

A computer network consists of a set of computers connected together both physically and conceptually. The physical portion of the connection consists of a network adapter of some sort, as well as the wire or other media used to transmit the network packets between machines. See Figure 10.1. The conceptual part of the connection consists of the software that lets the user access the network. This software includes not only the network drivers that communicate directly with the network adapter, but also programs that massage the network data so that it appears to the user as a disk drive, a printer, or an e-mail message.

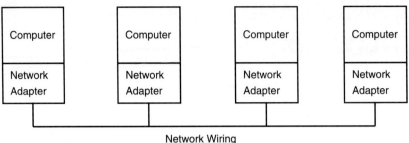

Figure 10.1
Hardware in a typical network.

There are many variables that go into designing a physical network. For example, the type of adapter card that you buy determines whether you have an Ethernet network, a Token Ring network, and so on. You can also choose the media that you use: Coax, twisted pair, radio waves, and so on. You can arrange the media in a variety of topologies: Bus, star, and ring topologies are the most common. You can also select the protocols used by the network. For example, Windows NT provides native support for the NetBEUI protocol. It can also support the TCP/IP protocol used by UNIX machines. Your specific choices for these different variables are determined by the size of your network, any existing wiring or networks with which you need to connect, the expected size of your network, and your personality and budget.

A typical, low-cost starting configuration for small to medium-sized networks consists of inexpensive Ethernet adapters connected with coaxial cable, as shown in Figure 10.1. Many machines come with Ethernet adapters already installed or wired directly onto the motherboard. Ethernet cards connected by coaxial cable implement a bus topology: Machines are connected one to another in a single, non-branching chain. It costs less than $200 per machine to create a network of this type, and the performance of the resulting network is very good.

A typical Ethernet network can handle 20 to 30 machines, depending on the applications that users are running. At some point however, the network slows down because users demand more data than it can carry. Ethernet networks have a maximum transfer rate of about one million bytes per second, although high traffic situations reduce this capacity due to collisions. Once the collection of users together demand more than the maximum carrying capacity of the network, network performance falls off rapidly.

At this point the network administrator will generally *segment* the network. Groups of related machines are placed on their own individual networks, or segments, and these segments are then connected to one another through a *router*. For example, all of the machines in the accounting department of a company might be on one segment, while all machines in sales are on another. When designed correctly, the majority of network traffic remains isolated on the local network segments. For example, people in the accounting department would make connections primarily to other accounting machines, and only rarely to sales machines. The router is able to detect the packets that must move between segments and transfers them appropriately. See Chapter 14 for more information on routers.

10.2   How NT Uses the Network

Windows NT is designed from the ground up to work with a network. It uses a network in a variety of different ways:

- Remote disk access: When you use the File Manager to connect to a remote disk drive, NT sends and receives data from the remote drive through the network. For example, if you copy a remote file to your local drive, your machine sends a request to the remote machine for the file, and the remote machine sends back packets of data that contain the file's contents.

- Remote printer access: When you print something on a remote printer, NT forms the data into packets and sends it out over the network to the machine sharing the printer. The remote machine spools that data and gives it to the printer. The printer may also send back status information over the network.

- Electronic mail: When you send an e-mail message to another user, NT places the message into network packets and sends them to the Post Office machine for your network. When you read e-mail, data is taken from the Post Office machine and sent to your machine over the network.

- Chat: When you form a chat connection with another user, your machine sends each character you type over the network to the other user's machine, and vice versa.

- Client/Server connections: Many applications support specific Client/ Server relationships between different machines on the network. For example, your network might have a machine acting as a database server for a number of clients. If you use an application capable of talking to that server, the application will send requests for data over the network to the server. The server processes each request and returns the result over the network as well.

If you do not take any special actions, NT will naturally use the NetBEUI protocol to transfer data between machines. What this means is that any packet of information that NT places on the network has an arrangement of bytes that conforms to the NetBEUI standard. All NT machines (as well as Windows for Workgroups machines) understand this standard, and can therefore accept packets of this type.

UNIX machines, on the other hand, will ignore all NetBEUI packets. UNIX machines instead accept packets formatted for the TCP/IP protocol, as do routers. By installing its TCP/IP package, NT can understand or generate TCP/IP packets as well. See Chapter 14 for details. A single network segment can support multiple protocols. For example, UNIX and NT machines can co-exist on a single segment without difficulty. The UNIX machines simply ignore the NetBEUI packets.

10.3 Network Configurations

You can use Windows NT to create any of three different network configurations: Peer-to-Peer, Client/Server, and Domain-Controlled. Each of the three configurations has its own advantages and disadvantages, as well as its own hardware and software requirements.

10.3.1   Peer-to-Peer Networks

In a Peer-to-Peer network, all of the machines on the net are equals. Any machine can share its hard disk or its printer. Any other machine on the network can attach to these shared devices. Peer-to-Peer networks have the advantage of initial simplicity. All you have to do is cable the machines together. If you give individual users administrative privileges on their own machines, then they can share their drives and printers as they see fit.

Peer-to-Peer networks provide the least expensive and simplest networking option, because you do not have to dedicate a machine to act as the server. Two problems arise from this simplicity however. Say you have 10 users on a Peer-to-Peer network and people keep their work on their local hard drives. If you are working on a project that requires you to share work with five other people, then you have to connect to five separate network drives and switch between all of them constantly. Also, to back up the network you have to attach to all 10 drives and work with each one separately. If you have 20 machines on the network the problems compound themselves further. As discussed in Section 1.4.4, this setup also tends to waste disk space. Each disk on the network will have unused space on it, but there is no way for anyone on the network to consolidate this space and use it efficiently.

A solution to this problem is to give one machine a large hard disk and create user directories on that hard disk for everyone on the net. Users can then store all their files on this single drive. One advantage of this arrangement is that everyone connects to a single machine to access any user file. Also, when you need to perform backups you can focus on this single machine rather than having to ferret out personal files scattered all over the network. Typically you would also locate the tape drive and any shared printers on this one machine to centralize all shared resources.

If the number of users on the net is small, the machine holding the large disk can still be used by someone as a normal machine. As the number of users grows, however, the load on that hard drive grows until the machine becomes so sluggish that no one will want to use it. At this point you generally make the jump to a server-based network.

10.3.2   Client/Server Networks

In a Client/Server network one or more machines on the net are dedicated to a server role, and each one runs some sort of special server software. An existing network might have servers from other vendors such as Novell. At a minimum the server does the same things as the central machine described in the previous section. It manages a hard disk that everyone shares, and it also manages shared printers.

A server may also support special server applications. For example, the server machine might run a database engine that is accessed by many different applications on the net. When a client application needs a piece of data from the database, it sends a message to the server and the server's database engine processes the request and sends back the result. Since database queries tend to be CPU and disk intensive, the server machine generally should be well endowed in terms of speed, memory, and disk space. On the other hand, user machines can often have less capability because they are off-loading the database tasks to the server.

10.3.3   Domain-Controlled Networks

The management of user accounts can become troublesome on Peer-to-Peer networks. An example helps to clarify difficulties that can arise. Say you have three machines on a Peer-to-Peer network. The machines are used by Bob, Sally, and Tom. See Figure 10.2. All three machines use NTFS, so it is possible to create file permissions on any file or directory.

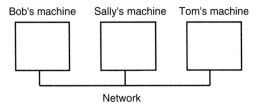

Figure 10.2
A simple Peer-to-Peer network. Sally wants to use file permissions to share a directory with Bob, but keep it secret from Tom.

Sally wants to create a directory and then set the permissions on it so that Bob can use the directory but Tom cannot. For this to work, Sally's machine has to have an account on it for Bob, and that account must have the same user ID and password that Bob uses on his machine. When Bob attempts to connect to the shared directory (e.g., using the **Connect** option in the File Manager), his machine will pass his user ID and password to Sally's machine, which will compare it with the ID and password in its account list to *authenticate* Bob. This works fine, and Bob is able to get to the directory because he has access to it. See also Section 11.2.

You can see what happens as the size of the network grows. For file permissions, printer permissions, groups, and so on to work properly, every machine on the net must have every user on the net in its account list. When a user wants to change his or her password, it must be changed on all the machines. It quickly becomes a major annoyance.

To solve this problem, the Windows NT Advanced Server implements a technology called *Domain-Controlled networks*. In this configuration, a designated server machine acts as the *Domain Controller*, providing account management services for all machines in the Domain. Only one account list for the network is managed on the Domain Controller, and it acts as a name server for all the machines in the Domain. Once it has been set up properly, any user can log onto any machine on the network. The Domain Controller greatly simplifies network administration and use.

Figure 10.3
The Welcome dialog for a machine on a Domain-Controlled network.

You can tell that a network has a Domain Controller when you log on. If there is a Domain Controller on the net, the **From** combo box in the Welcome dialog will contain the name of the current machine as well as the Domain Controller. When you log on with the local machine name, you are accessing the local account list. When you log on from the Domain Controller you are using the network-wide account list published by the controller.

10.4 Designing Your Network

No matter how big a network you are creating, from two machines to a thousand, it is worthwhile to spend some time designing the network. Even with a two-machine configuration, you will need to decide which machine is the e-mail Post Office, the names of the two machines, and so on. It is also a good idea to design for the future, making plans now for machines you may be adding over the next several months. Following is a list of some of the decisions you need to make.

- Who will be the network administrator, and what are his or her responsibilities? Make a list of all of the administrator's duties. It is important to pick someone who is able to fulfill all of the required responsibilities. A good network administrator, like a boy scout, is trustworthy, loyal, helpful, friendly, courteous, kind, obedient, cheerful, thrifty, brave, clean, and reverent. Generally, good administrators are also patient in the extreme and work well with people, and have wide-ranging experience with the operating system and networks in general. Look for these attributes when you pick your administrator.

- Do you want to use a Peer-to-Peer, Client/Server, or Domain-Controlled network? This decision is based largely on the size of the network and the available budget. You should strongly consider a Domain-Controlled network if you have more than five or so machines on the network. It greatly simplifies administration.

- If you are not using a Domain Controller or a server, would it be beneficial to designate one machine as the "central" machine to consolidate user files?

- Where should printers be located on the net, and physically in the building?

- Which machine should manage the e-mail Post Office? If there is a central machine or a server, use it.

- Which machine will contain the tape drive for backups? The administrator's machine is the logical location for the tape drive.

- What will each machine be named? What will your Workgroups or Domain be named?

- How many segments should the network have? On large networks the design of your segmentation scheme can require a great deal of thought. Which segments require their own servers? Where will the router(s) be located? Is a high-speed backbone required between segments? If you are designing a network requiring multiple segments and you have never done it before, you should research the problem carefully or hire an outside consultant to help with the design.

If this is your first network design, think about these questions, come up with some answers, and try it out. If it doesn't work, then change it. It will take a few iterations to learn what works and what doesn't at your particular site.

One good way to design a network is to draw pictures of it. Figure out how many machines, printers, disks, tape drives, and so on that you have and draw a picture of your proposed design. Figure 10.4 demonstrates a simple network that includes four NT machines, a printer, and a tape drive.

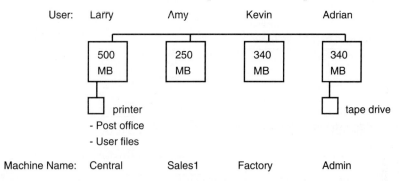

Figure 10.4
A typical small network.

Since Larry only uses his machine for an hour each day, the central 500 MB hard disk is placed there, and users share that drive for their personal file space. Larry's machine also acts as the print server and the Post Office. Adrian is the administrator, so her machine has the tape drive to allow her to do backups easily.

The name on each machine here tries to reflect function, but you can use any naming scheme that you like. You should also choose a name for the Workgroup holding these four machines. The default name is WORKGROUP, but you can also name it anything you like.

10.5 Setting Up Machines

With the design of your proposed network in hand, it is time to begin assembly. Start by installing network cards in machines that do not have them, and run your cables. Move printers and tape drives around as necessary.

The Network applet in the Control Panel is responsible for setting up a machine's network drivers and protocols, and also for interfacing with the Domain Controller and Workgroups. The network dialog is shown in Figure 10.5. Figure 10.6 shows the Domain/Workgroup Settings dialog. See also Appendix F.

A majority of the network installation happens during the installation of NT itself. The Windows NT installation program recognizes that you have a

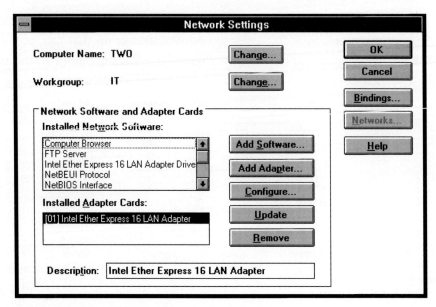

Figure 10.5
The Network dialog.

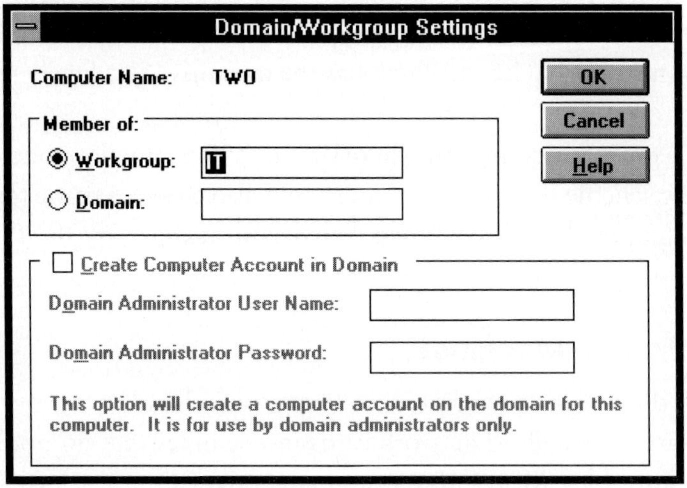

Figure 10.6
The Domain/Workgroup Settings dialog.

network card and configures NT for it. It also installs a number of modules that enable network capabilities. If you did not have a network card in your machine when you first loaded NT onto it, it is probably best to insert the card and reinstall.

You can use the Network applet to:

- Change the name of your machine
- Change the Workgroup name or join a Domain
- Change the software drivers and configuration information used by your adapter
- Add new software modules
- Change bindings

See Chapters 14 and 15 for examples of adding new modules, such as TCP/IP and the Remote Access Server (RAS).

Changing your machine's name is simple. Open the network applet and click on the **Change** button next to the current name of the machine. Type in a new name that does not conflict with any other name on the network. Anyone using drives or printers on your machine will have to re-do their connections after you make a change, so this is not something that you want to be doing arbitrarily.

NT allows you to create groups of machines called *Workgroups* on a network. Workgroups do nothing more than subdivide a large number of machines into smaller subgroups. For example, if you have a single network with 20 machines on it, it is likely that natural groupings exist for those machines. For example, 10 of the machines might be in the front office, five in manufacturing, and five in marketing. By grouping each set into its own Workgroup, you limit the number of machines that users have to sort through when they browse for disks and printers in the different connection dialogs. A Workgroup does not provide any sort of security: users can still browse through all the machines on the net.

If your network has a Domain Controller, you will add your machine to the Domain rather than to a Workgroup. See Chapter 13 for a discussion on Domains and Domain Controllers.

If you change your network card, or add a second card to your machine, you use the Network applet to change or add new drivers. In Figure 10.5, the **Add Adapter** button handles new adapters. It will ask you to choose the appropriate driver for the new card, and then ask for the location of the driver. To configure an existing card, click on the **Configure** button. You will see a dialog that allows you to modify things such as the interrupt line and I/O address for the card. To update existing drivers click on the **Update** button. You will see a dialog that asks you to enter the directory containing the new drivers.

Finally, the **Add Software** button lets you add different software components to the networking system. You will see many examples of adding software in Chapters 13, 14, and 15.

10.6 Administration of the Net

Connecting machines together with cable forms a physical network, but there are many other parts of the system that must be configured properly in order for the network to function usefully. The network administrator is generally responsible for performing this configuration work so that users don't have to think about it.

Once you have cabled your machines together, go around to each one and log on as the administrator. Check each machine's name and Workgroup to make sure it is correct. Use the User Manager (Chapter 2) to create users and groups on each machine so that everyone can log on. Go to the Print Manager of machines that have printers and share their printers on the network, and share the drives on any machines that need to share their drives. See Chapter 11. You may also want to configure each machine so it can use the printers and shared drives on the network, thereby saving users the trouble of creating these connections themselves. Create a central Post Office and make sure each user has a mailbox. See Chapter 12. You may want to create a short letter or report that tells each user what you have done, or hold a meeting to train people in different network capabilities. Things will go more smoothly if people using the net know what is going on. See Appendix F for more information.

Once you have completed all of these modifications, users should be able to use the network comfortably. You will find that network administration is comfortable as well: You can perform most routine administrative tasks remotely, so it is easy to fix or change things on the network from your office. For example, the Tape Backup program can back up any drive shared on the network from a single machine. The Print Manager can manage any printer on the network if it has proper permissions. The Event Viewer (Chapter 8) and Performance Monitor (Chapter 9) can both access remote machines. Once you have set up the network, try out some of these tools and make sure they perform as expected.

The NT Advanced Server offers a number of other remote network administration tools. See Chapter 13 for details. With a Domain Controller on the network, you can administrate any part of any machine on the network without ever leaving your office.

10.7 Examples

Every site has its own special situations and requirements. The purpose of this section is to show several typical configurations and demonstrate the advantages and disadvantages of each.

10.7.1   Two to Four General Users

If you have a small office with two to four Windows NT machines used by two to four people, then probably the easiest thing to do is build a pure Peer-to-Peer network. If the users are technically sophisticated and in a low-security situation, you can leave everything alone and people will work it out themselves. The users will share drives and printers with one another as necessary.

As the administrator, there are several things you can do to facilitate the process. You can give each user an account name, and maintain the account lists on all of the machines so that each machine knows about all the users. By keeping the account names and passwords on all machines synchronized, you make network authentication of user IDs transparent, and therefore disk drive and printer sharing are much easier. You can also make each user a member of the Power Users group, so that everyone is able to treat their machines as "their own" and handle many administrative tasks themselves.

If the users are not sophisticated, you will want to make them members of the Users group, and work with them to help them share drives with each other when necessary. You can also set up the printers so that the users do not have any trouble accessing them.

You should create a backup strategy that backs the entire network off to tape on a regular basis, so that no important information is lost.

10.7.2   Five or More General Users

As you add more users to the configuration described in Section 10.7.1, things can start to get confusing. Since each person has "their own" machine, each person keeps all their files on the local hard disk. The number of shared resources grows rapidly, so the users then end up connecting to a large number of drives to get anything done. This situation gets annoying and confusing very quickly. When you want to find something, there are many different drives that you have to explore, and there is no automated way to do that.

The solution to this problem is to centralize shared resources. At the very least, you will want to declare one machine to be the "home directory machine," and place everyone's home directory there. This arrangement has two important advantages:

- You have to back up only that one machine and you are guaranteed to have everyone's important data.
- Every user is required to connect to only one drive to access everyone else's information.

It may also be worthwhile to place other shared resources such as printers, CD-ROM drives, and the e-mail Post Office on that same machine so that all shared resources are in one place. Initially someone can use this machine as a normal workstation, but eventually it will become sluggish because of all the activity. At that point, upgrade it to a high-power server machine and lock it in a room somewhere.

As the number of users grows, you will find that the distributed account lists of a Peer-to-Peer network become unmanageable because they become desynchronized too easily. This is especially true if there are more users than machines and the users tend to move around a lot. Every user will have a different profile (desktop colors, preferences, etc.) on each different machine they use. You will also find that there are many tasks requiring you to run around and physically touch each machine to administrate it. For example, when a service fails to start, you have to go to the machine to debug the problem.

When these problems get frustrating enough, it is time to install the NT Advanced Server to act as a Domain Controller for your network. It will consolidate all user account information in one place and let you do many more administrative tasks remotely. See Chapter 13 for details.

10.7.3   Five or More Application-specific Users, Low Budget

If you have a large number of application-specific users and you want to create an economical network for them, you can create a Client/Server arrangement that minimizes the cost of the overall installation. For example, if you have 20 clerks who are doing order processing using a front-end application that talks to a database, NT can help.

Purchase one high-powered machine to act as the database engine and install a package like Microsoft's SQL server. This machine might be a DEC Alpha machine, or an Intel Pentium machine, or a MIPS RISC machine. It will be fairly expensive (in the $6,000–$10,000 range), but you get to divide that cost across 20 stations so the per-station cost is low.

Now purchase 20 low-end machines. These might be inexpensive 33MHZ 486SX machines with 150–200 MB hard disks, and they will cost less than $2,000 each. These machines can be low-end because all of the CPU and disk-intensive operations associated with the database will occur on the SQL server machine. The total cost of the network for 20 users will be less than $50,000, or $2,500 per station, and the performance will be extremely good. Each user will also have all the capabilities of an NT workstation available, so they can run word processors, spreadsheets, etc., if necessary.

As the administrator, you will probably want to use the NT Advanced Server on the main server machine to make account management and administration easier. If you place everyone's home directory on the central machine, then it will be the only machine you have to back up. When one of the workstations dies, you simply reload NT on it, reconfigure it, and it is ready to go.

10.7.4   Five or More Scientific Users

In an academic environment or an engineering firm, you frequently need to give each person a fair amount of computing power. There are two ways to accomplish this task: Either you can purchase an extremely powerful machine for each user, or you can purchase moderately powered machines for the users and create several "compute engines" on the network that share their performance. For example, Sequent and other manufacturers sell machines with large numbers of multiple CPUs combined in a single box along with vast disk arrays and other specialized hardware. Using specially designed applications, these machines can share their power on the network through RPCs.

For example, in an engineering firm, the company might design its own visualization library for wind flow analysis and run it on a machine containing 10 RISC processors. Each user machine would call this compute server to calculate wind flow and then display it on the local machine.

As the administrator of the network, you have the same responsibilities as described in the previous section. You will probably want to use the NT Advanced Server to make account management easier. You will want to centralize home directories to make backing up and machine replacement easier.

10.7.5   100 Users on 10 Machines

Say that you are administrating an academic network where 100 students need to share 10 machines. You definitely need to use the NT Advanced Server in this situation. Its advanced User Manager will allow you to create all the accounts and user profiles easily. You will also be able to allow certain groups of students to use the lab at certain times, using the logon hours facility in the Advanced Server. The Advanced Server will allow any student to log onto any of the available machines and see "one account" on all of them, since each user's profile moves from machine to machine.

You should plan on using one machine as the Domain Controller and home directory site for the network. This is the only machine you will ever need to back up. Set the permissions on the user machines' hard disks so it is impossible for users to create directories or change anything on the local machines. You will find that Windows NT is perfect in academic environments.

10.8 Conclusion

Once you have created your network, watch it over the course of a few weeks and see how it is performing. Ask users for comments and implement changes as necessary. As the net grows you will probably reorganize it to better meet user requirements.

You will find that the job of network administrator requires certain "people skills." Users can get very angry when the network prevents them from doing their jobs. You will get to answer lots of questions, and solve innumerable problems as they arise. This tends to make the job interesting. Your job as administrator will be easier if you can create and maintain a good rapport with your users, and act on the suggestions that they make to improve their access to the network.

Sharing Disks and Printers

11

Because NT is designed to work on a network, disk and printer sharing is built in. You can share complete hard disks and individual directories on the net, as well as any printer connected to the machine. Users of Windows NT and Windows for Workgroups machines can connect using their File Managers and Print Managers.

With all the freedom a network provides to share information and connect to it, one of the biggest issues in a business or academic environment is the security of information. This chapter discusses a number of security issues and describes how to ensure the security of your system. Appendix G also provides a security checklist that will inform you of possible security holes in Windows NT.

Both administrators and power users can share a directory or a drive. Administrators, power users, owners, and users with Full Control access to a printer can share it.

11.1 Sharing Disks and Directories

To share a disk or directory, log on as the administrator and open the File Manager. Display, for example, the contents of your C: drive, as shown in Figure 11.1. You can share either the entire drive, or any individual directory on this drive. In Figure 11.1 both Drive C: and the "indydemo" directory are currently shared, and the directory named "it" is selected. You can tell that the drive and directory are being shared by the small hands underneath the folder icons.

169

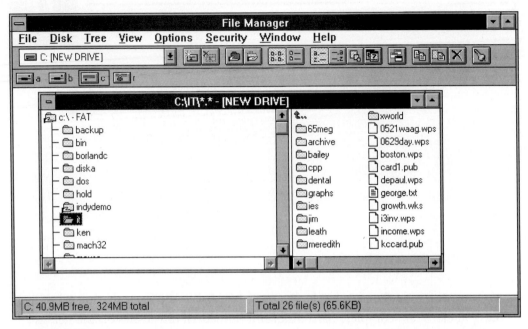

Figure 11.1
A typical File Manager display showing a shared drive and a shared directory.

If you want to share an entire drive, click on its folder at the top of the list of directories. If you want to share a directory click on its folder. Then choose the **Share As** option in the **Disk** menu of the File Manager. You will see a dialog like the one shown in Figure 11.2.

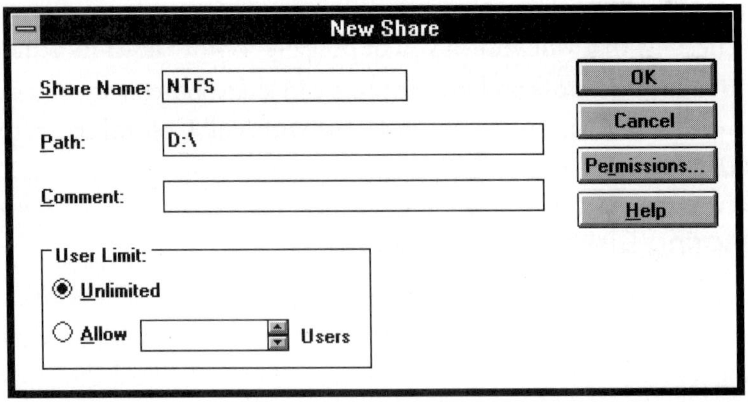

Figure 11.2
The New Share dialog.

In the New Share dialog, you specify the name of the drive or directory in the **Share Name** field. Users who connect to the drive will be able to use that name in two ways:

- They choose from the connect list using that name when they attempt to connect to the drive.
- When using UNC file naming, the name of the shared object is the name used in the path following the machine name (e.g., \\machine\sharename\dirname\filename).

The **Path** field is the path for the drive or directory on the local machine. This field gets filled automatically when the dialog appears. The **Comment** field is displayed as a description when people try to connect to the drive remotely. In the New Share dialog, you can also specify the maximum number of users that can connect to the shared drive or directory. This gives you a way to control the load that other network users can place on any machine.

The **Permissions** button in the New Share dialog gives you your first level of control over the security of the shared drive. Permissions are discussed in the following section.

If you want to modify the properties of a shared drive or directory, select the appropriate folder in the File Manager and choose the **Share As** option in the **Disk** menu again. You can share a drive or directory several times to give different people and groups different access to the drive. For example, you might want to give a certain group of users unlimited access to a drive, but let everyone else access it only one at a time. You do this by selecting the shared drive and pulling up its properties with the **Share As** menu option. A new button labeled **New Share** will appear in the dialog, allowing you to share the drive again. Each shared instance must have a different name.

Once you have shared a drive, people can immediately connect to it over the network. You can check on the status and usage of any shared resource using the Server applet in the Control Panel. See Section 7.1.5 for details. To stop sharing a directory or drive, select it in the File Manager and choose the **Stop Sharing** option in the **Disk** menu.

11.2 Security Issues with File Sharing

NT is a secure system. That is, if you have a Windows NT machine sitting on your desk, people cannot access your data and resources unless they have an account on your machine. That holds true even if the hard disk is formatted with the non-secure FAT file system. The account system keeps people out. [One caveat, especially for people using PC-style hardware to run NT: It is possible for someone with access to the physical machine to turn it off, turn it back on, and reboot with a different operating system, thereby gaining access to your data. The physical machine must be secure from physical tampering to ensure the integrity of Windows NT.]

If you use NTFS on the hard disk, you can provide a second level of security. With NTFS you can give users access to specific areas on the hard disk, and keep them out of areas where they do not belong. NTFS gives you more precise control over who can access different parts of the file system.

When you add a network card and connect a machine to the network, you open the door for many more people to access your data. It is important that you understand the security options you have to prevent unauthorized access to data over the network.

As discussed previously, file security hinges on the file system you use. The FAT file system is not secure, while NTFS is. If you are worried about the security of your data, then you should be using NTFS. You use NTFS to selectively give access to different parts of your drives. As discussed in Section 2.9, you can also use NTFS to protect the NT operating system itself from accidental or malicious tampering.

As with a lone machine, your first level of security on a network machine is the machine's accounts. Only administrators or power users are allowed to share drives. Normal users and guests cannot. When you log on as the administrator and share a drive or directory on the network, you have two further levels of security. First, you can limit the people who can actually connect to the shared drive. Second, you can control access to individual files and directories with NTFS. The **Permissions** button seen in Figure 11.2 enables the first level of security. Figure 11.3 demonstrates the Access Through Share Permissions dialog.

The dialog shown in Figure 11.3 controls who is allowed to connect to a shared disk resource. *Be sure to check this dialog every time you share something, because NT defaults to letting everyone connect.* In Figure 11.3, the default has been modified: Anyone can connect to the drive and read from it, but only the user Brain can fully access the drive. You can use this dialog to add or remove permissions, so each drive's access fits your security requirements. The dialog that appears when you click the **Add** button appears in Figure 11.4.

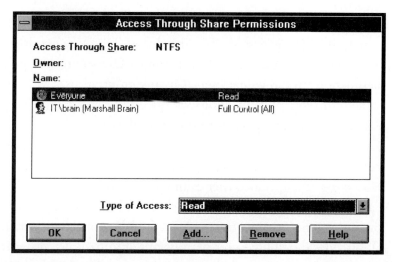

Figure 11.3
The Access Through Share Permissions dialog.

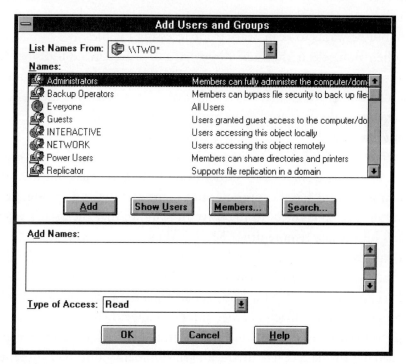

Figure 11.4
The Add Users and Groups dialog.

You can give connection permissions to the general groups shown in Figure 11.4, each of which is described in the dialog (Domains are discussed in detail in Chapter 13). You can also click the **Show Users** button to grant connection permissions to individual users. On any group or user, you can grant the following four types of connections:

- Read: connecting users can read files on the drive.
- Change: connecting users can read or modify files or directories.
- Full Control: connecting users can do anything on the drive.
- No Access: the specified user cannot access the drive.

On a single machine it is easy to see how NT's accounts keep people from logging on, but it is not so obvious how NT controls connections over the network. NT provides distributed user permissions automatically, using two different techniques. For example, let's say you have a network containing three different machines. Mary and Bob are the users, and there is one computer in each of their offices as well as a shared computer in the lab. Bob wants to share his "lab" directory on the network so he can access it from both his office and the lab, but he wants to keep Mary from accessing the files.

When Bob selects the "lab" directory and shares it, he uses the dialogs shown in Figures 11.3 and 11.4 to give only himself permission to connect to the drive. Note, however, that when Bob gives himself access to the "lab" directory, he is using the account list on his local machine. When Bob logs on to a different machine, he will be using a different account because each machine has separate account lists on a simple Peer-to-Peer network like this one. NT uses the following technique to authenticate Bob: If the account used on the connecting machine has the same account name and the same password as the account allowed to connect to the drive, it assumes that the user is valid and connects him to the remote drive. Mary is thus locked out, while Bob is able to move to any machine on which he has an account and access the drive. Note that all account lists must be synchronized for this system to work. The name of a user's account must be the same on all machines, and when users change their password on one machine, they should change them on all.

If the network has a Domain Controller, then the global Domain account list is used to provide access to drives, and the Domain Controller authenticates all access attempts. This is a much better system on larger networks because it avoids having to maintain many separate account lists on many separate machines. See Chapter 13 for details.

NTFS can provide a second level of control over the contents of any shared drive. Once a user gets authenticated and connected to a drive, that user can do anything to the drive if it is formatted with the FAT file system. If it is formatted with NTFS however, the user is limited by the same access controls that NTFS applies to local users. NTFS provides a very secure way to share drives on the network.

When you design your network, you will want to keep the different security options mentioned in this section in mind. If you have sensitive data that you want to protect, it is important to make sure it is shared on the network only in ways that are appropriate. Set up your connection permissions accordingly, and use NTFS to secure individual files. Also, make sure that the machine holding the sensitive data is physically secure. It does no good to secure the network if someone can walk off with the machine itself. You should also use the auditing features built into the File Manager to monitor the network for users trying to breach security. See Chapter 8 for details.

11.3 Sharing Printers

Chapter 3 discusses how to connect printers to individual machines and create them in the Windows NT Printer Manager. This section describes how to share printers over the network. Windows NT makes printer sharing extremely easy.

You can share a printer on the network when you create it. You can also modify the share status after creation using the **Properties** option in the **Printer** menu of the Print Manager. At the bottom of the Properties dialog you will find a **Share** section, as shown in Figure 11.5. You can specify the name that the printer will have on the network, along with its location. The location is simply a text string that helps network users find the printer when they want to pick up output. Once you have completed the Share portion of the dialog, click **OK** and the printer is available.

You can control the people who connect to the printer in much the same way you control a shared drive. The **Permissions** option in the **Security** menu makes this possible, as shown in Figure 11.6. Click the **Add** button and then select the group to which you want to give access. You can give permissions to individual users by clicking on the **Show Users** button. You can grant users the following four types of access:

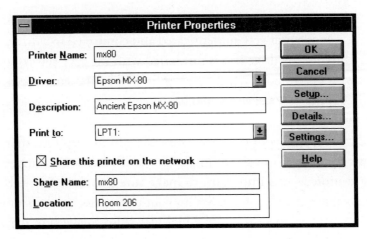

Figure 11.5
The Printer Properties dialog.

- Print: The user can print documents.

- Manage Documents: The user can print and manage (delete, move, etc.) documents.

- Full Control: The user can completely control the printer.

- No Access: The user cannot access the printer.

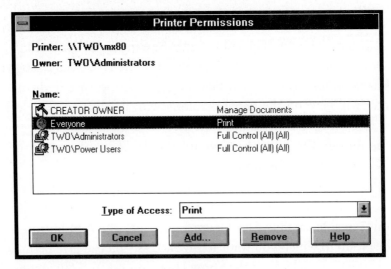

Figure 11.6
The Printer Permissions dialog.

Printers provide a way to leak secure information. If a user can print out a document that should not leave the site, then the system is not secure. Pay as much attention to the security of your printers as you do to the security of your drives. To watch printer accesses, you can enable the printer auditing features in the **Security** menu. Use the Event Viewer to view the different auditing events as described in Chapters 3 and 8.

To connect to a shared printer, open the Print Manager on the remote machine. Select the **Connect to Printer** option in the **Printer** menu and you will see a dialog like the one shown in Figure 11.7. This dialog displays a list of machines on the network, and you can double click on each of these machines to see the printers they currently share. Double click on the printer you desire. If the printer is on another NT machine, you will connect immediately. If the machine is not an NT machine, you may have to load the appropriate driver. Once you have connected to the remote printer, you can use it like any local printer.

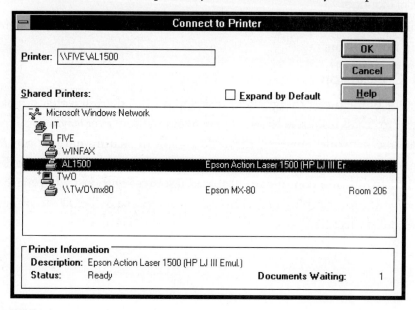

Figure 11.7
The Connect to Printer dialog.

Windows NT provides a tool that makes the remote administration of printers on the network extremely easy. Choose the **Server** option in the **Printer** menu of the Print Manager, shown in Figure 11.8. You will see a dialog listing all the machines on the network. Choose the machine you want, and you

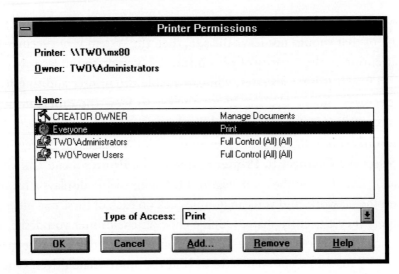

Figure 11.8
The Print Manager

can then perform any printer administrative task just as if the machine were sitting in front of you.

11.4 Conclusion

One of the nicest things about disk and printer sharing is that it makes it possible to access resources all over the network without ever leaving your chair. On a large network, however, the wide variety of sharing options can make things confusing for users. You may want to take this into account in the design of your network and consolidate all shared resources onto just a few machines. Not only will this simplify user choices, it will also make it easier to physically secure and protect hardware.

IMPLEMENTING ELECTRONIC MAIL   12

Windows NT provides an electronic mail, or e-mail, facility that lets everyone on your network communicate with one another. The NT e-mail system allows you to transfer simple text notes like any other e-mail system does, but also allows you to embed or attach complete documents, files, sounds, and a variety of other objects to any e-mail message that you create. The e-mail system works with all NT and Windows for Workgroups workstations.

Chapter 17 in the book "Using Windows NT: The Essentials for Professionals," describes how to use the Windows NT e-mail program. This chapter shows you how to set up and administrate the Post Office, the central machine that holds messages and routes them to different users as they are read.

12.1 Getting Started

You should plan for the e-mail Post Office when you design your network. The Post Office is located on one of the computers on the network and holds all the messages that any user generates. If you have a central machine acting as a server or resource-sharing machine, then this is a good place for the Post Office. Otherwise, any machine on the net can take on this role provided it has the disk space necessary to handle the job.

The Post Office by itself takes only about half a megabyte of space to create. However, if users get in the habit of sending graphics, documents, or digitized sounds through the mail, then the size of the messages that the Post Office holds can grow quite large. Make sure that the Post Office machine has the extra disk space necessary to handle the load. For a small network, the CPU usage of the Post Office will be almost imperceptible, so you can place it on a user's machine without worrying about bogging it down.

Generally a network should have just one Post Office. All users on the network then connect to it. If you want to create Post Offices for separate groups of users on the net, realize that these different groups will have no way to intercommunicate. The basic e-mail package that comes with Windows NT does not provide for the routing of messages between different Post Offices (although you can upgrade to other packages that do). You should also educate your users about the Post Office, and perhaps take the time to run mail the first time to make sure the user's machine is properly connected to the Post Office. Users need to know where the Post Office is located in order to properly connect to it themselves.

12.2 Creating a Post Office

Creating a Post Office is surprisingly easy. Before starting the installation however, decide on who will administrate the Post Office. Generally this will be the network administrator, but on a large network you may want to assign a separate person to Post Office administration. The administrator is primarily responsible for adding and deleting users from the e-mail system.

Go to the machine that will serve as the Post Office and click on the Mail application in the Main group of the Program Manager. Since this is the first time mail has been used, you will see a dialog like the one shown in Figure 12.1. [If you do not see this dialog, it means that someone has already run Mail on this system. To clear out the effects of their activity, use the Registry Editor (Appendix C) to find the `Mail` key in the HKEY_CURRENT_USER area. It is under `Software\Microsoft`. You should delete the `Custom Commands` key and `Custom Messages` key entirely, and delete every value in the `Microsoft Mail` key with the exception of `MigrateIniPrint`. When you restart the mail program, you will see the dialog.]

Click on the **Create a new Workgroup Postoffice** option and click **OK**. You will see a warning dialog like the one shown in Figure 12.2. Answer Yes. You will then see a dialog that lets you choose the location for the Post Office directory. You can choose any local drive or a drive on the network. You can also place the Post Office files inside of another directory if you choose to. Locate the Post Office directory in a place where it is certain to be backed up as part of your normal backup routine.

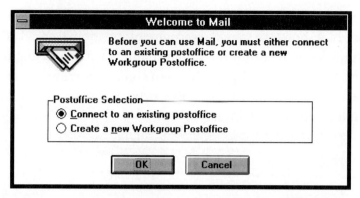

Figure 12.1
The opening screen for the mail program.

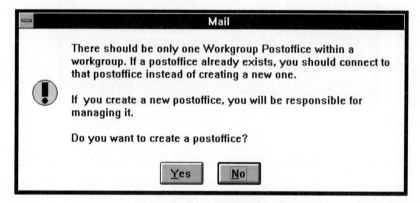

Figure 12.2
The Mail dialog.

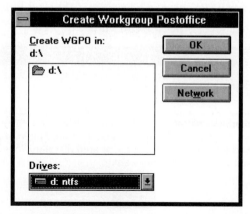

Figure 12.3
The Create Workgroup Postoffice dialog.

You will next need to create an administrative account for the e-mail system. Figure 12.4 shows the standard account information dialog. The **Mailbox** field holds the logon name for the administrator when connecting to the Post Office. The administrator also needs a password. Enter other information as appropriate. This is the only account that will be able to manage the Post Office in the future, so be careful with it.

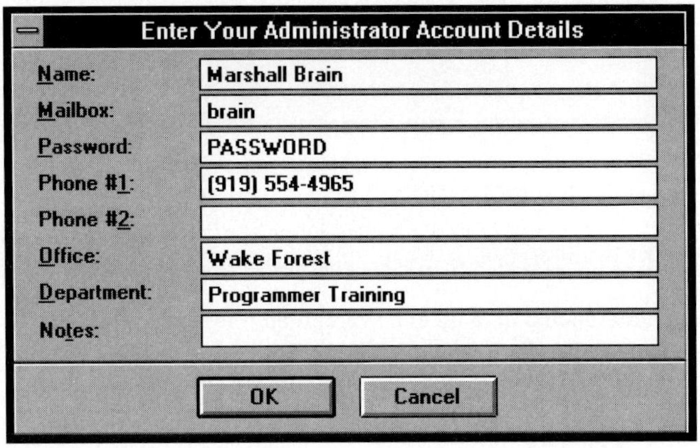

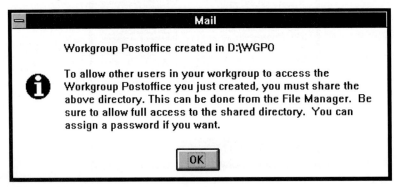

Figure 12.4
The Account dialog.

Once you have successfully created the administrative account, you will see a congratulatory dialog like the one shown in Figure 12.5, followed by the Postoffice Manager dialog like the one seen in Figure 12.6. In this dialog you add and remove users from the Post Office, and you also view statistics on Shared Folders and compress them if necessary. A Shared Folder is a collection of e-mail messages that several people can view.

Figure 12.5
The Success dialog.

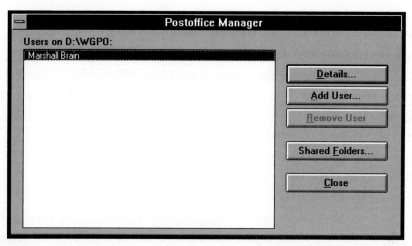

Figure 12.6
The Postoffice Manager dialog.

You can add new users at this point if you choose to, or exit the program and add them in later. Users can also add themselves: When they first start the mail program in their accounts, they have the option to create a new mail box. If you wish to add new users yourself, start up the e-mail program and choose the **Postoffice Manager** option in the **Mail** menu. You will see the same dialog shown in Figure 12.4. Enter all appropriate information for the new user and click **OK**. The new user can then attach to the Post Office and use the account immediately.

Once you have created the Post Office, exit the Mail program and find the directory it created. It is named "wgpo." Using the File Manager, share this directory with everyone on the network. They need Full Access permissions.

12.3 Centralizing Mail

The default behavior for the Mail program is Peer-to-Peer mode. It makes the assumption that each user sits on one machine exclusively. If your network is not set up that way, this behavior can be infuriating and confusing. This section explains how to convert the program to "centralized server" behavior.

When you, as the administrator, first run the mail program on a normal NT network and create the Post Office, the mail program stores two keys in the HKEY_CURRENT_USER area of the Registry (Appendix C) called WGPOMgr1 and WGPOMgr2. These keys mark the machine as the administration machine. Only on this machine can the administrator log in to manage the Post Office (add and delete users, compress folders, etc.). The **Postoffice Manager** option simply will not be available on any other machine on the network. Therefore, *create the Post Office from the machine that you plan to administrate it from as well.* There really isn't anything you can do about this limitation short of trying to modify the Registry on other machines to contain these two values. However, if you are using a Domain Controller with user profiles (see Section 13.4), then the ability to edit the Post Office will move with the user who created the Post Office.

You can create user accounts as an administrator, or users create their own accounts when they first run the mail program. In either case, when the user first runs mail it will create a personal message file for the user. The default location for this file is the `c:\winnt` directory. For example, when the user named "mary" first runs mail, NT will create a new file named `c:\winnt\mary.mmf` on the local machine. This is fine if Mary always uses the same machine, but if she ever tries to log on anywhere else, she is stuck.

To solve this problem, select the **Options** option in the **Mail** menu. Click on the **Server** button. Click the **Postoffice** check box. When you click **OK**, the system will move the `mary.mmf` file off of the local drive and onto the Post Office directory. Now Mary can access her mail from any machine she uses.

Administrative Strategy

Centralizing e-mail

If you are working in an academic environment where 100 students share 10 machines in a lab and therefore frequently move from one machine to another, be sure that they place their e-mail files in the centralized Post Office directory so that their e-mail accounts are not tied to specific machines.

12.4 Educating Users

After you have created the Post Office and added accounts for each user on the network, you will need to tell users how to connect to the Post Office. The first time any user runs the mail program on a machine, they will see the same dialog shown in Figure 12.1. Instruct each user to select the **Connect to**

existing Postoffice option. Immediately following this dialog, the Mail program will ask the user for the path to the Post Office directory. If you placed the Post Office directory in the root directory of a machine named "machine," instruct users to type **\\machine\wgpo** into the dialog.

Once the connection to the Post Office is correctly made, the user should be able to log in and send and receive mail normally. Chapter 17 of "Using Windows NT: The Essentials for Professionals" contains a complete description of how to send and receive mail.

You may also want to ask users to move their mail box file off to the Post Office directory so they can log in on different machines. See Section 12.3 for details.

Domains and Servers

13

As your Peer-to-Peer NT network grows, you will notice that administration becomes more and more difficult. For example, if you need to change the services provided by a machine, you have to walk to the machine to open its Control Panel and work with the Services applet. Account management also becomes a chore because each machine has its own account list and these lists need to stay synchronized for the security features of NTFS to work smoothly (see Section 11.2).

When you begin to notice these problems, it is time to install the NT Advanced Server on one of the machines on your network. The NT Advanced Server provides a number of capabilities that make the lives of both users and administrators easier. This chapter will introduce you to many of the Advanced Server's basic capabilities and show you how to take advantage of them on your network.

13.1 Capabilities of the NT Advanced Server

Microsoft sells Windows NT as two separate products. The normal form is Windows NT. The Windows NT Advanced Server is a second product that acts as a server on the network. The Advanced Server looks and works almost exactly like standard NT, but it contains extra tools and capabilities not found in the standard product. These tools make network administration easier. Normally the machine running the Advanced Server that acts as the Domain Controller is the central machine used by the administrator to control the Domain.

The most important feature of the NT Advanced Server is the concept of a *Domain*. When you load the Advanced Server onto a machine, the installa-

186

tion program will ask you if you want the server to become a new Domain Controller, or to act as a server under an existing Domain Controller. If this is the only Advanced Server machine on the network, then it must become the Domain Controller. A Domain Controller acts as a server for account information on the network. You can manage one account list on the Domain Controller and all other machines on the net can use that account information. See Section 13.3 for more information.

The Advanced Server implements a number of advanced user account features, such as restricting users to specific logon times or specific machines. You can also control the user's environment much more completely. For example, you can specify the program groups and enabled capabilities in the user's Program Manager and File Manager. See Section 13.4 for details.

The NT Advanced Server also provides a number of facilities that make network administration much easier. From the Advanced Server machine you can remotely access the Server applet, the Services applet, and the File Manager's drive sharing features for any machine that is a member of a Domain. See Section 13.5. With a Domain Controller in place, every machine on the network can be almost completely administered remotely.

The Advanced Server also has the ability to *replicate* information. That is, you can create a directory on the server and the server will automatically *export* it down to all machines on the network that have asked for copies. This is a good way to keep local copies of selected information on every machine on the net. See Section 13.6.

Other features are available as well. For example, the Disk Manager on the Advanced Server permits an advanced form of disk striping that provides error correction facilities for a Redundant Array of Inexpensive Disks (RAID) setup. You can also mirror disks. You can create global groups in the Advance Server User Manager. You can let Domains talk to one another using *trust relationships*, and so on. All of these capabilities together create a secure network that is much easier to manage and use, and also much more extensible, than a normal NT network. It is also possible to create a network that is very robust. For example, with multiple Advanced Servers on the network, account information will be copied among the different servers. If the Domain Controller machine goes down, another server on the net will take on the role of the controller so that network users can still log on to and access the network.

13.2 Implementing a Domain

A Domain consists of a Domain Controller and a set of workstations that are members of the Domain. A machine gains two things from becoming a member of a Domain:

- The Domain Controller provides account information. Users can log on to any machine in a Domain using their account information stored on the Domain Controller. The centralized account list causes users to see their accounts as exactly the same no matter which machine they log on to on the network. It also makes security features easier to manage, because file and printer permissions use a single, consistent account list.

- Machines that are members of a Domain can be completely administered remotely. The administrator never has to walk to a machine to make changes to its configuration.

Figure 13.1 shows a typical Domain-Controlled network consisting of a Domain Controller and four normal NT machines participating as members of the Domain. Far more advanced configurations are possible as well. For example, a single network can have two Domain Controllers with machines acting as members of different Domains. Or a network can have one controller and several other Advanced Servers acting strictly as servers. The additional servers provide redundancy. If the controller goes down, another server will pick up that role.

The Domain Controller's main job is to provide account services to its members. It also typically contains a large hard disk that gets shared on the network, and often controls printers as well.

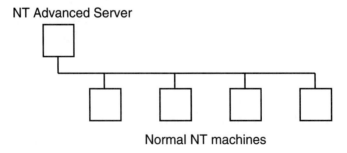

Figure 13.1
A typical small network with a Domain Controller.

The Domain Controller itself gets created during installation. When you install the NT Advanced Server (NTAS), it will ask whether you want it to be the Domain Controller, or to simply be a server in an existing Domain. If this is the first Advanced Server on the net, it must be the Domain Controller. You specify the name of the Domain on this machine, and all other machines that want to belong to its Domain refer to that name as well.

Machines become members of the Domain using the Domain/Workgroup Settings dialog as shown in Figure 13.2. You get to this dialog by clicking on the Network applet in the Control Panel of each machine and then clicking on the **Change** button located next to the Workgroup name.

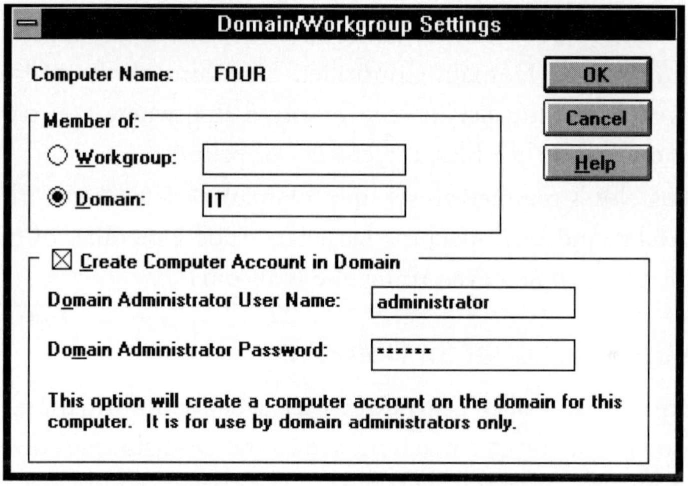

Figure 13.2
The Domain/Workgroup Settings dialog.

Click on the **Domain** radio box and then enter the name of the Domain. You must then move down into the **Create Computer Account in Domain** area, choose the **Create Computer Account in Domain** check box, and enter the name and password for a Domain administrator. This step authenticates the machine to the Domain Controller: Only an administrator on the Domain can make the machine a Domain member.

Once the machine is a member of a Domain, its behavior will change very slightly. The biggest difference a normal user sees is that the Welcome dialog at logon allows the user to choose either the local machine's account list, or the Domain Controller's account list. Once a machine becomes a member of a Do-

*Administrative
Strategy*

Domain Controllers provide security

The installation of a Domain Controller significantly improves the security of your network because no workstation can function as a member of the Domain without having the administrator password. In a network lacking a Domain Controller, anyone can connect a machine to the network and take advantage of certain services. This is not the case with a Domain Controller in place.

main, you normally pare down its local account list to the point that it contains only an administrator account for emergency use. Therefore all users are forced to log on through the Domain Controller. This same choice of local vs. Domain-Controlled account lists is seen in any dialog where you try to change permissions on objects like files, directories, or printers.

Nothing else is required to set up a Domain. Once a network has a Domain Controller, and each machine has been made a member of the Domain using the Network applet, everything else is automatic.

13.3 The User Manager for Domains

A Domain Controller centralizes user account information. Whenever someone wants to log on to a machine within the Domain, they do it using the account list on the Domain Controller. The Domain Controller is therefore acting like an account server for the entire network. This configuration has several advantages:

- A user can log on to any workstation within the Domain.
- The logon ID and password for the user are uniform on all machines, so disk and printer sharing is easier.
- Using a concept called a *profile*, the Advanced Server can keep track of any changes that the user makes to his or her desktop and remember those changes. Users get their same desktop no matter where they log on.
- You, as the administrator, have much more control over user accounts, and you can create and manage them all in one place. For example, if you want to disable all accounts between 2:00 a.m. and 6:00 a.m. to perform backups, you can do that.

These capabilities are not monumentally significant on a three-machine network, but can be extremely important in large networks. For example, say you are administrating the network for a student lab in a university setting. Five hundred students need to share 100 Windows NT machines. You absolutely do not want to have to keep track of separate user lists containing 500 names on 100 different machines. The Domain Controller solves this problem by consolidating all account information in one place. You also want users to be able to log on to any of the 100 available machines. The Domain Controller handles this as well, making the account list available on all machines. But the Domain Controller also allows the students to modify their desktops, and those modifications follow them around the network as well. If the user directories for all students are located on a central server, then as far as the students are concerned every single machine in the lab is exactly the same.

You will find that the extended user management features in the Advanced Server are located in two different places: The User Manager and the Profile Editor. The Advanced Server's User Manager looks just like the normal User Manager described in Chapter 2, but contains several extensions. The Profile Editor is a completely new program in the Administration Tools group of the Program Manager.

The Advanced Server's User Manager contains three new buttons. The first one allows you to set the user's logon hours. Figure 13.3 shows the Logon Hours dialog. In this dialog you use the mouse to drag over ranges of hours. You can also click on the top and left edges to select entire days and times. Once you've selected a range, click on the **allow** and **disallow** buttons to enable and disable those times. For example, if certain users should be able to log on only between 8:00 a.m. and 5:00 p.m. for security reasons, it is easy to implement that behavior in this dialog. Or you might allow certain students to use a lab only in the morning, while others can use it only in the afternoon.

The second new button allows you to limit users to a small number of specific workstations. This capability is intended to give a specific user access to a small number of specific machines. For example, if you have a guest account you might restrict its use to three different machines. Figure 13.4 shows the Logon Workstations dialog. Type up to eight machine names into the available slots. The indicated user will be able to log on to just those machines.

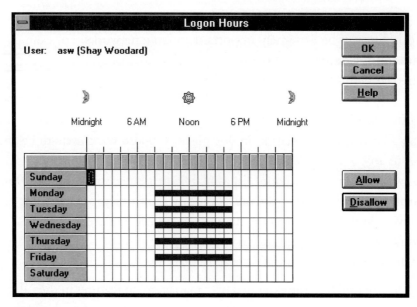

Figure 13.3
The Logon Hours dialog.

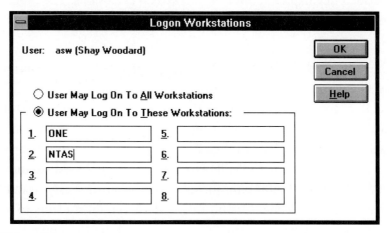

Figure 13.4
The Logon Workstations dialog.

The third new button displays account information, as shown in Figure 13.5. This dialog lets you set an expiration date for an account, and also lets you mark accounts as global or local. The distinction between local and global accounts here has to do with trust relationships between Domains.

Administrative Strategy

Tight security with the Advanced Server

If you want to have total control over how certain users use your network, you can take advantage of the features of the Advanced Server to implement a tight security barrier. For example, you can place five workstations in a locked and guarded room. You can then limit logon hours for the users in question to the hours that the room is open, and you can specify that the users can access only those five machines. There is then no way for those users to access the network except through those five workstations.

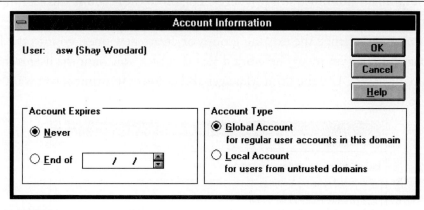

Figure 13.5
The Account Information dialog.

13.4 User Profiles

If you click the **Profile** button in the advanced User Manager, you will see the standard dialog that lets you set the user's home directory and logon script. However, the dialog also contains an additional field used to specify the user's *profile* file. The profile contains information about the user's desktop: Things like the user's color choices, preferences, program groups, and so on. Normally this information is stored in the Registry (see Appendix C) on the local machine, but in an Advanced Server network this approach is not acceptable because the user's desktop needs to move with the user's account from machine to machine. The Advanced Server can therefore store user profile information in special files that are kept on a globally available network drive (e.g., the server's drive). When the user logs in, the profile is retrieved from this drive and used to create the desktop. The user's desktop is therefore the same no matter which machine in the Domain the user logs on to.

The Profile Editor is used to create user profiles. Profiles can be either mandatory (unchangeable) or personal (changeable). To use the Profile Editor, you set up the Program Manager so that it looks just like you want it to look when the new user logs it. The Profile Editor then creates a snapshot of that desktop configuration, and lets you customize several other features as well.

You will probably want to create a new dummy account, called "profile" or something similar, so you can play with its desktop. Create this account and give it Domain Administrator privileges. Log on to the account and set it up so it looks the way you want it to look when a user logs in. For example, make any color changes, change the existing groups or create new ones, go into the File Manager and log on to any network drives to which you want the user to have automatic access. Use the Print Manager and connect to printers you want the user to have.

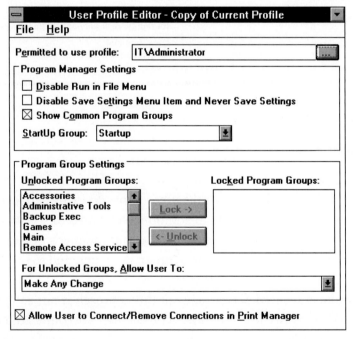

Figure 13.6
The Profile Editor.

Now start the Profile Editor, as shown in Figure 13.6. You will find this application in the Administration Tools group of the Program Manager. In the Profile Editor you can enable and disable a number of capabilities in the Program Manager and File Manager. For example, you can limit the user's access to one or two programs, and eliminate the possibility of accessing any others. When you are done, use the **File** menu to save the new profile.

In order to let the user access the new profile, you have to do three things:

- The user's name or group must appear in the **Permitted to Use Profile** field in Figure 13.6.
- The profile must be saved on a drive that is accessible to the user on the network.
- You must specify the path to the file using a UNC file name (e.g., \\server\c\profiles\jane.usr) in the Profile dialog of the User Manager.

Personal profiles should end with a `.usr` extension, while mandatory profiles should end in `.man`. Figure 13.7 shows several different possibilities for creating user profiles.

You can see that user profiles have a great deal of power, and can be used in many different permutations. You will want to play with them and read the additional documentation supplied with the Advanced Server to gain a full understanding of their capabilities.

13.5 The Server Manager

The Server Manager gives you additional remote administration capabilities in the NT Advanced Server. This application is located in the Administrator Tools section of the Program Manager. When you run it, you will see an application that consists of a menu bar and a list, as shown in Figure 13.8. The list represents the machines that are under the administrative control of the Domain Controller. The Domain Controller can manage both workstations and other NT Advanced Servers within the Domain.

The **Computer** menu contains all the important functions in this application. For example, to add a machine to the list of machines administered by this Domain Controller, choose the **Add to Domain** option in the **Computer** menu and type in the name of the machine you want to add. Similarly, to remove a machine from the Domain, select it in the list and choose the **Remove from Domain** option.

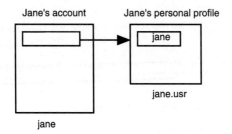

Jane has a personal profile named jane.usr

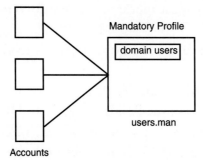

Three accounts use the same unchangeable, mandatory profile

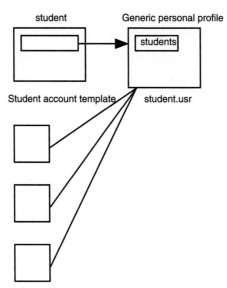

Individual student accounts

Individual student accounts are copied from an account template.
The system copies and creates individual .usr files from the standard
profile named "student.usr" each time it creates an account from the template

Figure 13.7
Different user profile possibilities.

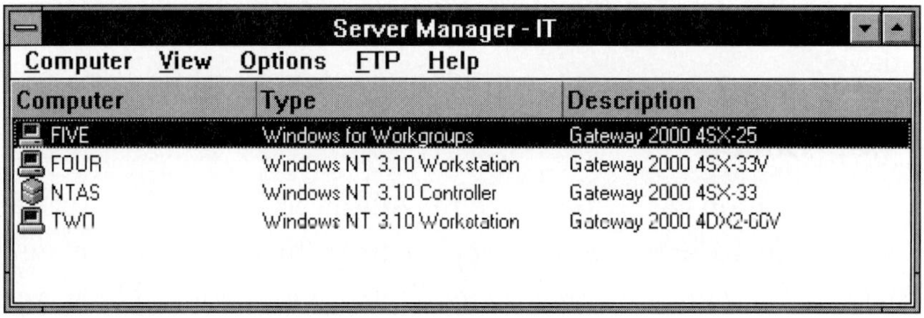

Figure 13.8
The Server Manager application.

The most important parts of the Server Manager are its remote administration facilities. It provides four:

- The **Properties** option emulates the Server applet in the Control Panel. See Section 7.1.5. Select a machine in the list and choose this option. You can use any of the dialogs found in the Server applet as though you were sitting in front of the machine itself.

- The **Shared Directories** option in the **Computer** menu lets you see and modify the drives and directories that each machine shares. It lets you modify the shared drives remotely. Select a machine in the list and choose this option. See Chapter 11 for more information.

- The **Services** option lets you see the same Services dialog that you would see using the Services applet in the Control Panel on the remote machine. See Section 7.1.6. Select a machine in the list and choose this option. The ability to remotely start and stop services is a major convenience, especially when a service on a remote machine is not starting properly.

- The **FTP** menu lets you adjust the FTP server on any NT machine within the Domain. Select a machine in the list and choose this option. See Section 14.4 for more information on FTP servers.

The **Computer** menu also contains a **Send Message** option. With this option you can broadcast messages to all users connected to the specified machine. For example, say you are administrating a machine named "bigdisk2" remotely over the network, and you want to change the share permissions on one of its drives. If you select that computer in the list and choose the **Send Message** option, then the message you create will get broadcast to anyone who has a connection to "bigdisk2" (for example, because they have a connection to one of its drives).

13.6 Replication

The replication facility built into the Advanced Server allows specified directories and files to be *replicated*, or copied, from the server down to individual workstations that have requested the replicated information. The server is referred to as an *exporter*, while the workstation acts as an *importer* of the data. If you look at the directory tree on the Advanced Server, you will find a directory named `c:\winntas\system32\repl\export` (provided you installed the Advanced Server in `c:\winntas`; adjust accordingly if you installed it elsewhere). On every NT workstation you will find a corresponding directory named `c:\winnt\system32\repl\import` (provided you installed Windows NT in `c:\winnt`; adjust accordingly if you installed it elsewhere). Once you have properly configured the exporter and importers, then every file placed into or modified in the exporter directory will get copied to all of the corresponding import directories on all of the subscribing workstations.

You use the replicator when you have files or applications that are frequently read by all users. For example, say you have an application in your company that makes a large number of read accesses to a certain file. If the file is stored on a server, it can create a lot of network traffic. If it is replicated to all workstations, however, each machine can access it off the local drive rather than burdening the network and the server. Whenever the file needs updating, you change it in the export directory on the Advanced Server and the file is automatically replicated to all relevant machines. This facility is also frequently used when the Domain Controller is managing a number of other servers, or for scripts such as logon scripts and `at` command scripts that you want to have on the local machine even if it becomes accidentally disconnected from the network.

There are several hoops to jump through when implementing the replicator service. First of all, on the Advanced Server machine you must create a new account that is a member of the Backup Operators group. You might call this account "DirReplicator," "Repl," or something similar. Set the **Password Never Expires** option in the User Manager window for the account. Also make sure that the account allows all logon hours.

Now go to the Services applet in the Control Panel of the Advanced Server. Find the Directory Replicator service as shown in Figure 13.9. Click the **Startup** button and modify the **This Account** field to contain the new replicator account you just created, as shown in Figure 13.10. Set the Startup Type to Automatic if you plan to use this service on a regular basis. Start the service by clicking the **Start** button. The replicator account will automatically be given the "Log on as Service" right and added to the Local Replicator group.

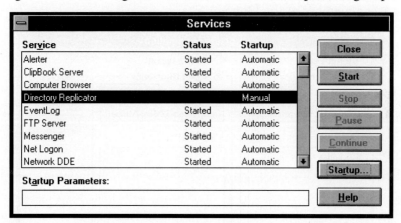

Figure 13.9
Enabling the Directory Replicator Service.

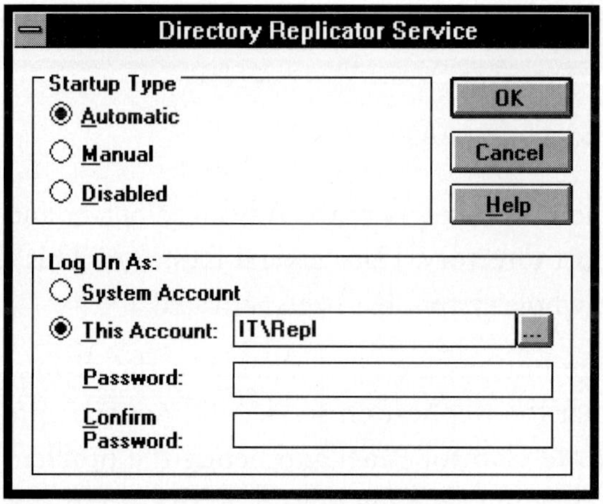

Figure 13.10
Setting the account for the Directory Replicator Service.

Now open the Server applet in the Control Panel of the Advanced Server. Click on the **Replicator** button and you will see a dialog like the one shown in

Figure 13.11. Click the **Add** button on the Export side of the window and add the name of each workstation that you want to export to. If you leave the Export list blank, it will by default export to all machines in the local Domain (the members of the local Domain being determined by the list of machines in the Server Manager shown in Section 13.5). On the import side of the dialog, add the name of the server itself if you want to test things out. Again, if you do nothing and leave the list blank the server will automatically import from itself because it is a member of the Domain.

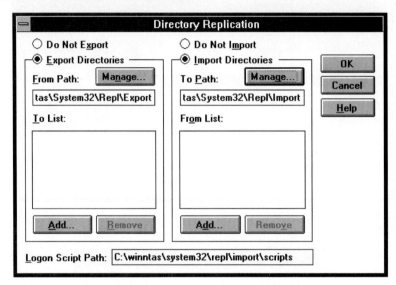

Figure 13.11
The Directory Replication on NTAS dialog.

Now go to the File Manager of the Advanced Server and create a new directory in the export directory. Place several files in it. This directory will get exported once the whole system has been activated.

If the **Manage** buttons are not available in the dialog shown in Figure 13.11, it means that the Replication service did not start properly. Go to the Services applet in the Control Panel and debug the problem. Otherwise you should be able to click the **Manage** button on the export side and see a list of directories. This list by default contains all the subdirectories in the `c:\winntas\system32\repl\export` directory. As you add new directories to the export directory with the File Manager, they will automatically show up in this list.

If you wait a few minutes, the export directory will get copied to the import directory on the server without your intervention. If you add a few more files to the export directory, they will get copied eventually as well. It probably will take 30–60 seconds for the copy to take place. This proves that everything is working properly.

You have several options when managing export directories. You can select the **Wait Until Stabilized** option on any subdirectory: This option causes nothing from the directory to be exported until you have left the directory alone for more than two minutes. This feature ensures that a directory does not get copied in a partial state while you are adding files to it. You can also turn on or off the copying of sub-trees within an export subdirectory. The **Add Lock** button allows you to temporarily lock an export directory. It will not export its contents while it is locked.

Using the replication service

Use the replication service to copy files automatically from the server to all client machines in the Domain. You use this service for two reasons:

- To copy files that are needed frequently in a Read Only fashion, and would therefore create too much network traffic if accessed over the network.
- To copy files that you want to have on the local machine in the event that the workstation gets temporarily cut off from the network. For example, logon scripts are frequently copied using the replicator service because a machine cannot function properly without them. By making sure that the replicator service gives each machine its own private copy, you ensure that each machine will still work properly if cut off from the network.

To enable the replication capability on a remote workstation in the Domain, start the Directory Replicator service on the remote machine, giving it the replicator account on the Domain Controller as its service logon account. Once the service starts, everything in the server's export directory should copy itself over automatically to the remote machine's import directory after a few minutes. You may want to use the **Replicator** button in the **Server** applet to customize things. For example, you can lock or remove import directories by pushing the **Manage** button.

13.7 Conclusion

This chapter really only scratches the surface of the Advanced Server's capabilities. When you have multiple Advanced Servers on a network, many interesting possibilities present themselves. For example, two different Domain Controllers on different communicating networks can form "trust relationships" with one another to validate user IDs back and forth between the Domains.

You will want to study the documentation for the Advanced Server carefully to fully appreciate and understand all the possibilities and ramifications.

CONNECTING TO TCP/IP MACHINES

14

The TCP/IP network protocol is one of the oldest and best established networking schemes in widespread use today. It has been used as the primary interconnection mechanism on UNIX machines for many years. It is also the basis of the Internet and other worldwide networks. Implementations of TCP/IP exist for virtually every system available.

If you have UNIX machines on your network, or if you want to interconnect with a wide variety of disparate machines, the TCP/IP protocol provides an easy avenue for communication. It also allows you to directly connect your network into the worldwide Internet. In this chapter you will learn how to activate TCP/IP networking on an NT workstation so you can communicate with other TCP/IP machines.

14.1 Overview of TCP/IP

TCP/IP is a two-part system for interconnecting machines using networks such as Ethernet. It is one of many protocols available for this purpose. For example, Windows NT and Windows for Workgroups natively use a protocol called NetBEUI. If you have a network with NT workstations on it, and if you have done nothing special with the networking portion of the system following installation, then by default the system uses NetBEUI to send and receive information packets between the NT machines.

The TCP/IP network protocol, along with NT's TCP/IP package, allows you to communicate with other machines on the network that rely on TCP/IP for their network communications. The NT package includes the client-side applications that you find with most TCP/IP packages: TELNET (to log on to remote machines or connect to sockets), FTP (to copy files from remote machines), and so on. It also includes an FTP server. These facilities will be important to you in any of the three following cases:

- If you have (or want to have) one or more UNIX machines on your network, and you want to be able to use telnet, ftp, rcp, and so on from your NT workstation to communicate with the UNIX machines, you need TCP/IP. For example, if you want to be able to log on to the UNIX machine from your NT workstation over the network, loading the TCP/IP protocol package for NT enables these capabilities. These same facilities allow you to communicate with appropriately equipped OS/2 machines as well.

- If you want to connect to the Internet and use the TELNET and FTP facilities of TCP/IP to connect to other machines, you need the TCP/IP package. If you want to create an FTP presence on the Internet with an NT machine, you need the NT FTP server.

- If you have created an NT network that has grown so large that network traffic is becoming unacceptable, you may want to consider adding a router and TCP/IP to segment the network.

These different situations are shown in Figure 14.1. In the first case, in which one or more NT machines want to be able to FTP with UNIX machines on the network, TCP/IP is useful because it is the protocol that UNIX machines use. The same holds true for Internet connections, because the Internet consists largely of UNIX machines. In the third case, TCP/IP is useful because it is *routable*. The routability of TCP/IP packets allows you to divide your network into several segments and isolate local traffic to separate segments. To understand these different uses of TCP/IP, it is helpful to understand a little about TCP/IP itself.

Let's say you have a simple network consisting of two NT machines connected by Ethernet using the standard NetBEUI protocol. Machine 1 has a printer attached, and shares it with Machine 2, as shown in Figure 14.2. When Machine 2 wants to print something, it sends the data for the printer over the network.

If you were to look at the network packets sent by Machine 2 as the packets travel over the network, you would find that they look something like those shown in Figure 14.3. A packet, while traveling on the wire between machines,

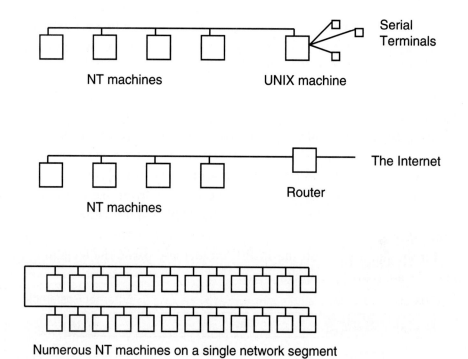

Figure 14.1
Different networking scenarios that require TCP/IP.

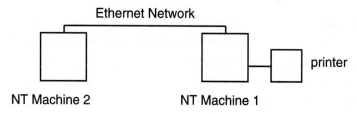

Figure 14.2
A simple network using NetBEUI to share a printer.

consists of preamble and postamble bytes added by Machine 2's Ethernet card, as well as the data itself. The data portion of the packet contains header information that allows NetBEUI drivers to recognize the packet's recipient. When the Ethernet card on Machine 1 sees the packet, it strips off the preamble and postamble and delivers the data to the network card's driver for delivery to the appropriate receiver.

In the case of TCP/IP packets, the data segment of the packet shown in Figure 14.3 contains an additional TCP/IP header. This configuration is shown

Ethernet Preamble   Ethernet Postamble
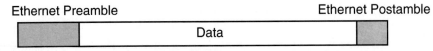

Figure 14.3
A typical data packet as it travels over the wire between computers.

in Figure 14.4. The TCP/IP header contains a variety of information. Most importantly, the header contains an ID that marks the packet as a TCP/IP data packet. The header also contains the TCP/IP address of the sender and intended receiver, checksum information (the value used to make sure the data is transmitted without error), and so on. The TCP/IP driver that you load when you install NT's TCP/IP package looks at the TCP/IP information of any packet that arrives on the network and uses it to decide if it should accept the packet. If it should, it strips off the TCP/IP header and passes the remaining data on to the appropriate recipient driver.

Ethernet Preamble   Ethernet Postamble
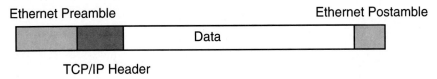

TCP/IP Header

Figure 14.4
A typical TCP/IP packet.

Whenever a UNIX machine sees a packet on the network, it examines it first to see if it is a TCP/IP packet. If it is, it then looks at the TCP/IP header to decide if it is the intended recipient of the packet. If the UNIX machine is the recipient, it strips off the TCP/IP header and delivers the data packet to the appropriate driver on the machine.

By installing TCP/IP software on your NT workstation, you give your workstation the ability to send and receive TCP/IP packets. In order for your machine to correctly communicate in this realm, it must have a corresponding TCP/IP name and address. Naming is one of the most important parts of the TCP/IP installation process, because it ensures that your machine does not conflict with other machines on the network. If you are working in a large organization, you will get your machine's name from your company's network administrator. If you are creating a small, isolated network of your own, you can create an arbitrary naming scheme. If you want to hook your network onto the Internet, you will need to follow the Internet naming scheme, and you will receive very specific instructions from the provider of your Internet feed. See Section 14.6.

A TCP/IP name consists of both an *Internet Domain Address* (or the "Fully Qualified Domain Name") and an *Internet Protocol (IP) Address*. The IP address is a set of four integers ("octets") with values ranging between 0 and 255 (e.g., 152.16.240.6). This number, if you are connected to the Internet, is unique on the Internet and has a format that is well established. For example, numbers of the format 128.109.xxx.xxx are used by many machines operating within the state of North Carolina. However, North Carolina State University grew to have such a large network that it now uses a different address of the form 152.1.xxx.xxx. The entire IP address number space has been carefully divided and organized like this throughout the world to avoid confusion.

If you are on an isolated network of your own, you can create your own IP addresses, but when you connect to the Internet you will be given specific numbers to use. For example, a large company obtaining an Internet feed might be told to use 192.175.xxx.yyy for its IP addresses. The "xxx" value would represent subnets (segments) within the company, while the "yyy" value would represent individual machines. A smaller company might be assigned the number 128.5.49.yyy, and use a different value in "yyy" for each machine.

The Internet Domain Address is an English name for each machine. Again, if you are on an isolated network you can make up names. If you are connecting to the Internet you apply for a name. For example, all machines at Interface Technologies are in the "iftech.com" Domain and individual machines tack on their *host name* to this Domain name. The result: machines with names like "itgate.iftech.com." There is a one-to-one correspondence between names and addresses. For example, the machine named "itgate.iftech.com" might have the IP address 128.5.49.3. No other machine on the Internet has that name or number.

This may all seem rather arcane, but you must figure it out before you attempt to install the TCP/IP package on an NT workstation. Otherwise, tremendous network confusion is the result. If your machine is attached to a network in a large company, you will want to talk with the network administrator so the name and address for your machine are correct and do not conflict with other machines on the company's network. If you are creating an isolated TCP/IP network in a small company, you will need to create a Domain name for the company (choose something with a "company.com" format), along with names for individual machines. Limit names to 10 characters. You will also want to select a numbering scheme. Two numbers to totally avoid are 127.0.0.1 (used for loopback) and 255.255.255.255. Also, the use of 0, 1, or 255 in any octet is not recommended because these values have special meanings. Starting with 128 is safe. If you decide to connect to the Internet you will eventually have to rename and renumber every machine, but that is easy to do.

One final detail to consider before you begin TCP/IP installation is called Domain Name Services. Your machine needs a way to associate Internet Domain Addresses (e.g., itgate.iftech.com) with IP addresses (e.g., 128.5.49.3). This association is done either by using a local *Hosts* file that contains the associations, or by talking with a *Domain Name Server* somewhere on the net. The Hosts file is a text file that contains an entry for every machine on the network. It looks something like this:

127.0.0.1	localhost	loopback	
128.5.49.3	itgate.iftech.com	itg	itgate
128.5.49.4	one.iftech.com	one	
128.5.49.5	two.iftech.com	two	

The first field on each line is the IP Address, the second field is the Internet Domain Address, and the remaining fields are synonyms. So, for example, "itg" is a synonym for "itgate.iftech.com." A Domain Name Server contains equivalent functionality, but centralizes all naming tables in a single machine that shares its information on the network. If your network already contains UNIX machines, then it is likely that there is already a name server on the net and you will want to attach to it. If you are creating a simple network of your own, you will want to use local Hosts files because of their simplicity.

One of the most significant advantages of TCP/IP is its routability. A *router* is a device that sits between two separate network segments, as shown in Figure 14.5. It examines the TCP/IP header in each packet and decides whether or not a packet on one of the segments should be copied to the other segment. In the diagram below, an administrator has created two separate subnets (128.57.49.xxx and 128.57.50.xxx) and would configure the router to recognize and route packets appropriately. If a machine on Network 1 sends a packet to another machine on Network 1, the router would ignore it because both machines have the same subnet number. On the other hand, the router would detect a packet on network 1 intended for network 2 because of the difference in the subnet number. It would echo the packet onto network 2 so the appropriate machine can receive it.

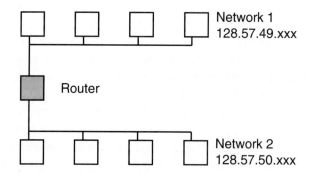

Figure 14.5
A router between two networks.

As you can see, large network administration can become very complicated very quickly. But on small isolated networks, it is very easy to enable the TCP/IP capability and use it to interface to UNIX or OS/2 machines. The following sections show you how to do this.

14.2 Installing the TCP/IP Package

Before you begin installing the TCP/IP package, you should decide on your goals, and then make a map of your network so you can name your machines. For example, say you have a situation like the one shown in Figure 14.6, with a UNIX machine and several NT machines on a network. You want to allow the NT machines to connect to the UNIX machine with the TELNET and FTP programs.

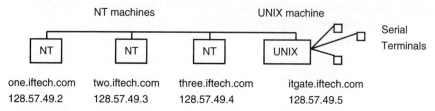

Figure 14.6
A simple TCP/IP networking scenario.

You will need to determine the IP address and Internet name address of the UNIX machine. Probably the easiest way to do this is to look in its `/etc/`

When you begin to design large networks, you will commonly use two different pieces of equipment to connect your network segments together. The first is called a *bridge*. You use a bridge to connect two segments that have the same type of network adapters, but have different physical media. For example, if you have two Ethernet segments that communicate over different media (e.g., one segment uses coax, while the other uses twisted pair), you would use a bridge to connect them. The bridge echoes all packets between the two segments, so any traffic on either segment appears on both. Bridges therefore do nothing to solve traffic problems.

A *router* is used to subdivide networks into segments in order to lower the total amount of network traffic on the individual segments. For example, if you have a large, single-segment Ethernet network that is demonstrating poor performance because of excessive network traffic, you can split the network into subnets and connect the subnets back together with a router. The segmentation localizes network traffic to appropriate subnets. You have to be careful when you create the subnets so you avoid placing machines that frequently talk to one another on different subnets. Machines that frequently talk to one another must reside on the same subnet, or the segmentation accomplishes nothing.

Routers also connect segments that use totally different signaling systems. For example, if you wanted to connect one network that uses token ring adapters to another network that uses Ethernet cards, then you would use a router. In larger networks (e.g., at a university or large company), you often see routers connecting machines in individual departments onto some sort of high speed backbone network.

Obviously the topic of routers and large-scale network design could fill an entire book. You can learn a great deal on your own by reading up on the subject and by contacting manufacturers of routing equipment to request sales literature.

`hosts` file. You will also need to select IP addresses and names for each of the NT machines. See Section 14.1 for more information on naming. You will then have to create Hosts files for the NT machines so they know about the UNIX machine. Once you install the TCP/IP package on the NT machines and implement the Hosts file, they will recognize and connect to the UNIX machine.

The installation of the TCP/IP package assumes that the NT machine you are using has a network card, and that the network portion of NT was installed during the initial installation of Windows NT. If the network portion did not install initially, reinstall NT with the network card in the machine. The addition of the TCP/IP package will not affect the normal NetBEUI printer and disk sharing mechanisms in any way.

Start the installation process by logging on as the administrator and selecting the Network applet in the Control Panel. You will see a dialog box like the one shown in Figure 14.7. Click the **Add Software** button. You will see a dialog like the one shown in Figure 14.8. Choose the TCP/IP protocol and click on the **Continue** button. In the following dialog select the directory containing the TCP/IP package. This will generally be the install directory on the NT installation CD-ROM or diskette drive.

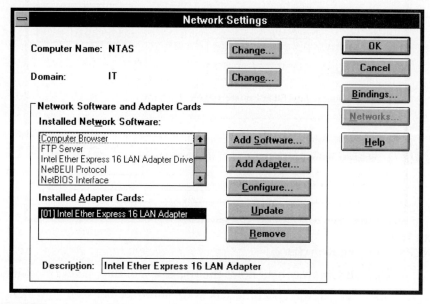

Figure 14.7
The Network Settings dialog.

Now if you click on the **OK** button in Figure 14.7, the configuration dialog shown in Figure 14.9 will come up automatically. The dialog in Figure 14.9 shows you the different pieces of information required to configure your machine for TCP/IP.

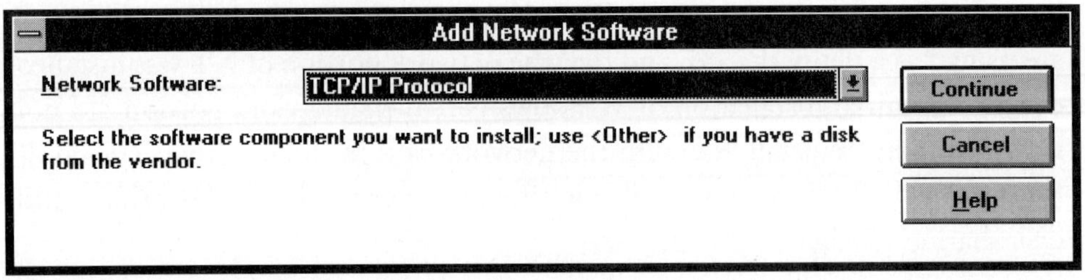

```
┌──────────────────────────────────────────────────────────────────┐
│ ▬                         Add Network Software                      │
├──────────────────────────────────────────────────────────────────┤
│                                                                     │
│  Network Software:      │TCP/IP Protocol                      ▲│   ┌──────────┐ │
│                                                               ▼     │ Continue │ │
│  Select the software component you want to install; use <Other>  if you have a disk  └──────────┘ │
│  from the vendor.                                                   ┌──────────┐ │
│                                                                     │  Cancel  │ │
│                                                                     └──────────┘ │
│                                                                     ┌──────────┐ │
│                                                                     │   Help   │ │
│                                                                     └──────────┘ │
└──────────────────────────────────────────────────────────────────┘
```

Figure 14.8
The Add Network Software dialog.

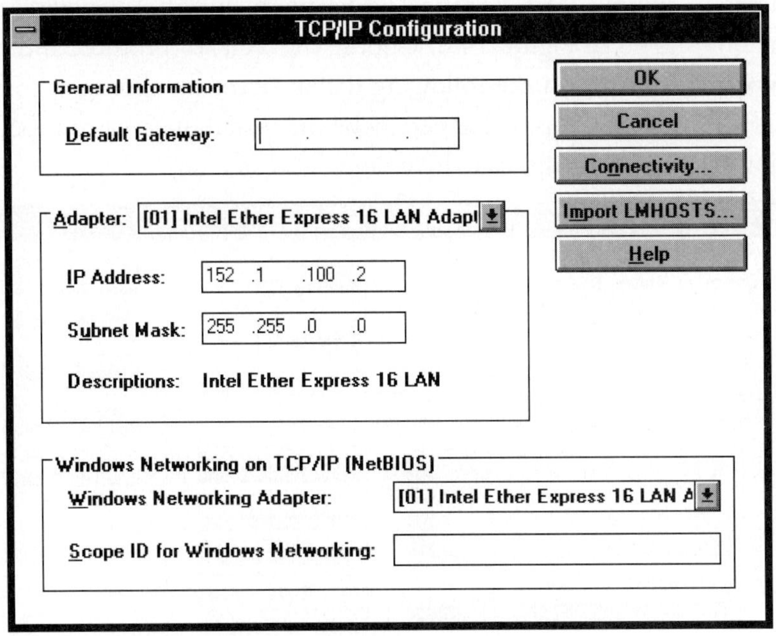

```
┌──────────────────────────────────────────────────────────────────┐
│ ▬                        TCP/IP Configuration                       │
├──────────────────────────────────────────────────────────────────┤
│  ┌─General Information────────────────────────┐   ┌───────────────┐ │
│  │                                             │   │      OK       │ │
│  │   Default Gateway:   │     .     .     │    │   └───────────────┘ │
│  │                                             │   ┌───────────────┐ │
│  └─────────────────────────────────────────────┘  │    Cancel     │ │
│                                                     └───────────────┘ │
│  ┌─Adapter: [01] Intel Ether Express 16 LAN Adapt ▲▼┐ ┌───────────────┐ │
│  │                                             │   │ Connectivity...│ │
│  │   IP Address:   │152 .1    .100 .2 │         │   └───────────────┘ │
│  │                                             │   ┌───────────────┐ │
│  │   Subnet Mask:  │255 .255 .0   .0  │         │   │Import LMHOSTS..│ │
│  │                                             │   └───────────────┘ │
│  │   Descriptions:  Intel Ether Express 16 LAN │   ┌───────────────┐ │
│  │                                             │   │     Help      │ │
│  └─────────────────────────────────────────────┘  └───────────────┘ │
│                                                                      │
│  ┌─Windows Networking on TCP/IP (NetBIOS)──────────────────────┐    │
│  │                                                              │    │
│  │   Windows Networking Adapter:  │[01] Intel Ether Express 16 LAN A▲▼│ │
│  │                                                              │    │
│  │   Scope ID for Windows Networking: │                    │    │    │
│  └──────────────────────────────────────────────────────────────┘   │
└──────────────────────────────────────────────────────────────────┘
```

Figure 14.9
The TCP/IP Configuration dialog.

The **Default Gateway** field holds the IP address of the *gateway* machine for your network. The gateway machine acts as the interface between your network and the wider Internet. Your network administrator will be able to supply you with this address if there is a gateway machine. If you are working on an isolated network, leave the fields blank as shown. In the **IP Address** field, enter the address you have chosen for the machine. In the **Subnet Mask** field enter a mask that indicates the IP Addresses you want your machine to ignore. In Figure 14.9, the administrator chose the value 255.255.0.0 for the mask. This choice dictates that the first two values of any IP address received must be the same as the machine's IP Address, or the machine will ignore the packet. If the mask's value is changed to 255.255.255.0, then the first three values in the IP Address of any packet received must match the machine's or the packet is ignored.

Once you have finished with the configuration dialog, click on the **Connectivity** button in Figure 14.9. You will see a dialog like the one shown in Figure 14.10. This dialog allows you to select whether you want your machine to use a local Hosts file or a remote Domain Name Server for your name server. If there is a name server on your network already, then you can use it. You will probably want to have the machine look at its local Hosts file, and then at the name server, so you can modify the local Hosts file for special situations as the need arises.

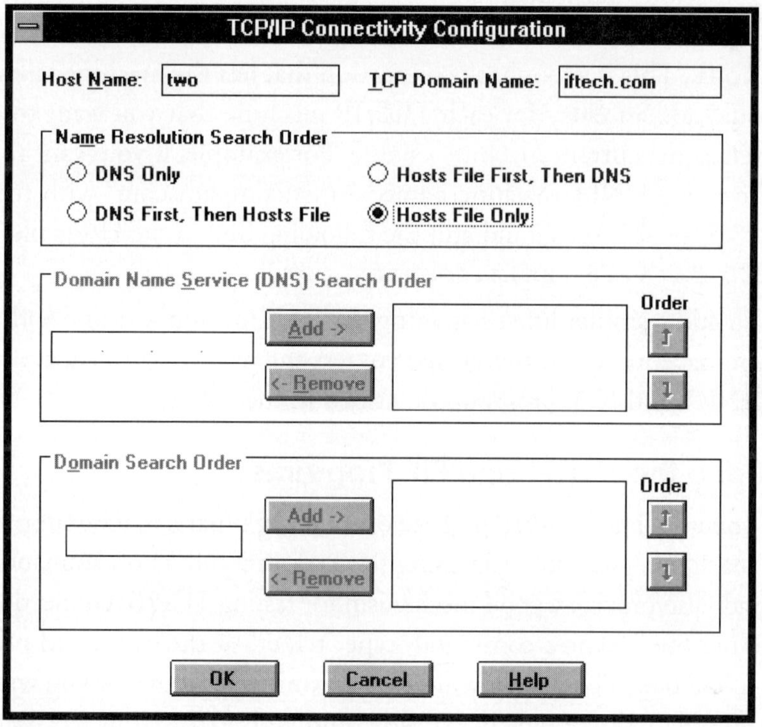

Figure 14.10
The TCP Connectivity Configuration dialog.

For now, select the **Hosts File Only** option (see Section 14.5 for a further discussion of Domain name services). Click the **OK** button, and click the **OK** button on the Network dialog as well. NT will question you about the lack of a default gateway if you left the gateway field blank. If that is what you intended to do, click the **No** button. NT should install the TCP/IP module without complaint and ask you to reboot the system.

You now need to edit the Hosts file so the NT machine knows about the names of any other TCP/IP machines on the net. Alternatively, you can simply memorize the IP Address of each machine and use these addresses to form connections. However, the English name made available by the Hosts file is generally much easier to remember. NT created a stub Hosts file for you when it loaded the TCP/IP package. It can be found in the NT `system32` directory inside of the `drivers\etc` directory. If you have trouble finding the file, use the **Search** option in the File Manager and look for "Hosts" in the Windows NT directory on your machine.

The stub file created by NT during installation contains an entry for `localhost`. This is a loopback connection that lets the machine talk to itself. You should add an entry for each TCP/IP machine that you want to connect to, as well as the current machine's name. For example, if you want to be able to connect to a UNIX machine named "unix.company.com" with the IP address 128.54.6.16, you should add the following line to the Hosts file:

```
128.54.6.16  unix.company.com
```

Also add a similar line containing the local machine's name and address. Once you have massaged the Hosts file, test the new TCP/IP capability using the TELNET and FTP programs described in the next section.

14.3 Using the TELNET and FTP Programs

If you install the TCP/IP package on a network that has, for example, several UNIX machines, you can begin using the `telnet` and `ftp` commands. These commands also provide a good mechanism for testing TCP/IP connectivity.

To use the `telnet` command, type "telnet" at the command prompt of an MS-DOS box. The system will open a terminal window for you with a "telnet>" prompt. You can type the `open` command, followed by the name or IP address of the machine you want to connect to. For example, if you have a machine named "unix.company.com" on your network, type the following at the telnet prompt:

```
telnet> open unix.company.com
```

If the TCP/IP package is working correctly and the Hosts file is in order, then you should see a standard logon prompt for the machine named unix.company.com (Note that you cannot telnet to other NT machines). If there is a problem, you should fall back to the IP address and see if that works. For example, if the IP address for unix.company.com is 128.52.45.6, you can type the following:

```
telnet> open 128.52.45.6
```

If this works, it means that there is a problem with the Hosts file. If it does not work, it means that something is wrong with the TCP/IP functionality on your machine, or on the remote machine.

To use the `ftp` command, open an MS-DOS window and type `ftp` followed by the machine name. For example:

```
c:\> ftp unix.company.com
```

If everything is working correctly you will see a prompt asking for your ID and password. If you do not have an account on the machine, you can often log on as "anonymous" and gain some sort of access to the files on the machine. Once connected, FTP provides a number of its own commands. The three most commonly used are `ls` (to list files on the remote machine; `dir` also works), `get` (to copy a file from the remote machine to your machine) and `put` (to copy from your machine to the remote machine). For example, you might type `ls` to find out that a file named "demo.txt" is available, and then type `get demo.txt` to copy it over. Other UNIX commands like `cd` and `pwd` (print working directory) also work. If you are transferring a binary file, be sure to type `binary` before the transfer so that all eight bits of each byte transfer properly. When you are done with FTP, type `quit`.

14.4 Creating an FTP Server

By creating an FTP server, you allow UNIX users and people on the Internet to connect to your machine to download files. NT allows you to create an FTP server on any NT machine that has the TCP/IP package installed. In addition, you can manage all the FTP servers in a Domain using the Advanced Server. See Section 13.5 for details.

Start the installation process by logging in as the administrator and selecting the Network applet in the Control Panel. You will see a dialog box like the one shown in Figure 14.7. Click the **Add Software** button. You will see a dialog like the one shown in Figure 14.8. Choose **FTP Server** and click on the **Continue** button.

You will see an information dialog telling you the following:

The File Transfer Protocol relies on the ability to pass user passwords over the network without data encryption. A user with physical access to the network may be able to examine user passwords during FTP validation. Are you sure you want to continue?

What this means is that when a user connects to an FTP server and logs on, the user's password is passed across the network in an unencrypted form. Anyone who happens to have a network analyzer attached to the network can theoretically intercept such a packet and learn the user's password. If you are trying to create a totally secure network, then this is probably an unacceptable risk.

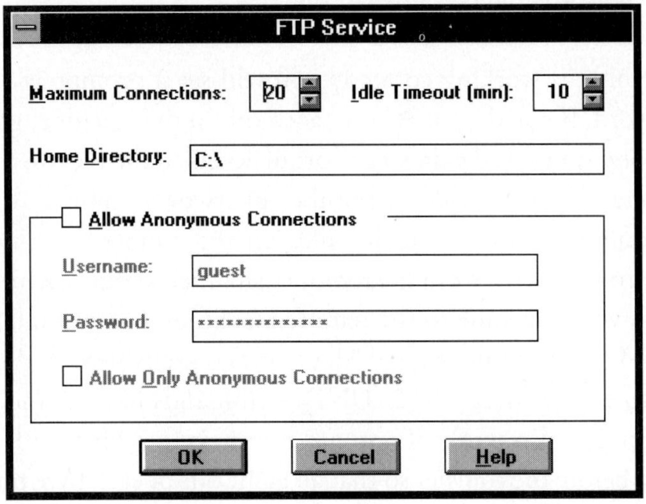

Figure 14.11
The FTP setting dialog.

Once you have loaded the FTP server, you will see a dialog like the one shown in Figure 14.11. This dialog allows you to set parameters for the new server. You can set the following:

- Maximum connections: The maximum number of users that can connect to the server at any one time (You would be amazed at how many connections a popular server on the Internet will generate).
- Idle timeout: The number of minutes that a user can remain idle before the FTP server drops their connection.
- Home directory: Specifies the initial directory for anyone logging on. If you are allowing anonymous **FTP,** then you will probably create a specific directory that contains the information you want to publish.

- Allow anonymous connections: In this section you can specify the account name and password used when someone uses the name "anonymous: to login. By default, anonymous users are logged in under the "guest: account, but you can change this to any account. You can also specify that only anonymous logons are allowed.

Once you have set everything up properly, reboot the machine and your FTP server will begin service.

The Control Panel contains an FTP applet that lets you control the server. It shows you all the users connected to the FTP server, and allows you to disconnect any individual or the whole group. The **Security** button lets you restrict FTP users to a certain partition, which can be useful if you are using non-secure file systems.

Administrative Strategy

Partition security

    If security is even vaguely important to you, you will want to place the home directory for the FTP service on an NTFS partition, and then wire the permissions so the anonymous user has no access outside of that directory tree. You also want to give an FTP user Read Only access. Create an account called "anonymous" and use that when creating permissions.

    If you place the home directory for an anonymous user on a FAT partition, then an anonymous user can access any part of the file system. You can use partition security found in the FTP applet of the Control Panel to limit the access of these users.

14.5 Using a Domain Name Server

If your network contains an existing TCP/IP Domain Name Server (generally on a UNIX machine), you can connect to it quite easily using the dialog shown in Figure 14.10. In the **Domain Name Service Search Order** section type the IP address of the machine providing name services. Click the **Add** button to add it to the list. If there is more than one provider on your network, you can add up to three IP addresses. The search order is from top to bottom in the list. To change the order, click on one of the addresses and then click the up or down arrow buttons to move it.

You must also choose one of the four options in the **Name Resolution Search Order** radio box. For example, if you request the **Host file first, then DNS** option and type a command like `telnet unix.company.com`, the system will first try to find that machine name in the local Hosts file. If it finds nothing it will send a request to the Domain Name Server.

At the bottom of Figure 14.10 you will also notice a box labeled **Domain Search Order**. This is a convenience feature. If your TCP Domain name is "company.com," and you have a machine named "unix," it can be bothersome to have to continually type things like "ftp unix.company.com." Therefore, the system allows you to type "ftp unix" and automatically appends the TCP Domain Name (shown at the top of Figure 14.10) to the name for you. The **Domain Search Order** box lets you add other TCP Domain Names to the search. When you type "ftp unix," the system will try all the different Domain names in the **Domain Search Order** box, in the order specified, in its attempt to find the machine named "unix." In a large company or university with many TCP Domains, this facility can save a lot of keystrokes.

14.6 Connecting to the Internet

This chapter has mentioned the Internet in several different places. One of the biggest advantages of having the TCP/IP protocol on your machine is that it gives you the potential to connect into the worldwide Internet. Full connections to the Internet are not cheap, but they can provide you with an ocean of information.

The Internet is made up of thousands of machines and millions of users, all interconnected by a TCP/IP network. It contains many millions of megabytes of information, almost all of it free for the taking. Government agencies, universities, and most large companies have direct Internet connections, and thousands of smaller sites have e-mail and news connections. Connecting your company to the Internet makes all of this information available. By creating an FTP server for your company, you make it possible to publish your own information on the network.

Most machines on the Internet are UNIX machines, and you connect to them directly using TELNET or FTP just like you would if they were on your own local network. The Internet also provides wide-ranging e-mail services, as well as a set of user forums known collectively as NetNews. Generally when you obtain a connection to the Internet, you get 1) e-mail alone, 2) e-mail and Net-News, or 3) a full connection that provides total TCP/IP connectivity. Prices rise accordingly. NetNews and e-mail can come via the network, or through a modem using a facility called UNIX to UNIX Copy (UUCP).

What many companies end up doing initially is using a UNIX machine for their Internet connection. NT users can connect to that UNIX machine from their NT workstations to read their mail and news, and then connect directly to Internet machines with the `ftp` and `telnet` commands.

You can connect to the Internet at several different levels. Generally a connection is referred to as a "feed." For example, you can get a UUCP mail feed for less than $50 a month. This feed provides total e-mail connectivity with all Internet users. At your end you will need a modem and a UUCP package. You can obtain a third-party UUCP package for NT and hook it up fairly easily, although the configuration of UUCP software is something of a black art that takes getting used to. Contact a local University's computer center, or services such as UNIX to UNIX Network (UUNET) in Falls Church, VA, (800-4UU-NET3) for information. UUCP connections can provide NetNews as well.

Getting a full TELNET and FTP connection to the Internet is generally not quite as easy or inexpensive. What you have to do is connect your local network into the global TCP/IP network. This can be done in a variety of ways, but probably the most common is to use a T1 phone line connected to a router on your network. If you are a small company, you can see the problem: Routers are not cheap, and neither are T1 lines. There are less expensive solutions however. For example, you can obtain a 9600 baud modem connection from your network to the Internet. This option is relatively inexpensive. With a full connection like this in place, you can FTP to any machine anywhere in the world that is connected to the Internet. Again, contact a local university or UUNET for information.

14.7 Conclusion

The TCP/IP package provided by Windows NT opens up the possibility of heterogeneous network design. You can use it to connect your NT machines to your existing UNIX network, or to the worldwide Internet.

OTHER CONNECTIONS

This chapter discusses several different ways to connect Windows NT to other systems. The Remote Access Server (RAS) lets you create the equivalent of a network connection using a serial line. It makes it easy to participate in the Windows NT network via modem. Section 15.2 briefly describes other connection possibilities.

15.1 Implementing RAS Connections

It is fairly common these days for people to have laptop computers that they take with them when traveling. It is also common for people to have a machine at home, or at a remote office, and for these people to need files and other resources from the network at the main office. One of the problems with creating a large and sophisticated network is that these remote users usually feel left out. Once a person leaves the office, the network resources become unavailable.

Windows NT supports a new facility called RAS that allows any authorized user to form a remote network connection. If the remote workstation is running Windows NT, there is no functional difference between a standard network connection using a network adapter card and the serial connection formed by RAS. The File Manager connects to the drives in exactly the same way, and the Print Manager connects to printers as well. In fact, if you take a computer that is on the network, disconnect it, move it 200 miles away and then dial in via RAS, all of the connections that the user had to network drives and printers will be restored as though nothing had happened. The only perceivable difference between a network connection and a RAS connection is the speed degradation. If the remote machine is dialing in using a 2400 baud modem, you will not want to blithely copy a 2 MB file from a network drive, because it would take several hours to complete the transfer. But for small text files and minor print tasks, the performance is quite acceptable.

Administrative Strategy

Solving booting problems

If you disconnect an NT machine from an Ethernet network and find that it will not boot, or that it is *extremely* sluggish when booting and logging on, try attaching an Ethernet terminating resistor directly to the network card and see if that helps.

Another use of RAS is to form temporary network connections for machines lacking network cards. For example, say an employee is frequently on the road with a portable computer. When she comes into the office, she would like to connect to the network to do some printing and file copying. The normal solution to the problem is to use floppy disks, but this is inconvenient. An expensive solution to the problem is to get a network adapter that connects via the portable computer's parallel port. Whenever she comes into the office, the employee can hook into the network at full speed. An extremely inexpensive alternative, however, is to connect the portable using RAS and a null-modem cable. This configuration is not as fast as a network adapter. Its speed is limited to perhaps 5Kbytes per second, so a 1 MB file which cannot be compressed takes three to four minutes to transfer. However, the cost of the serial cable is very low. RAS also contains an automatic compression facility that roughly doubles the perceived speed of a RAS connection.

RAS also allows other operating systems to use the system. For example, Microsoft sells RAS clients for Windows for Workgroups machines. If you have a portable computer running Windows for Workgroups, you can connect to an NT network using RAS and access all drives and printers.

To enable RAS connections, you must create a RAS server, and then load RAS client software onto the remote machine. The RAS server should have a network card so that it is a full participant in the office network, along with an available COM port. The RAS client can be any NT machine that has a free COM port. You must then hook up any equipment necessary to create the connection. For example, if you plan to use a pair of 9600 baud modems for RAS communications, connect them to their respective machines using the appropriate cables.

To load the RAS server, open the Control Panel and select the Network applet. Click the **Add Software** button. Select the Remote Access Server and click the **Continue** button. The system will load the files from the specified drive, and the Add Port dialog shown in Figure 15.1 will appear. Choose the port to which you plan to connect your modem.

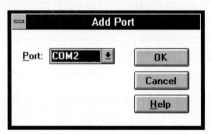

Figure 15.1
The Add Port dialog.

The Configure Port dialog is shown in Figure 15.2. In it you can choose the type of modem, and the way you plan to use RAS on the workstation. Generally a machine is either a server or a client, but there are situations where a machine needs to play both roles and NT allows this. The **Settings** button on this dialog reveals a Settings dialog (Figure 15.3) that lets you customize the behavior of the modem you are using.

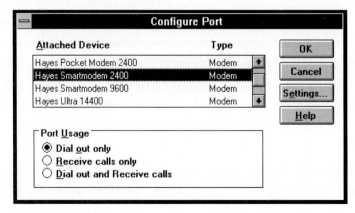

Figure 15.2
The Configure Port dialog.

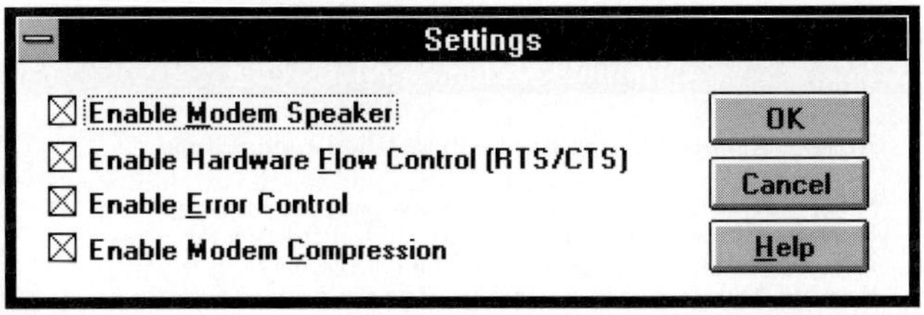

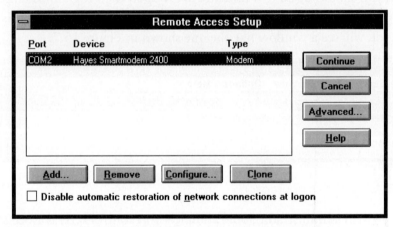

Figure 15.3
The Settings dialog.

The Remote Access Setup dialog shown in Figure 15.4 allows you to configure additional ports. You will find an **Advanced** button (Figure 15.5) whose dialog lets you control the remote user's access to the network. For security reasons you may wish to allow the remote user to access only the resources available on the server itself. Otherwise you can let the user access the entire network. The advanced options are available only on ports that receive calls.

Figure 15.4
The Remote Access Setup dialog.

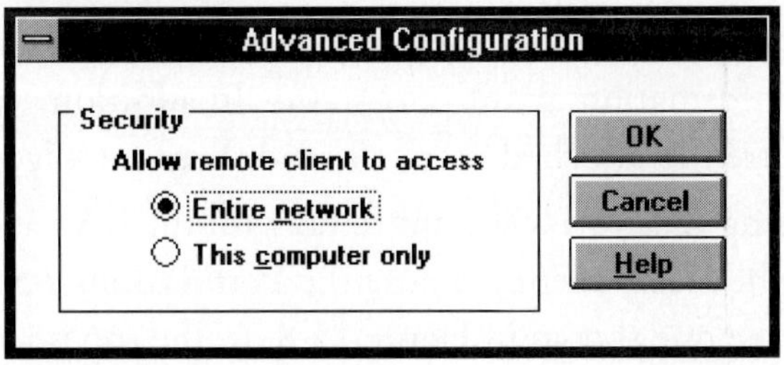

Figure 15.5
The Advanced Configuration dialog.

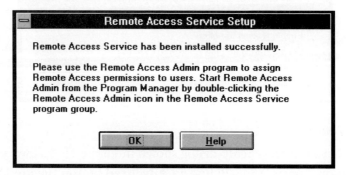

Figure 15.6
Successful completion of the RAS installation.

Once you have successfully completed the installation of the RAS server, you will see a dialog like the one shown in Figure 15.6. When you click the **OK** button, you should be able to find a RAS group in the Program Manager, and inside of it find the RAS administration application. When you start this application you will see a window like the one shown in Figure 15.7.

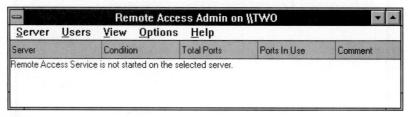

Figure 15.7
The RAS Administrator application.

The RAS administrator application lets you control several aspects of the RAS server. It allows you to enable and disable the server so you can prevent people from attempting to log on. You can also control the security of the server. For example, you can specify the user accounts that are allowed to dial in. You can gather information about port status. In addition, you can get information about currently attached users, or send them messages.

The first thing that you will want to do with the RAS administrator is set permissions. In the **Users** menu, choose the **Permissions** option and you will see a dialog like the one shown in Figure 15.8. In the top portion of the dialog you indicate the users that should be able to access RAS. Click the **Grant All** button to grant all users access to RAS, or select individual user names and click the **Grant Dialin Permissions to User** check box.

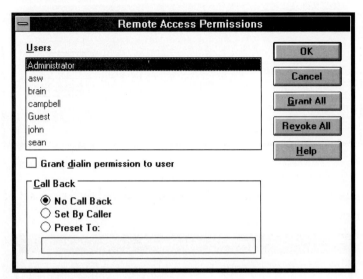

Figure 15.8
The Remote Access Permissions dialog.

At the bottom of the dialog you can set the call back mode. The **No Call Back** option accepts the call when the user dials in and connects it immediately to the RAS server. The **Set By Caller** option lets the remote user enter his or her phone number. The RAS server then hangs up and calls the remote site. This is a good way to minimize phone charges, especially if the remote user is having to call from a pay phone or hotel. The **Preset To** number is a security feature. When the remote user dials in, the server authenticates the account, and then calls back using the preset number. This step ensures that only calls from a certain location or secure phone line are permitted.

Once you have set up permissions, start the RAS server with the **Start Remote Access Server** option in the **Server** menu. You will see a dialog like the one shown in Figure 15.9. Simply enter in the name of the machine holding the server that you want to start.

Once you have started the RAS server, users can dial in. You have two different ways to find out about the current connections. In the **Server** menu there is a **Communications Ports** option that lets you view the different ports available. For example, by clicking the **Port Status** button you can view a variety of information about the port as shown in Figure 15.10. You can also send messages to remote users or close a connection. The **Active Users** option in the **Us-**

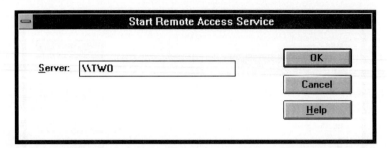

Figure 15.9
Selecting the RAS server that you want to start.

ers menu does the same thing, but the list is presented on a per-user basis rather than a per-port basis.

Port Status			
Port:	COM2		OK
Server:	TWO		
Modem Condition:	Normal		Reset
Line Condition:	Waiting for call		
Port Speed (bps):	2400		Help

Incoming

Bytes:	0
Frames:	0
Compression:	0%

Outgoing

Bytes:	0
Frames:	0
Compression:	0%

Errors

CRC:	0	Framing:	0
Timeouts:	0	Serial Overruns:	0
Alignment:	0	Buffer Overruns:	0

Figure 15.10
The Port Status dialog.

On any client machine, use the Network applet in the Control Panel to load the Remote Access Service software. Configure its port as you did for the server side, and when the installation is complete you should find a new RAS group and icon in your Program Manager.

The first time you run the client, you will be asked to enter the phone number and name of the RAS server, as shown in Figure 15.11. If you click on the **Authenticate using current user name and password** check box, then the ID and password of the current user will automatically get passed to the server whenever you call it. Otherwise the system will prompt you for an ID and password and use it for authentication. Click on the **Advanced** button to see specially customized settings, as shown in Figure 15.12.

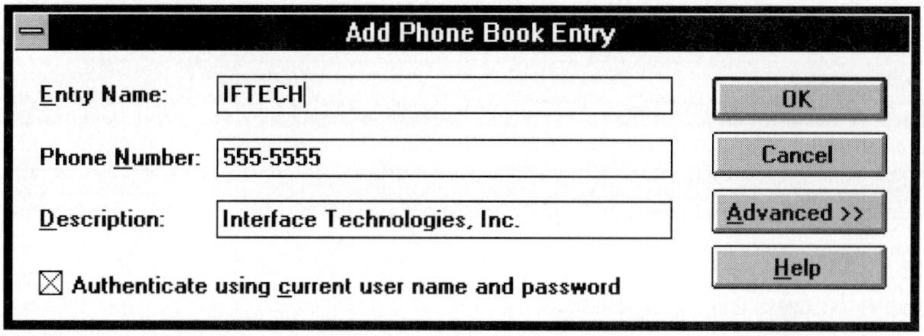

Figure 15.11
The Add Phone Book Entry dialog.

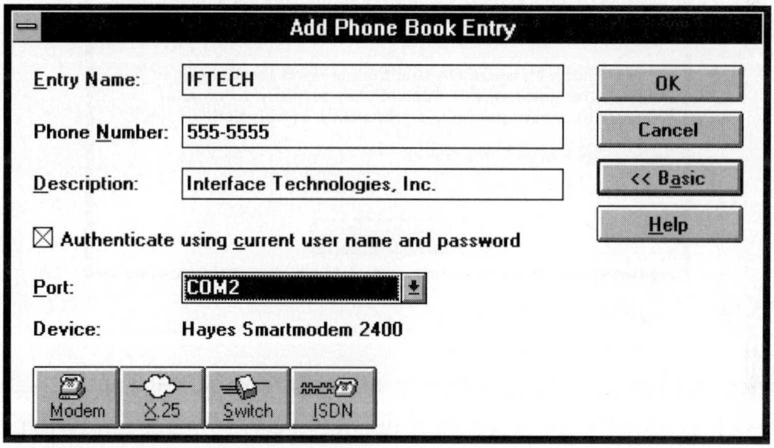

Figure 15.12
The Advanced Add Phone Book Entry dialog.

Once initialized with a phone number, the Remote Access client application appears as shown in Figure 15.13. You can add new phone numbers, edit or delete existing entries, or copy an entry to create a new one. When you want to connect to an RAS server, double click on one of the listed entries, or select an entry and click the **Dial** button.

The program will dial and connect you to the remote server. Upon your initial successful connection you will see a dialog like the one shown in Figure 15.14. You can specify that the client application automatically minimize itself after a successful connection, and you can also eliminate the Connection Complete dialog in the future.

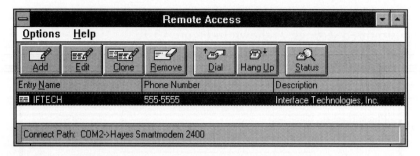

Figure 15.13
The Remote Access client application.

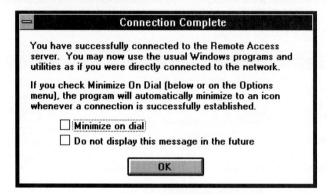

Figure 15.14
The Connection Complete dialog.

Once you have formed a successful connection, you should be able to use the network as though you were there in the office. Connect to drives using the File Manager. Connect to printers using the Print Manager. Although a little slower, you can still participate in the network as though you were there. While you are connected, the Remote Access Monitor is available to show you the current state of the modem connection, as shown in Figure 15.15. If you do not see it, you can call it up manually by clicking on its icon in the RAS group in the Program Manager.

Figure 15.15
The Remote Access Monitor.

15.2 Other Connections

Windows NT can natively connect to a variety of systems, and third party software allows you to connect to many other systems as well. This section briefly highlights some of these different connections.

As discussed in Chapter 1, Microsoft sells an intermediate product between Windows 3.1 and Windows NT called Windows for Workgroups. Windows for Workgroups machines on an NT network can share in a number of the facilities that NT provides:

- Windows for Workgroup machines can access drives and directories shared by NT machines, provided that the drive or directory allows access by "Everyone." A Windows for Workgroups user simply attaches to the drive with the File Manager. A Windows NT workstation can similarly attach to drives shared by Windows for Workgroups machines. If the person sharing the drive on the Windows for Workgroups machine has password-protected the connection, you will have to know the password to connect. Note the NTFS partitions shared with Windows for Workgroups machines will abbreviate long file names to conform to the 8-dot-3 naming standard required by Windows for Workgroups.

- Windows for Workgroups machines can share printers and NT machines can connect with them. When you connect to such a printer, the system will require you to select an appropriate driver for the printer. When NT machines share printers with other NT machines, this step is not necessary. Similarly, a Windows for Workgroups machine can connect to a printer shared by a Windows NT machine, provided that the NT machine shares it with everyone.

- Windows for Workgroups machines can join a Post Office created on an NT network.

- Windows for Workgroups users can "chat" with NT users using the Chat application.

The option of using Windows for Workgroups on an NT network gives users with low-end machines the ability to participate in the network. The NT machines will lock out the Windows for Workgroups users on any secured device or service.

NT machines can communicate with OS/2 machines in two different ways. If an OS/2 machine has the TCP/IP package, then NT clients can use the TEL-NET and FTP programs (Chapter 14) just as they would with any UNIX machine. OS/2 can also interoperate with Windows NT when running the OS/2 LAN Manager.

There are many other connection possibilities that are provided by third party distributors. For example, you can connect to Internet e-mail feeds using third party UUCP packages, as described in Chapter 14. UNIX machines can share their drives, or mount drives from other UNIX machines, using a system called Network File System (NFS). By purchasing a third party NFS package you can further integrate NT into an existing UNIX network.

15.3 Conclusion

Windows NT is truly a huge and powerful system. On a stand-alone machine it provides a modern and complete operating environment that is very secure and totally robust. On a network of NT machines its power is magnified by disk and printer sharing, along with a number of built-in networking facilities that new applications can use to create enhanced capabilities.

The ability to work with a wide range of other systems is also an advantage. You can integrate NT into your existing network and quickly communicate with UNIX machines, OS/2 machines, and Windows for Workgroups users. Windows NT makes it possible to design networks that completely accommodate the needs of all users in a secure and reliable way.

Securing Files on Windows NT

The NT security system is available on any drive formatted with NTFS. It lets you pick a file or directory and specify the people who can access it. You can also determine exactly what those people will be able to do to the file, and you can audit, or monitor, people who access given files or directories. The following exercises will help you to find and understand the security features made possible by NTFS.

To try out the security system, open the File Manager and find a drive formatted with NTFS. Create a new directory called `test` and in that directory create three files named `file1`, `file2`, and `file3`. It does not matter what the files contain: create a simple test file with Notepad and copy it to create the three files.

Click on the `test` directory to select it. Now choose the **Owner** option from the File Manager's **Security** menu. A dialog similar to the one shown in Figure A.1 will appear and tell you that you are the owner of the directory (the person who creates a directory or file owns it initially). You can use this dialog to check the ownership of any file on the system. If you have the privileges to do so, you can take ownership of files or directories with the **Take Ownership** button.

As the owner of a file or directory you have the right to set permissions on it. To set permissions, choose the **Permissions** option in the **Security** menu. You will see a dialog similar to that shown in Figure A.2. This dialog shows you the permissions that are currently set for the directory. For example, the dialog in Figure A.2 shows that the test directory has permissions set for the Creator of the file, Everyone, and for Brain. Since Everyone has access, and since that

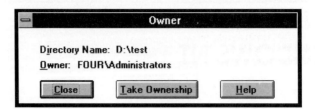

Figure A.1
The Owner dialog.

access is Full Control, anyone anywhere on the net can access this directory and
change it or any file in it as they please.

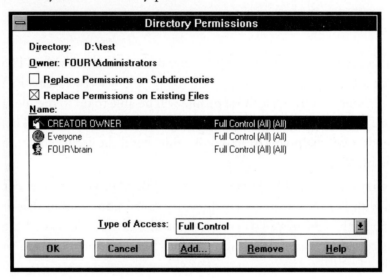

Figure A.2
The Directory Permissions dialog.

To make the access to this directory more selective, click on Everyone and
click the **Remove** button. Now only the Owner and the user Brain can access
the file. To add another person or group into the access list, click on the **Add**
button. You will see a dialog like the one shown in Figure A.3. The list shows
you a variety of groups to whom you can give access. For example, you can give
access to everyone, to interactive users (all users on this particular machine), to
users who are members of the Power Users group, and so on. Clicking on the
Show Users button will include a list of individual users on this machine as
well (the **List Names In** combo box at the top of the dialog lets you include
user lists from different Domain Controllers on the net). To give a particular

group or user your permission to access the `test` directory, click on one of the groups or users and then click the **Add** button.

Now choose the type of access you want to give them from the combo box at the bottom of the dialog. You have the following choices in the list: No Access, List, Read, Add, Add and Read, Change, and Full Access. Pick one at random and press **OK** to return to the Directory Permissions dialog.

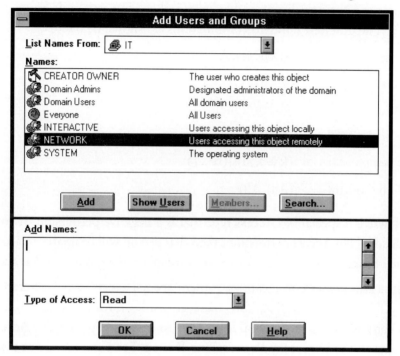

Figure A.3
The Add dialog.

What were all those different types of access? There are six access bits that can be set on any file or directory, as shown below:

- Read (R): The user can read the file.
- Write (W): The user can write to the file.
- Execute (X): The user can execute the file.
- Delete (D): The user can delete the file.
- Change Permissions (P): The user can change the access privileges on the file.
- Take Ownership (O): The user can take ownership of the file.

These bits are normally set in combinations. The different access types such as **List**, **Read**, **Add**, and so on in the **Add** and **Directory Permissions** dialogs are simply collections of common access bit patterns for the directory (first set of parenthesis) and the files in the directory (second set of parenthesis). For example, the **List** access type lets the user read and "execute" the directory (which allows you to CD into it), but do nothing to the files inside the directory. The user can therefore get a directory listing and see what is there, but cannot do anything with the files. The different standard combinations are shown below:

List	(RX)(None)
Read	(RX)(RX)
Add	(WX)(None)
Add & Read	(RWX)(RX)
Change	(RWXD)(RWXD)
Full Control	(All)(All)

There is a special **No Access** type that is a negative permission. If you give an individual **No Access** permissions then that person will be unable to access the specified file or directory even if they are a member of a group that has access.

It is also possible to create your own "special access" types where you set whatever access bits you like. You create the list both for the directory and the files it contains using the **Special Directory Access** and **Special File Access** Access Types in the **Directory Permissions Dialog**. See Figure A.4. For example, if you create a directory that contains executables, and you want to allow people to execute those files but not copy them, you can give the directory RX permissions and the files X permissions.

The Directory Permissions dialog has two check boxes at the top that let you percolate permissions set on a directory down through the directory tree to all files and subdirectories that it contains. If you do not set that check box, then any new files or directories created in that directory will inherit the permissions you set, but all existing files will retain their current permissions.

You can set permissions on individual files in the same way you set permissions on a directory. Select the file(s) and then choose the **Permissions** option in the **Security** menu.

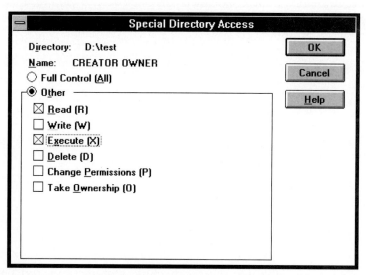

Figure A.4
The Special Access dialog for directories.

If you log on as the administrator, you can use the **Audit** option in the File Manager's **Security** menu as well. By enabling certain types of auditing in the Audit dialog, you cause the system to generate events that you can later view in the Event Viewer's security log. This facility gives you a way to monitor user activities and find people who are trying to breach security.

As the administrator, you have complete control of any NTFS volume. You can take ownership of any file and then manipulate its permissions in any way you like. There is nothing a user can do to prevent you from accessing a file. Use this power wisely.

INSTALLING NT

Windows NT is available for several machine architectures and has a huge number of installation options. In general, you should read the Microsoft installation documentation before you perform the install. However, if you choose the express setup option, your decisions are minimized and the whole process is relatively straightforward.

Installation on a PC compatible is probably, and ironically, the most difficult because of the millions of possible machine configurations. On a workstation, the NT install program can make a number of assumptions about the hardware, and the user will almost certainly be creating a "pure NT machine" (a machine that runs only NT). If you are installing on a PC you have several decisions you need to make before starting the install:

- Do you want a pure NT machine, or one that can boot both NT and DOS?
- Do you want your hard disk formatted for the FAT file system or NTFS? If the machine can swap between DOS and NT then the DOS partition will have to remain a FAT partition. You can format your other partitions and drives with NTFS however. If you do that, the partitions will become invisible to DOS, so there is a trade-off. There is a definite convenience factor to being able to see all files from both DOS and NT. On the other hand, NTFS partitions will be secure and more robust.
- Will your machine reside on a network? If so, you need to find out what kind of network card you have and get NT drivers for it if NT does not

ship with those drivers. You need to figure out the machine's name and find out about Workgroups and Domains on the net (See Chapter 10 and Appendix F for details). If you plan on connecting to a network, make sure the network card is in the machine when you install NT, so the install program can configure NT.

Special pieces of hardware such as scanners and multi-media cards may also need NT drivers. You will have to acquire these drivers from the manufacturer if they do not ship with NT properly.

If you choose to create an NT-only machine rather than a dual-boot machine, you should empty and reformat the hard disk before installing Windows NT, and then convert it over to an NTFS disk during the installation process for maximum security.

Before starting the installation process on any machine, you need to have several things ready:

1. Find a diskette suitable for your boot drive. On any RISC workstation and on most high-end PCs, the boot drive requires a 3.5-inch diskette. On some PCs however, the 5.25-inch drive is the boot drive so you need a blank diskette of that size. Do not start the installation process until you have found a diskette of the proper size.

2. Decide where you want to install NT. The default is a directory called `c:\winnt`.

3. Decide on the type of file system you want to use. Unless there are good reasons to do otherwise (e.g., you need the dual boot capability), then you should use NTFS for its security and reliability.

4. Decide on the computer's name. If it is installing on a Peer-to-Peer network you need to know the proper Workgroup name for the machine on the network. If you are installing on a Domain-Controlled network, you need to know the name of the Domain, and the account name and password for an administrator's account.

5. If you are going to install a printer during the installation of NT, you need to know the name of the printer and what port to attach it to. It is just as easy to install a printer after you install NT, so you can easily ignore the printer installation step during your first install without penalty.

6. If the machine is installing on a network, you need to know the name and manufacturer of your network card, as well as pertinent information such

as its I/O address and interrupt number. If you plan on using the machine on the network the card should be in place when you install NT.

The installation program will ask you questions, and the above information will allow you to answer them. Eventually the installation program will allow you to set the time, date, and time zone for your machine, and will then use the floppy disk that you supply to create an Emergency Repair Disk (ERD) for your machine. This ERD disk is useful in the following situations:

- You accidentally delete or corrupt files in NT that prevent it from booting.
- You accidentally set permissions on the NT directories that prevent it from booting.
- You forget your administrator password.
- A power failure or glitch corrupts a system file.

In any of these situations, you can boot up the setup program and use the ERD to repair the damage. See Section 4.4 for details.

The installation program will create an *administrator account* on the machine, and it will give you the opportunity to create a user account as well. This user account will need some tuning later, as described in Chapter 2. You might want to consider giving both of these accounts null passwords initially and then changing them to something else immediately after installation. That way, if you have to reload the account information with the ERD you know the password. The alternative is to reinstall NT from scratch.

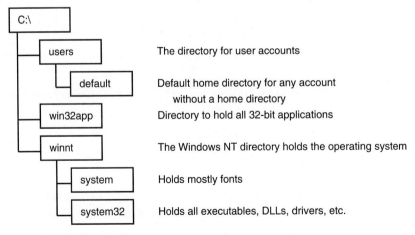

Figure B.1
Directory structure.

After you reboot following the installation, you will find that the directory structure looks like Figure B.1.

Your machine will have an administrator, user, and guest account. If you installed a printer it will be ready to use, and if you installed a network card you can access the network immediately to share files and directories.

Proceed to Chapter 1 to begin administering your new machine.

THE REGISTRY

If you are a former Windows 3.1 user, then you are probably familiar with the concept of an `.ini` file. You may be wondering what happened to `win.ini` and `system.ini`. If you are a former UNIX user, then you are probably familiar with the user information in `/etc/passwd` along with all the other configuration information in the `/etc` directory and various dot files, and are wondering where similar information gets stored on an NT workstation. The answer to both of these questions is "The Registry."

The registry is a database used by Windows NT to centrally store most application, user, and system information. The registry is generally invisible, but NT does supply a tool called `regedt32.exe` that lets you browse through and modify registry entries. It is normally dangerous to modify anything, because random changes can make the system unstable. However it is interesting to look around and see what is there.

If you start up the registry editor, you will see four icons or four windows. These icons represent the four different parts of the registry:

- HKEY_CURRENT_USER: Profile information for the current user, such as Program Manager groups, screen colors, etc. See Chapter 13 for a discussion on profiles.

- HKEY_USERS: Default profile information and profile information for all currently active users with local accounts on this machine.

- HKEY_LOCAL_MACHINE: Information about this machine.

- HKEY_CLASSES_ROOT: Information used by the File Manager and Object Linking and Embedding (OLE) to open applications. For example, this section associates different file extensions with applications.

If you open one of the icons, you will find that the registry has a hierarchical structure like a directory tree. When you get down to a leaf of the tree, it consists of a key name and one or more values. You can double click on any value to edit it. You can also add and delete keys and values.

It is interesting to browse through the entries in the Registry and see what is there, but in general it is not a good idea to modify anything unless you have specific instructions guiding you.

One of the most common reasons to use the registry as the administrator is to change the system's environment variables, particularly the PATH variable. Users can do this individually, but if you want to change it for all users then you need to use the registry. Take the following steps:

1. Start the program named REGEDT32.EXE by typing `regedt32` in an MS-DOS window. You may want to create an icon for it in the Administration Tools group of the Program Manager.
2. Open the HKEY_LOCAL_MACHINE portion of the registry.
3. Go down to the System/CurrentControlSet/Control/SessionManager/ Environment section.
4. Double click on the variable named Path and modify it.

When the machine boots, the PATH variable can also be modified by the file `autoexec.bat` in the root directory. If this file contains a statement such as the following, it is appended to the value of the PATH variable found in the registry:

```
PATH = c:\bin; c:\local\bin
```

The registry has security options similar to the File Manager or Print Manager. You can audit events, set permissions, and take ownership of keys. Read Appendix A and Chapter 11 on the File Manager and then apply this information to the Registry Editor.

There are several interesting registry values that you tend to run across by accident and may find useful. For example, you can add a legal notice to your machine by going into the HKEY_LOCAL_MACHINE\Software\Microsoft\Windows NT\CurrentVersion\WinLogin Key and changing the Legal

Notice Caption value (double-click on it) to be the caption you want in the legal notice dialog. Also change the Legal Notice Text value to the body of the dialog.

By exploring the registry, you can find other values like this and experiment with them. The NT Resource Kit comes with a useful tool that explains every key and value in the registry.

CONTACTING THE AUTHORS — D

Windows NT, like all operating systems, will change over time. We want to keep your copy of the book current by providing you with correction and update pages via electronic mail. If you find errors in the book, or if you have any questions, comments, or suggestions for improving the book, we would like to hear from you. Your comments will help us improve later editions, and we'll post your corrections so other readers can take advantage of them.

You can contact the authors either by U.S. mail or by electronic mail. Electronic mail is preferred. The U.S. mail address is:

Interface Technologies
P.O. Box 841
Zebulon, NC 27597

To send suggestions, comments, or corrections via electronic mail, address e-mail to:

comments@iftech.com

To ask a question, send e-mail to:

questions@iftech.com

To request a list of the available update and correction pages, as well as free supplements, send e-mail to:

info@iftech.com

In the last case, the message can contain anything or nothing at all. The mail system will send an automated reply with a list of topics and further instructions.

These e-mail addresses are on the Internet and will suffice on mail systems connected directly to the Internet. If you are using CompuServe, you can add the prefix "INTERNET:" to the address to get your message onto the Internet. For example:

INTERNET:comments@iftech.com

Other mail services such as MCImail, as well as many PC bulletin boards, also offer Internet access. See the documentation for your specific system for details.

A ROAD MAP FOR MIGRATING UNIX ADMINISTRATORS

If you are a seasoned UNIX administrator moving to Windows NT, then you have a bit of adjustment ahead of you. UNIX is a venerable and well-established operating system that has existed, in the time domain of computers at least, forever. It uses a pleasant and forthright text-based system for recording and manipulating administrative information. As an experienced professional, you know where all the important files are located, and you know exactly what will happen when you wiggle certain characters in those files. Like anything else, you are comfortable with UNIX because you understand how it works.

Windows NT is going to feel uncomfortable initially because it is totally new and different. The administrative interface is completely graphical, and the tools you use to manipulate things are scattered far and wide. You will have that feeling of despair that comes from knowing how to do something in one culture, but not another. It is like traveling in a foreign country: Of course you know how to use the bathroom, but how do you find out where it is? It can be very frustrating.

This appendix is designed to help you map your UNIX knowledge onto the Windows NT operating system. Each section takes a topic familiar to you and shows where to find it in NT.

E.1 Logging On

If you want to be the administrator on a UNIX machine, you log on as "root." On an NT machine you log on as "administrator" instead, or you grant administrative privileges to your personal account in the User Manager. See

Chapter 2. Generally the latter option is a bad idea. There are many advantages to having a mental distinction between your user account and your administrative account.

If there is a Domain Controller (Chapter 13) on your network, the **From** field of the logon dialog lets you choose between logging on to the local machine with local account information or with Domain account information from the Controller. Generally you will use the Domain accounts.

In UNIX you can bump up your user privilege by typing "su." There is no easy way to do this in NT. You have to log out and log back in. You can also change who you are in UNIX. This again is not possible in NT.

To log off, select the **Log Off** option in the **File** menu of the Program Manager, or press Ctrl-Alt-Del and click the **Log Off** button.

E.2 Changing the Administrative Password

To change your password, either use the User Manager or press Ctrl-Alt-Del while you are logged on and click the **Change Password** button in the dialog that appears.

E.3 Getting a Command Prompt

If you are a long-term UNIX user, it often seems easier to simply type in little commands than to use a mouse all day long. To get to a command prompt in NT, open the Program Manager, open the Main group, and double click on the MS-DOS prompt. Type "help." Or, again in the Main group, double click on the command Help application to get help on DOS commands. For those who wish to have the comfort of a few familiar UNIX command line utilities, don't fret. Many UNIX tools like `tar`, `vi`, `emacs`, `make`, and others can be found as shareware or commercial packages. See Chapter 7 in "Using Windows NT: The Essentials for Professionals" for more information on MS-DOS commands and scripts.

E.4 Creating a Simple Text File

In UNIX you would probably use `vi` or `emacs` to create a simple text file. In NT type "start notepad" at a command prompt, or open the Accessories Group in the Program Manager and click on the Notepad icon. See Chapter 8 in "Using Windows NT: The Essentials for Professionals."

E.5 Creating User Accounts

When you create an account in UNIX you have to create a directory for the user, change ownership of it, and then modify the `/etc/passwd` file to create the new account. In NT you use the User Manager located in the Administrative Tools groups of the Program Manager. See Chapter 2.

E.6 Home Directories

User home directories can be located anywhere in both UNIX and NT. NT, however, will create a directory on the system's hard drive named "users" for holding the home directories. A subdirectory called "default" is automatically created under "users" for use as the default home directory for guest accounts. The "users" subdirectory is a good place to put new home directories as well. See Chapter 2. Keeping all home directories in one place makes backing up the system easier.

E.7 File Security

In UNIX, file security is determined by the permission bits (rwxrwxrwx). In NT, permissions are instead set using Access Control Lists, which are much more precise. See Appendix A for a discussion and some exercises.

E.8 Disk Management

If you want to partition disks, create stripe sets, or create volume sets, you do it using the Disk Manager. It is located in the Administrative Tools group of the Program Manager. See Chapter 6.

E.9 Mounting Remote Disks

In UNIX, each machine has a single directory tree onto which all local and remote drives are mounted. NT instead uses the concept of "drive letters," with one letter being used for each local or remote drive. You mount remote drives in NT by "connecting" to them in the File Manager. See Chapter 5 in "Using Windows NT: The Essentials for Professionals," or Chapter 11 of this book.

E.10 Talking to Floppy Drives

In UNIX, floppy drives are mounted into the directory tree like everything else. In NT they have their own separate drive letters, generally A and B.

E.11 File Names

In UNIX, file names can be quite long, and can contain almost any character anywhere. In NT, several different file systems are used and they restrict things differently. If you are using NTFS, file names are just as flexible as they are in UNIX. However, if you use floppy disks, or a hard disk partition formatted with the FAT file system, files must conform to the 8-dot-3 naming convention. File names can have up to eight alphanumeric characters, followed by a period, followed by up to three alphanumeric characters. Because you often want to copy files from NTFS partitions to floppy disks, there is a built-in tendency to make your file names conform to the 8-dot-3 standard despite the flexibility of NT. If you *do* copy a long file name from an NTFS partition to a floppy disk, NTFS will automatically truncate and mangle the file name to fit it into the 8-dot-3 format.

E.12 NFS

When you want to share a disk or directory with another UNIX machine, you typically do so with NFS. In NT you share disks using the **Share** option in the File Manager (see Chapter 11). If you have a network containing both UNIX and NT machines and you want to mount an NT disk onto a UNIX machine, you need to buy a third party package to do it. One such shareware package for NT is called SOSSNT. You can get it from many bulletin boards. We use it in our office to talk to our UNIX machine.

E.13 UUCP

UUCP connections are possible in NT, but you must buy a third party or shareware package. UUPC is the name of one shareware package that is available on Compuserve. Be sure to get the NT version.

E.14 Daemons

In UNIX, daemons are background processes that run all the time. In NT the equivalent functionality is provided by "services." The Service Manager is located in the Control Panel. See Section 7.1.6.

E.15 Printer Drivers

In UNIX, printer drivers (if you want to call them that) are found in the `/etc/printcap` file. In NT you install printers using the **Create Printer** option in the Print Manager. See Chapter 3.

E.16 Sharing Printers

To share printers over the network from an NT machine, use the **Share** option in the Print Manager. See Chapter 11.

E.17 Using Remote Printers

Connecting to a remote printer is extremely easy in NT using the **Connect** option in the Print Manager. See Chapter 6 of "Using Windows NT: The Essentials for Professionals."

E.18 Changing the Screen Resolution

With today's UNIX workstations, the screen resolution is usually determined by the X Server and it is not easily adjusted in most cases. In NT you can usually change screen resolution by changing screen drivers. Use the Windows NT Setup icon in the Main group of the Program Manager. See Section 7.2.

E.19 Installing Device Drivers

Unlike UNIX with its `/dev` subdirectory, Windows NT device drivers are not mapped into the file system so cleanly. Drivers are loaded and configured in one of four different places in NT.

- The Print Manager handles printer device drivers.
- The Windows NT Setup application (see Section 7.2) manages the drivers for the screen, the keyboard, the mouse, any SCSI devices, and tape drives.
- The Network applet (see Chapter 10) handles the network card.
- The Drivers applet handles all other device drivers for add-on hardware such as sound cards. You can add, remove, or modify driver settings in this applet. See Chapter 7.

E.20 Terminals

All UNIX machines are able to support the attachment of external terminals so that multiple users can log on to the machine simultaneously. NT is strictly a one-user-at-a-time system. Many UNIX gurus will scoff at this limitation, but before you do consider this. At North Carolina State University there is a huge UNIX network with about 1,000 workstations on it for student use. All the workstations are UNIX machines from DEC, Sun, HP, etc. However, they have all been configured so that only one user at a time can access each one. You cannot `rlogin` to them, or `ftp` to them, or `rcp`, or `rsh`. This is a fairly common way to configure workstations on a large network because if you don't, mayhem results (especially in an academic environment). This is exactly the configuration supported by Windows NT. It's not that crazy.

E.21 Changing the Name of the Machine

You change the name of an NT machine on the network using the Network applet in the Control Panel. See Section 10.5.

E.22 Changing the TCP/IP Name and Address

In NT you can look at or change the TCP/IP address of the machine in the Network applet of the Control Panel. Select the TCP/IP software module from the list. This is also where you install TCP/IP support. See Chapter 14.

E.23 Using FTP and Telnet

Once you have installed the TCP/IP section in the Network applet of the Control Panel, you can use the `telnet` and `ftp` commands like you would on any UNIX machine. See Section 14.3.

E.24 Setting Up E-mail

In UNIX, you get e-mail "for free" when you create user accounts. In NT you set up e-mail separately. See Chapter 12.

E.25 Using Talk

The `talk` command in UNIX is replaced by Chat in NT. Double click on the Chat icon in the Accessories Group of the Program Manager. See Chapter 18 in "Using Windows NT: The Essentials for Professionals."

E.26 Sending Messages to Users

In Unix you can use the `write` and `wall` commands to send messages to users. In NT, you send messages to users on the network with the `net send` command. See Section 7.1.6. If you are using a Domain Controller, you use the **Send Message** option. See Section 13.5.

E.27 Finding the System Load

In UNIX you would use the `w` or `uptime` commands to find the system load. In NT use the Performance Monitor tool in the Administrative Tools group of the Program Manager. See Chapter 9.

E.28 Killing Off Processes

To kill off a process in UNIX you would use the `ps` command to get the list of processes and then use the `kill` command to kill the process. In NT you double click on the background on the screen. You will get a task list and can click on any task to kill it. If you have the Software Developer Kit (SDK), look for an application named `pview` to view processes and kill them off individually.

E.29 Shutting Down a Machine

You shut down an NT machine by selecting the **Shutdown** option in the **File** menu of the Program Manager, or by pressing Ctrl-Alt-Del while logged in and clicking the **Shutdown** button.

E.30 Tape Backup

In UNIX you can use the `tar` or `dump` commands to perform tape backups. In NT you use the Tape Backup tool in the Administrative Tools group of the Program Manager. See Chapter 4. The `tar` command is also frequently used to save subdirectory trees to a single file. In NT you most commonly use a shareware archive program, for instance pkzip, available on most bulletin boards. In NT the `compress` command is `compress` and the `uncompress` command is `expand`.

E.31 System Log Files

All system log files in NT are consolidated under the Event Viewer found in the Administrative Tools group of the Program Manager. See Chapter 8.

E.32 Setting Time and Date

In UNIX you use the `date` command to set the time and date. In NT use the Date/Time applet in the Control Panel. See Section 7.1.2.

E.33 UPS Devices

Configure UPS devices in NT using the UPS applet in the Control Panel. See Chapter 5.

E.34 Virtual Memory

Changing virtual memory size in UNIX is not easy. In NT it is painless. Use the System Applet in the Control Panel. See Section 7.1.1.

E.35 Task Priority

To adjust the priority assigned to different tasks in NT, use the System applet in the Control Panel. See Section 7.1.1.

E.36 Terminal Program

If you want to pull up a simple vt100 terminal to dial out to another machine, use the Terminal application in the Accessories group of the Program Manager. See Chapter 11 of "Using Windows NT: The Essentials for Professionals."

E.37 CRON Jobs

UNIX has a facility called CRON that schedules background tasks for automatic execution at set times. In Windows NT the `at` command handles the same functionality in combination with the Schedule service. See Section 7.1.6.

A NETWORK CONFIGURATION CHECKLIST

Let's say you have a network at your company, that you are the network administrator, and that you are about to install a new NT machine onto the net. You cannot simply install the Windows NT files onto the hard disk and walk away. There are many pieces you have to touch if you plan on letting anyone sit down and use the machine in the near future. This checklist is designed to remind you of all the things you might want to adjust before you allow other people to turn the new machine on and begin using it.

If you do not have a Domain Controller (Chapter 13) on the network and you plan to stay sane running a network full of NT machines, then you need to make up a master list of all your NT users, and you need to use the same account names for each person on every machine. If Mary Jones has an account "mjones" on her machine and she wants an account on a new machine, be sure to call it "mjones." Tell Mary to keep all her passwords synchronized as well. When she changes one, she should try to change them all. It's also nice to keep groups synchronized, but not as important. By keeping all user account names identical on all machines, you make it easier for people to share files with one another over the network. See Section 11.1 for details.

Here are the steps you should take whenever you install a new machine on the network:

1. Install the network card in the machine *before* installing Windows NT. Make sure the interrupt addresses and I/O addresses of the card don't conflict with anything else. Have the documentation for

the card in your hand during the installation process, just in case you need it.

If for any reason you want to partition the C: drive, do it *before* installing NT because you cannot do it afterwards. See Chapter 6. All other drives should be partitioned *after* installation.

2. Figure out the name for the machine on the network. If your network has a Domain Controller (Chapter 13) find out the name of the Domain Controller, or if you are using Workgroups on the net instead, find out the name of the Workgroup for this machine. File this information to avoid future naming conflicts.

3. If the network is a TCP/IP network, figure out the new Host name, the Domain name, the IP address, and the subnet mask for the new machine. If there is a Domain Name Server on the net, find out its IP address. If there is a gateway machine, find out its address. See Chapter 14. Have all of this written down on a sheet of paper that you can later file, along with the names from Step 2.

4. If you need to install NT on the system, then proceed with the installation process. See Appendix B. Many systems come with NT pre-installed, however, and these folks can proceed to Step 5.

During the installation you can use the express or custom setup, as you prefer. NT will ask you for the machine name and so on. Once NT is installed, boot the machine and log on as the administrator. Use the File Manager and make sure that you can see all the drives you expect to see on the local machine. Try connecting to a network drive to see if the network is responding. If something is wrong, fix it.

5. Log on as administrator and begin adjusting the machine. Start by going to the NT Setup application in the Main Group of the Program Manager. If you want to change the screen driver to get better resolution, do it here. See Section 7.2 for details.

6. Open the Control Panel application in the Main group of the Program Manager. Open the Network applet. Check that the machine name and Domain/Workgroup name are correct. See Sections 10.5 and 13.2 for details.

If the machine is going to interface with TCP/IP machines, load the TCP/IP package. See Chapter 14. Use the names from Step 2 to fill in the blanks.

If the machine is going to act as a RAS server or client, load the RAS package. See Chapter 15.

Close the Network applet.

7. Open the Services applet and set to *automatic* any services that need to start when the machine boots. Be sure that the Schedule, Alerter, Messenger, and Directory Replicator services are on if you need them. See Section 7.1.6.

8. Open the Server applet and start the directory replicator if you plan to use replication. See Chapter 13.

9. Open the System applet and adjust the virtual memory size and tasking preference. See Section 7.1.1.

10. Open the UPS applet and install the UPS if you are using one. See Chapter 5.

11. Open the User Manager and create any local accounts and groups that you need on this machine. If you have a Domain Controller you will probably omit this step. If not, create an account for each user who will need to log on to this machine. As mentioned at the beginning of this appendix, it is wise to keep all accounts synchronized, so use standard names for each user.

    If you are using the replicator, set up the local replicator group properly while you are in the User Manager. See Chapter 13 for details.

12. Open the File Manager and share any drives and directories that you plan to share with the rest of the network. See Chapter 11 for details.

13. If this machine will have any printers directly attached to it, open the Print Manager and install the printers. See Chapter 3. If you plan to share the printer on the network, do this as well. See Chapter 11.

14. If the machine has a tape drive, run the Tape Backup program in the administrator group and make sure that the drive is working properly. If not, see Section 4.2.

15. If you have other drives in this machine other than the C: drive, use the Disk Manager (Chapter 6) to partition and format them as appropriate.

16. If you need to install any odd devices like sound cards, scanners, etc., install them following the manufacturer's instructions.

17. Log out as the administrator.

18. If you want to provide truly exemplary service for your users, you can now log on as the user and set up a few things they will need.

    Go to the File Manager and connect to any system-wide file servers that the user will need. See Chapter 10.

    Go to the Print Manager and connect to any printers that the user might need. See Chapter 3.

    Go to the Mail application and connect the user to the Post Office if you have one. See Chapter 12 for details.

    Open the Control Panel and set up any user preferences that might be desirable (colors, fonts, etc.). Also go into the System applet and set any required environment variables. If you have a Domain Controller, you can do a lot of this work remotely using profiles. See Chapter 13.

    Log out.

Now your users can use the machine. You may want to write up an instruction sheet to help them get started and tell them what you have done, or hold a meeting or a training session on network resources. You will be amazed at how much more smoothly things go when people know what is going on.

Security Issues on NT Workstations

This appendix summarizes a number of different security issues in the Windows NT operating system. They are collected together here to act as a security checklist for an individual machine or a network. If you, as a system administrator, are concerned about the security of your network, you may want to run down this checklist so you are aware of all the potential security holes in NT.

If you are not concerned about security right now, you may want to take a second look at the issue. Here are some things to think about:

- If your machine is secure, then no one can look at any file on the machine unless they have an account. This means your work is private, just like the papers in a locked filing cabinet are private.
- If your machine is secure, it means you are immune to viruses.
- If your machine is secure it means no one using your machine can do anything that causes the operating system to fail. For example, a normal user cannot accidentally erase a file that disables the entire system.

If you are coming from a PC environment, then these are probably novel concepts. You are used to every machine being wide open and you have built a mind set around that. You may want to consider taking the time to change your mind set and take advantage of all the security features that NT has to offer.

G.1 Security Immediately After Installation

Immediately after installing Windows NT there are three security concerns you should eliminate.

1. The installation program automatically created a guest account, but the account has a null password. Either delete the account or change its password.

2. The system directories under `c:\winnt` have read and write permissions for everyone, so any user can damage the system. Change the permissions on this directory to read and execute only. See Appendix A.

3. Several parts of the system allow the Everyone group to do things. For example, after initial installation Everyone can shut down the machine. The Everyone group also has access to all files on the hard disk. You will want to remove this group from everything. This applies after formatting a partition also.

The Everyone group, especially on a Peer-to-Peer network with multiple account lists, is rather interesting. Here is how it works. When a user tries to connect to or access an object that has Everyone permissions set on it, NT tries to authenticate the user on the machine possessing the desired object. The user's ID and password are compared against the account list, and if the user is known the system lets the user access the desired object. If the user is not known, the system then tries to authenticate the user as a guest. If the guest accounts on both machines have the same password, then the user is authenticated. However, if either machine does not have a guest account, or if either guest account is disabled in the User Manager, or if the guest accounts on the two machines have different passwords, the user does not get authenticated and is denied access. On a Domain-Controlled network there is only one guest account, so if it exists and it is enabled, authentication is guaranteed.

By eliminating the guest account, you eliminate a good portion of the "everyone" capability. To eliminate the rest of it, remove the group from all files, printers, and so on.

G.2 Physical Security

If you have an NT machine sitting out in an open room, then there are several ways that a person can easily attack the security of the system:

- If the machine is a PC-style machine based on the Intel x86 architecture, a user can reset the machine, stick a bootable MS-DOS disk in the floppy drive, and boot MS-DOS. If the hard disk is formatted with the FAT file system, it is an open book. If its formatted with NTFS, then the person would have to have a program capable of decoding the file system and reading it, but such a program would not be impossible to create.

- On any type of machine, if the user has a set of NT installation disks, they can reinstall NT and in so doing essentially negate all the passwords and permissions. Even if the disk is formatted with NTFS, they can log on as administrator and take ownership of all the files.

In other words, a determined user who has access to a machine with floppy drives simply has to turn the machine off and turn it back on to get in. The only way to prevent this is to remove any floppy drives from the machine. A determined user, given enough privacy and time, could theoretically walk in and install a new drive if the case is not locked. You can lock the case, however, to prevent that. The best bet is to place a locked and cabled machine having no floppy drives in a secured room. You can then safely say that the machine is as physically secure as possible.

You can easily monitor reboot attempts after the fact by enabling the reboot event auditing capability in the User Manager. If you disable the reset switch and on/off switch of the machine, turn off the floppy drive device (see Section 2.8), and remove the Shutdown Workstation right from all users, you also greatly limit the probability of a casual security breach.

G.3 Passwords

The easiest way for someone to get into an NT system is through inadequate password protection. If one of your users has an easy-to-crack password, or leaks their password accidentally, then security is breached. There are two approaches to lessening this problem. First, in the User Manager, you can force users to create good passwords and change them frequently. Second, you can secure the files on the disk with "fire walls" of file permissions, so that someone who breaks into an account has only limited access to the rest of the system's files.

You can enforce user password behavior using the principles described in Section 2.7. For example, you can force users to create passwords eight characters long, and you can also force users to change their password every week, or even every day. The latter option creates its own problems however, because users find it hard to remember their current passwords and end up writing them down to remember them.

As long as you use NTFS on your hard disks, you can prevent any intruder from getting very far by using file and directory permissions that keep users out of directories where they do not belong. See the following section.

G.4 System Integrity and File Security

Probably the best way to make your system completely vulnerable to an intruder is to use the FAT File System on your hard disk. A FAT hard disk is totally insecure, so anyone who manages to log on to the system, even if it is through the guest account, can see the entire file system. You should use NTFS on your hard disk, and you should do the following with its permissions.

- Mark all operating system directories so they have only read and execute permissions for users. There's a lot to be said for making those directories read and execute only for the administrator as well. You can always change them to writeable if you ever need to do so. Making them Read Only means that you can't accidentally damage or destroy something when you are logged in as the administrator.

- Limit all users to their own home directories. Change the permissions so that a user can see and write to only his or her home directory. You can then allow users to share their files themselves by granting file administration privileges. See Appendix A.

By taking these two simple steps, you limit all damage from a leaked account password to the minimum area possible, with the exception of the administrator account. You will have to protect the administration account religiously yourself. Never give it out for any reason to anyone, and change the password frequently.

Whenever you format an NTFS partition or share a directory, the drive will initially give permission to Everyone. You will want to check permissions on any drive or directory immediately after sharing or formatting.

G.5 Printers

Printers seem innocuous, but if you have sensitive information or trade secrets on your network you want to prevent people from printing out that material. You can do this by carefully controlling printer access:

- Limit printer access to only those people who need to use them.
- Audit printer usage in the Print Manager so you know who is printing what.
- Do not give out power user rights to anyone, because power users can create printers and share them on the network. Also do not give out full control access privileges on a printer.
- Restrict printing hours to normal work hours in the Print Manager.

G.6 Security Logs

The Security log made available by the Event Viewer helps to track security-related information. You must do two things to make this log worthwhile:

- You must turn it on and specify that it record events performed by users. You control this in the User Manager, the Print Manager, the File Manager, and the Registry Editor.
- You must make sure that if the log overflows the system shuts itself down. You control this behavior in the Event Viewer.

The log is only worthwhile, however, if you look at it. Look especially for repeated unsuccessful attempts to log on to an account, repeated attempts to shutdown or restart a computer, failures to access files that you know are important, and excessive printing.

G.7 Tapes

Tape drives offer an amazingly convenient way to walk away with a complete copy of your workstation's files. Any user can use the Tape Backup program to back up files that they have access to. This can make a tape drive as dangerous as a floppy disk or printer in terms of allowing critical data to walk off site. In addition, any member of the Administrator or Backup Operators group can back up the entire drive. You want to be extremely careful when choosing people who will have these rights.

Once you create the tapes, you need to be careful where you put them. If someone picks them up and walks off with them, they potentially have a complete copy of your network. You can limit this problem somewhat by choosing the **Restrict Access to Owner or Administrator** check box when creating the backup tape, but this is a fairly soft form of enforcement. Physical security in the form of a safe or other locked enclosure is your best bet.

G.8 Portables

Let's say you have an Ethernet network, and someone walks into your office with a portable computer and connects into the network. What are they able to do?

If your network has a Domain Controller and all the machines on the network are members of the Domain, the intruder will be able to do very little unless he or she knows the administrative password of the Controller. The Domain Controller basically locks out anyone who has not been made a member of the Domain, and the administrator password is required to do that.

If your network is a basic Peer-to-Peer network, and if each machine has guest accounts with null passwords, then the intruder can access any disk or printer where the group Everyone has access. If you change the Guest account's password, then that password will control access to directories marked Everyone, and the intruder will need to know that password. Unfortunately, a guest password like that is common knowledge, so its not that hard to obtain.

If you are worried about security, install an NTAS Domain Controller to control access to the net. See Chapter 13. If you are required to use a Peer-to-Peer network then eliminate the Guest account completely on all machines and use private groups that you have created yourself to control access to different resources.

G.9 The Registry

The registry contains a great deal of sensitive information, and if it is damaged then the system can be disabled. You therefore want to use NTFS and the security measures available in the **Security** menu to keep unauthorized users out of the registry.

G.10 Mail

The mail program has several security holes. Do not use the standard NT mail program if security is important. Several problems are listed below:

- It is possible for any user to create an e-mail account with any name they like. This means that you can have unidentified e-mail messages traveling through the system.

- The WGPO directory has to have Full Control permissions assigned for everyone. This means that any user can erase all or part of the directory and destroy the e-mail system.
- Users can move their e-mail directories into the WGPO directory, and once there they can be copied by anyone. It is not clear that a valid encryption technology is used on these files.

If you need a relatively secure e-mail system, you would be better off hooking a UNIX machine into your network and letting it handle e-mail and FTP locally and on the Internet. See Chapter 13.

G.11 FTP

As mentioned in Section 14.4, FTP clients pass unencrypted passwords on the network. Anonymous FTP accounts create a security hole which you may want to eliminate.

INDEX